ROSALIND MILES

Danger! Men at Work

Illustrated by Christine Roche

Futura
Macdonald & Co
London & Sydney

A Futura Book

First published in Great Britain in 1983
by Futura Publications, a Division of
Macdonald & Co (Publishers) Ltd
London & Sydney

ISBN 0 7088 2371 8

Filmset, printed and bound in Great Britain by
Hazell Watson & Viney Ltd, Aylesbury, Bucks

Futura Publications
A Division of
Macdonald & Co (Publishers) Ltd
Maxwell House
74 Worship Street
London EC2A 2EN
A BPCC plc Company

Rosalind Miles teaches English and Communication
Studies at the Lanchester Polytechnic, Coventry.

For
John, Geoffrey, Peter, Raymond, Jonathan,
Tom, Hugh, DP, all my Davids, Ian,
Michael and Ben –

it's been a pleasure to work with
you

CONTENTS

FOREWORD

So many working girls have encouraged and assisted me with this book, that writing it has brought me friendship and understanding beyond anything I imagined when I began. To all those who have so freely shared their experiences with me, a special thank you. Many have asked not to be identified, for obvious reasons, so where I have used a first name only, it is fictitious – real people are identified by the addition of their surnames.

I would like to thank those organizations and individuals whose co-operation has made this book possible: the staff at the Equal Opportunities Commission and the National Council for Civil Liberties, Lloyds Bank, Coventry, the Statistical Services Division of the Alfred Marks Bureau, and *Chief Executive Monthly*. I am very grateful to Edith Lowy of Bruno Electrical Ltd, Bernadette Lawrence of Aquarius Metals, Sue Hackett of Thames TV, Elizabeth Cutler of New York City, Suzanne Hunter, Wendy Curme, Doreen Parfitt, Beverley Bruges, Avis Lingard and Sue Campbell, and above all to Malinda Coleman of Brussels, whose sisterhood has never failed me.

I am deeply indebted to all my legal beagles who have guided me through the thickets of the law, especially Lord Scarman, Helen Grindrod Q.C., David Pannick, barrister and Fellow of All Souls College, Oxford, and Mr D. F. Tandy of Penmans, Coventry. It would be a poor return for their generosity if they were held responsible for any misunderstandings that remain, or for any of my opinions.

Names of women have been changed to protect the innocent. Those of men have been disguised to protect the guilty. The insight I have had into the working lives of women today has shown me that, contrary to popular masculine belief, many women have never had it so bad. For every example of bullying, harassment, obstruction

9

or dirty tricks of one sort or another that I have mentioned here, I could have included literally hundreds of others. If this is the masculine idea of the equality that women are supposed to have, it's back to the drawing-board, boys.

This book is written for women, by a woman, and speaks to women throughout. If men find any of it incredible, irritating or insulting, I'd like to say I'm sorry. But I'm not. I'm sorry for all the women struggling away under the adverse circumstances of having to work for them. That's why I wrote it. To men who don't like it, I can only say that there are *millions* of books that have been written for you. This one simply tries to come in from the other side.

To working women throughout the world then, keep working on it – and on them. That's a full-time job in itself!

Rosalind Miles

1

What It's All About

If the Good Lord had intended us to have equal rights to go out to work, he wouldn't have created man and woman –

Patrick Jenkin, Secretary of State for Social Services, BBC TV, 1980.

Why this book?

Many people today think that the battle for sexual equality is over and won. The activities of women's groups, the withdrawal of some of the grosser inequalities, and a few famous victories emptily trumpeted by the ever-attentive media, have combined to create the impression that the doors of the world of work stand wide open for women now – all they have to do is to bring home the bacon. The media have even developed this newfound female freedom into one of the sillier stereotypes: 'Bell was a high-flying career girl – quick, clever and beautiful . . . the successful career girl living the life she had always wanted', drivelled *Woman* in its February issue, 1982. So fixed is this idea of the modern girl swinging her way through her work, that 'the world's greatest weekly for women' finds it necessary to insist that whatever the cost, there's no turning back: 'Beneath her glittering professional appearance was a vulnerable heart but her career was what mattered after all. Just so long as she could keep going.' The liberated woman, so the message goes, has burned her bridges along with her bras – but she has got her career. 'She sighed, then turned to her work again, her determination redoubled.'

If only life were like that

The reality of women's working lives could hardly be more different from this. For the majority of 'career girls', work is not a territory where they roam free developing their strength and skill, but a jungle in which they are always in danger from hostile natives. Helen was embarked on a successful career with the Civil Service when a promotion brought her into contact with Jackson, whose sexual attentions rapidly became noticeable and persistent. Despite constant discouragement Jackson continued to pester Helen with direct offers of sex, with jokes and innuendoes, so that she was heartily relieved when his promotion removed from her work life a problem which she had been unable to deal with successfully. Jackson's replacement, however, had heard on the office grapevine of Helen's steadfast resistance to his predecessor, and took upon himself the challenge of thawing out the 'ice maiden'. He repeatedly propositioned her, in increasingly coarse and aggressive terms, and began leaving nude pictures, copulating figures, etc, on her desk. Eventually he began to harass her physically, brushing against her and touching her bottom and breasts – at the same time he began to phone her at home to make obscene suggestions. At this point Helen complained to their immediate boss, whose reaction was 'What the hell are you bleating about? It's all part of office life – you're an attractive woman, you should expect it. Any man in his right mind would want to rape you!' Helen pursued her case up the management ladder and took it to her Head of Section – now her former adversary Jackson. On receiving Helen's complaint, Jackson sacked her.

What price equality?

Helen's last resort was the Industrial Tribunal, which ruled in her favour. Janice was not so lucky. While working as a secretary in a mechanical engineering firm, she became interested in the firm's operations and asked to be considered for a better job. She was told that she could never be promoted without the necessary technical qualifications, and was refused day-release in order to study for them, even though the young men from the firm who applied all automatically received this. Undeterred, Janice studied mechanical engineering in her own time, attending night school three days a week until she gained the required practical and theoretical knowledge. At the next reshuffle Janice was made redundant, on the grounds that she was now over-qualified for her secretarial post, and the firm could not afford to pay her at a level commensurate with her new status. 'You've priced yourself out of the market, girl', the management representative observed with satisfaction. Janice was advised that an appeal to the Industrial Tribunal would have little chance of success, as she would find it hard to prove that she had suffered discrimination on the grounds of her sex, or that her 'redundancy' was a disguised dismissal for getting above herself. She is still unemployed after eighteen months.

Just unlucky?

Helen and Janice both had bad work experiences, where male colleagues opposed and damaged them in different ways. But they are only two individuals – are these isolated cases in any way typical? What is the reality of the work situation for women? A mass of statistical evidence returns a quick answer to that question – it's a man's world, and one in which men show little signs of being ready to relinquish their traditional dominance and control. So far from being the haphazard and random behaviour of a few errant male chauvinists, discrimination is systematic, structural, and institutionalized in the work pattern of this country.

Women's work

All the available information about women's position in the labour force shows that they are concentrated in industries and occupations which have been female ghettoes since time immemorial, while the high-status, high-income jobs remain an almost exclusively masculine preserve. Women manual workers are largely employed in personal services like catering, cleaning and hairdressing – non-manual women workers find themselves clustered in the equally traditional female occupations of secretarial, clerical, and related tasks. Lynne, a twenty-year-old hairdresser described her choice of job in these terms: 'Well, a couple of my friends had gone into it, it seemed an obvious job for a girl, really.' Lynne's response is fully borne out by Department of Employment statistics:

Occupational distribution of women workers

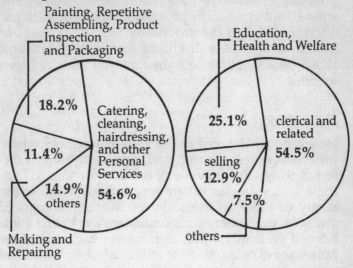

Painting, Repetitive Assembling, Product Inspection and Packaging

18.2%

11.4%

Catering, cleaning, hairdressing, and other Personal Services

14.9% others

54.6%

Making and Repairing

Manual

Education, Health and Welfare

25.1%

clerical and related

54.5%

selling 12.9%

7.5%

others

Non-manual

SOURCE: Department of Employment, New Earnings Survey 1980, Part E, table 135

In other words

What this means is that if you are female, your significant work decision has been taken for you, at the moment of birth. Over half of you will find yourselves pressured, sucked or directed into service or clerical work – usually at an age where you are unaware that there could be other options. All too often these two jobs are the only work possibilities held up to girl school-leavers. Lynne's experience was typical in this respect, too – she chose hairdressing because she could not stand the 'secretarial and book-keeping' course to which she had been allotted by the school 'careers' teacher (appropriately enough, one Hobson). This systematic direction of women into predetermined work areas not only keeps wages low in the female sector – it severely hinders and reduces women's chances of gaining entry into other jobs. The structured inequality of women's work opportunities emerges clearly from a Department of Employment survey of the field of work overall:

What way out?

As this shows, women's work is heavily concentrated in the unskilled and semi-skilled areas, from which it is difficult to escape. Janice's experience of being refused the training which would have lifted her out of the secretarial rut is duplicated on a larger scale through a variety of industries and concerns. In 1977-8 women were still only 0·2% of total craft trainees, and 1·8% of technician trainees. Those few girls who do break through this institutionalized discrimination do so by the rare combination of personality and good luck. Lynn B, who is now working a four-year apprenticeship towards becoming a master farrier, attributes her success to 'just being cheeky enough to ask for the job'. Even so, she had to work in the forge for six months beforehand, to prove that she could stand the heat and the hard work, and handle both horses and customers. Barbara, now a qualified bricklayer, and Karen, a motor mechanic, both owed their start to a family business – Barbara persuaded her father to take her on in his construction firm as an apprentice, while Karen was born in the Orkneys, and had to help her father, the lifeboat

Women as a percentage of the industrial labour force of Great Britain, 1980

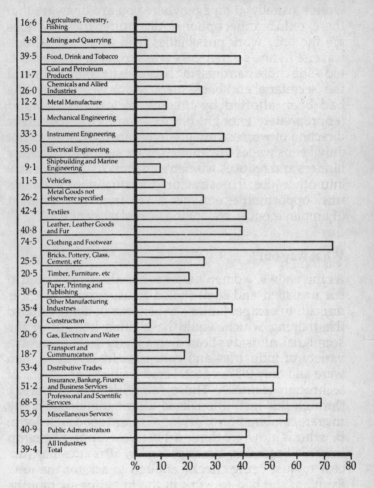

	%
Agriculture, Forestry, Fishing	16·6
Mining and Quarrying	4·8
Food, Drink and Tobacco	39·5
Coal and Petroleum Products	11·7
Chemicals and Allied Industries	26·0
Metal Manufacture	12·2
Mechanical Engineering	15·1
Instrument Engineering	33·3
Electrical Engineering	35·0
Shipbuilding and Marine Engineering	9·1
Vehicles	11·5
Metal Goods not elsewhere specified	26·2
Textiles	42·4
Leather, Leather Goods and Fur	40·8
Clothing and Footwear	74·5
Bricks, Pottery, Glass, Cement, etc	25·5
Timber, Furniture, etc	20·5
Paper, Printing and Publishing	30·6
Other Manufacturing Industries	35·4
Construction	7·6
Gas, Electricity and Water	20·6
Transport and Communication	18·7
Distributive Trades	53·4
Insurance, Banking, Finance and Business Services	51·2
Professional and Scientific Services	68·5
Miscellaneous Services	53·9
Public Administration	40·9
All Industries Total	39·4

SOURCE: as Fig. 1.

engineer, to service the electric generator before hydro-electric power came to the Islands. Such unusual courses for young women are still discouraged – Ann, who had just completed a four-year training in mechanical engineering did so in spite of 'careers guidance' at an earlier stage: 'The careers lady at school only offered me teaching or nursing!'

Once in, what then?

For all its difficulty, gaining entry to a training scheme may be the easiest thing a girl has to face. Breaking into a traditional male stronghold carries with it certain obvious drawbacks and penalties – the woman pioneer is heavily outnumbered by the men already in possession. Their responses will be various, and impossible to predict, but one thing is certain – they will be totally unused to dealing with women, either on an institutional or a personal basis. Rita and her friend at Chatham Docks successfully broached a previously exclusive masculine preserve when they applied to become slingers as soon as the Sex Discrimination Act was passed. Both now successfully run teams which secure crates with cables for the cranes to shift the cargo. But neither has persuaded the authorities to issue the regulation garments in anything other than man-size: 'The overalls and boots are made for men, and they just don't fit us!' On a more personal level, Sandra ran into trouble after coffee-time on her first day when she went to work as the only female trainee brewer in a factory of one hundred and fifty men. The nineteenth-century 'brew-house' was without sanitary facilities, and the custom had been for the lads to take a stroll along the canal bank, where there was not even a bush in sight by way of cover. Rigorous self-control and a lunch-time visit to the neighbouring pub solved this difficulty – but Sandra afterwards discovered that her 'mates' had been making a book on her possible reactions when she learned of the situation!

I suppose you think that's funny

Sandra thought herself lucky that her work-mates' response to her was one of humour and curiosity. Sue became the first woman coastguard in April 1979 by dint of her experience and qualifications as a radar plotter, and ground-to-air control in the Fleet Air Arm. But even after a career in the WRNS, Sue warns that a women who takes on 'a man's job' has to be emotionally tough, and prepare herself for hostility. Jenny did not have Sue's background and maturity when, on the basis of outstanding O-level results, she was accepted as the only girl on an electrical engineering training course. She was therefore quite unable to understand or to cope with her workmates' aggression, which intensified as she both persevered in the face of their enmity, and achieved consistently good results in her work. Harassment escalated from exclusion and isolation to verbal abuse, and finally to attacks upon her work itself – these culminated when an electrical system which she had spent months in making was destroyed immediately before a key assessment of the students' progress. Jenny's repeated appeals for help to her supervisor were brushed aside on the grounds that 'the lads were only playing about – she had to learn to cope'. Undermined and demoralized, Jenny left. Her defection was held to demonstrate the unsuitability of appointing a girl to the training scheme in the first place. Jenny has subsequently been unable to find a post of any kind in this field, and had been on Social Security ever since.

The higher, the fewer

It is all too often hard and painful for women to get one foot on the ladder of opportunity – and things do not get any easier the higher they climb. For a start, things get even lonelier – although nearly half the workforce now is composed of women, only 12½% of managers are female, while for senior or general managers, the figure for women drops to 8%. Even on this higher level, the distribution of women in management reflects the distribution of women through the workforce in general, with women largely represented in and confined to specified and traditional female roles:

Women as percentage of managers in different occupations in Great Britain:

Occupation	% Managers women
Farmers, foresters, fishermen	10
Miners and quarrymen	0
Gas, coke and chemical makers	0
Glass and ceramic makers	0
Furnace, foundry and rolling mill workers	0
Electrical and engineering workers	2
Engineering and allied trade workers	2
Woodworkers	2
Leatherworkers	3
Textile workers	12
Clothing workers	13
Food, drink, and tobacco workers	3
Paper and printing workers	8
Makers of other products	15
Construction workers	1
Painters and decorators	2
Drivers of stationary engines, cranes, etc.	0
Transport and communication workers	1
Warehousemen, storekeepers, packers and bottlers	2
Clerical workers	15
Sales workers	26
Service, sport and recreational workers[1]	47
Administrators and managers[2]	9
Professional, technical workers, and artists[3]	37

1. Includes publicans, stewards, housekeepers, matrons, proprietors and managers of guest houses and hotels, restaurants, cooks, hairdressers, beauticians, manicurists, launderers and dry cleaners.
2. Administrators and managers include personnel managers, of whom 31% in the sample were women.
3. Includes nurses, primary and secondary schoolteachers, social workers.
SOURCE: OPCS, Census 1971, Great Britain, Economic Activity *Part II, Table 8.*

Once again the subtle discriminatory pattern emerges of women bunched together in the service roles and industries – clerking, selling, cleaning, nursing and teaching. Recent research from a Manpower Research Group at the University of Warwick underlines this picture of women's management opportunities as occurring almost entirely in office, retail or catering work (see opposite).

Service with a smile

This funnelling of women with management ability into the service areas of employment has a series of effects. It preserves the division of the labour market into 'men's work' and 'women's work', and as a result holds down both salary and status. Glenda works as the Bar Manageress at a plush country hotel outside Stratford, where she has a staff of thirty people running three bars at lunchtime, evening, and throughout the day for residents. Her salary, however, is less than two-thirds that of the Maitre d'Hotel who, despite his gradiose title, is in effect the manager of the restaurant which has ten waitresses, and opens only at night. And as a man, he is spared Glenda's occupational hazards, which routinely range from a boozy businessman pushing his room-key across the bar at her all night, to outright grabbing and groping from over-confident Lotharios. 'If it weren't for the foot of copper between me and them', she says, 'there'd be murder done here – every night!'

The ambitious beginner

Glenda is at least able to pass on her experience of negotiating these pitfalls to the up-and-coming young women whom she is training for a career in hotel management. Others have no model, no support and no assistance. Isla is one of the only women journeymen compositors working in the jealously-guarded print industry. She has completed her four-year apprenticeship, when she was honoured with the traditional 'banging-out' ceremony, and is now studying for her

Managers by Managerial Classification and Sex, and for Females by Part-time or Full-time Status (%)

	General	Production	Site	Transport	Warehousing	Office	Retail	Catering	Farm	Officers and Others	Total %	Total No.
Male	95	99	99	96	97	85	60	58	94	80	82	2,149
Female full-time	3	1	1	3	3	13	34	37	5	13	16	413
Female part-time	2	–	1	1	–	2	5	5	2	7	3	74

SOURCE: National Training Survey tapes, Manager's subset. Table taken from 'British Managers: A Study of their Education, Training, Mobility and Earnings', Geoffrey Crockford and Peter Elias, Manpower Research Group Discussion Paper no. 13, May 1981, University of Warwick.

21

HNC, which she hopes will lead eventually to progress within the industry and a job in management. Isla thinks that it is girls' narrow ambitions, rather than masculine prejudice, that account for so few females training for these highly-skilled and very well-paid jobs in printing – 'Women's expectations, and those of their families, are set too low', she says. Like Isla, Pennie is a pioneer in a man's world, as one of the first women station masters on British Rail's Southern Region. She too is ambitious to further her career: 'There are lots of opportunities for me to progress up the BR ladder, and I'd like eventually to specialize in, say, marketing or industrial relations.' But both these women, to succeed, will have to go it alone. As they were the first women in their field, so they will be the solitary pace-setters all along the line.

The loneliness of the long-distance woman

The woman would-be manager, going it alone, is by definition an outsider trying to get in, with all the problems that that entails. She has, single-handed, to take on and break down discriminatory attitudes and practices which are enshrined in established custom whose origin is often lost in the mists of time, but treasured the more keenly for all that. Geraldine was the first woman in the ring of the London Metal Exchange in 1977, dealing in lead, silver, zinc and other metals. Despite previous experience of dealing, she reported that 'it was very difficult to get the Committee of the London Metal Exchange to let me trade. When they eventually consented, there was a lot of opposition from the men.' Although her male colleagues, in Geraldine's view, 'got used to it in time', she remains, like all pioneering or exceptional women, highly visible.

The problem of visibility

The trend-setting or achieving woman inevitably

receives a great deal of attention, and far more than would be given to a man in her position. This leads not only to a loss of privacy, but to an increase in stress and strain in addition to doing the job – 'It's like living in a goldfish bowl', 'You feel you are always on display', are typical comments on this from women who have undergone it. The new man is allowed to settle down and work his way in, but the new woman continues to be subjected to a microscopic scrutiny, and to a period of proving herself which extends beyond her to her whole sex. Linda worked strenuously in the lower management echelons of a manufacturing firm for five years without any promotion or increase in salary, while men who were appointed long after she had been outstripped her time and again. 'I never got past being treated as a probationer,' she complained bitterly. 'It was always, "Let's see what you make of this one". And whatever I did, it was "You bloody women are all the same".'

The token woman

The solitary woman in the management arena is vulnerable in several ways. She is judged more harshly than male colleagues, a factor that most women seem to accept stoically as a fact of life: 'You have to be twice as good as a man, and work twice as hard, to get anywhere', was the most common observation made by women workers during interview. Mistakes are highlighted, passed around and enjoyed among male colleagues, where not positively engineered – one girl trainee manager was sent to Scotland on a wild-goose-chase to the Jock Strap Manufacturing Company, and became so alienated by the non-stop persecution of the ensuing hilarity and ribaldry that she left the firm. Conversely, any successes receive a good deal of attention but are usually ascribed not to merit, but to favouritism, 'tokenism', or senior management's generous desire to encourage the newcomer.

Jenny K, who presides over the careers of more than

5,000 workers (the majority of them women) as the General Secretary of the National Association of Probation Officers, summed the situation up sadly, as follows: 'Women have to work on the principal that no one thinks they can do the job – they have to work very hard to establish themselves initially, whatever profession it is.'

Women are, however, advised against placing too much faith in the power of hard work to get them on. Avis was placed in charge of a new promotion to launch water-beds in this country, and exerted herself so effectively that within a year she had built up a sales network covering all the major outlets, while the company's order books were filled for the next eighteen months. She was then made redundant, as her services were no longer needed – she had, in effect, worked herself out of a job, while four men whom she had hired and trained were kept on. What angered her most, however, was the retrospective denial of her work. 'The worst work experience is non-recognition,' she insists. 'Their promotions are still my promotions, their ideas are my ideas, they are still using all my sales material. But it's as if I never existed.'

And higher still

Despite her own mauling in the business jungle, Avis was still prepared to describe both selling and catering management, her two main areas of work experience, as 'equal opportunity occupations'. Theoretically at least, personal success need not be determined by sex. The same cannot be said of the professions, where gross discrimination is entrenched and institutionalized, and the admission of women is proceeding at such a snail-slow pace that it will be another century before this is fully achieved. Consider, as an example, the situation in the legal profession in the key decade between 1967 and 1977:

24

Solicitors holding practising certificates:

Year	No. of Male Solicitors	%	No. of Female Solicitors	%	Total no. of Practising Solicitors
1967	22,168	97·3	619	2·7	22,787
1968	22,893	97·1	681	2·9	23,574
1969	23,664	97·0	743	3·0	24,407
1970	24,563	96·8	803	3·2	25,366
1971	25,421	96·5	906	3·5	26,327
1972	26,194	95·7	1,185	4·3	27,379
1973	27,442	95·5	1,299	4·5	28,741
1974	28,287	94·8	1,563	5·2	29,850
1975	29,471	94·3	1,779	5·7	31,250
1976	30,680	93·5	2,132	6·5	32,812

The same absurdly slow progression towards equality may be detected in the other arm of this ancient, traditional and lucrative profession:

Barristers in practice 1955-1978:

Year	No. of Male Barristers	%	No. of Female Barristers	%	Total no. of Practising Barristers
1970	2,437	94·3	147	5·7	2,584
1971	2,547	93·8	167	6·2	2,714
1972	2,723	93·3	196	6·7	2,919
1973	2,898	92·4	239	7·6	3,137
1974	3,125	92·6	252	7·4	3,377
1975	3,388	92·9	258	7·1	3,646
1976	3,568	91·9	313	8·1	3,881
1977	3,740	91·8	336	8·2	4,076

SOURCE: *Women in the Legal Services (EOC, 1978), table 2, and information supplied by the Senate of the Inns of Court and Bar.*

Some advances have obviously been made in this over-manned profession, where in 1967 only 2% of women were solicitors, although solicitors' activities touch the lives of women at so many different points. But an increase of 4% to 6·5% in a decade can hardly be seen as satisfactory progress. Women appear to be faring better at the Bar, with a 2% increase of membership over the solicitors' branch of the profession. But a proportionate share of 8% remains frankly derisory as a representation of women – and as women made up 3·2% of Barristers in 1955, it has taken *over twenty years* to achieve this miserable 5% increase in membership!

Discrimination in the legal profession against women is felt from the judges, who in 1982 believe that a female hitch-hiker is 'asking for' rape, down through the lecturers in law schools who still think that the highest compliment payable to a promising female student is that she 'has a mind like a man's'.

It spills over even into the ancillary services – Anita, Lesley and Joan are, most unusually, employed as barristers' clerks in a set of London chambers, but are at a loss as to how they penetrated this traditional male bastion – chambers still fill vacancies with 'someone's nephew, or the son of a friend', they say, in preference to women.

Even at the secretarial level, several young women every year are discouraged, in a thoroughly legal and civilized fashion, from proceeding any further in a solicitors' or barristers' office because they have expressed a continued preference for coming to work in trousers, rather than a skirt. Even with this minimal involvement of women, the law is still doing better than accountancy. In 1980, only 4% of all chartered accountants in this country were women. Recent research has highlighted the patchy and inadequate presence of women in all fields where professional regulations and requirements can be invoked to keep them out:

And as women are so sparsely represented in the professions in the first place, they are even more thin on the ground nearer the top – even in the so-called 'women's professions'. Men vastly outnumber women as Heads of Social Service Departments, schools and

Female membership of selected professional Institutes and Associations, 1980:

Professional Institute or Association	*Total no. of members*	*No. of female members*	*% women*
Hotel Catering/ Institutional Management	20,963	9,398	44·8
Institute of Personnel Management	22,790	6,830	30·0
British Medical Association	44,041	12,094	21·5
Institute of Health Service Administrators	3,062	439	14·3
Institute of Bankers	107,588	14,000	13·0
The Law Society	49,806	5,833	11·8
The Chartered Insurance Institute	54,887	5,302	9·7
The Royal Town Planning Institute	6,921	490	7·1
The Rating and Valuation Association	5,479	325	5·9
Association of Certified Accountants	23,000	1,164	5·0
Institute of Chartered Accountants	71,926	3,011	4·2
Institute of Marketing	21,766	528	2·4
Institution of Chemical Engineers	12,527	219	1·7
British Institute of Management	64,794	1,018	1·5
Royal Institution of Chartered Surveyors	42,228	468	1·1
Institution of Works Managers	21,985	200	0·9
Institute of Building	28,000	120	0·4
Institute of Mechanical Engineers	74,218	246	0·3
Institution of Production Engineers	18,965	44	0·2

SOURCE: figures supplied by the individual institutes of membership numbers as at January 1981.

colleges, while in 1974 women formed only 8% of the Bar Council, 1% of the Institute of Directors, and 12% of Medical Consultants. Individual women may break through these barriers – Beryl was elected to the Council of the Institute of Quantity Surveyors in 1976, and is now Chairman of their Practice Advisory Panel. Speaking from the basis of her own deservedly successful career, Beryl states that 'the prospects of a woman in surveying are as good as in any other profession'. But her belief is flatly contradicted by the figures above from the institutes themselves.

Equal opportunities?

Under the Equal Pay Act of 1970, a woman was given the right to equal pay with a man for a job involving work of 'the same or broadly similar nature', or for a job that had been rated as the equivalent of a man's under a job evaluation scheme. This Act has simply failed to have its intended effect. The fourth report of the Equal Opportunities Commission covering 1979 showed that after an initial increase in women's wages, differentials between male and female earnings have actually started to *widen* again. Between 1970 and 1975, the average gross hourly earnings of women increased from 63·1% to 72·1% of men's. By April 1977, this was 73·6%. But by 1980 women were earning on average only 72% as much as men.

This differential between male and female earnings goes right down the line to the bottom – ten in every hundred women full-time workers earned less than £50 a week, while not one in a hundred men was so low paid.

So this is equal pay

This widening gap between male and female earnings shows the inadequacy of the Equal Pay Act. It has, in brief, had a 'once and for all effect' – it led to an initial improvement in women's wages, which in itself produced a startlingly sudden backlash as men recovered from it

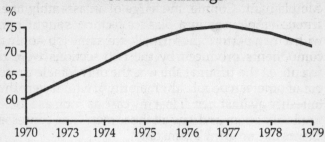

Women's earnings as a proportion of men's earnings

The 1980 figures confirm this trend:

Average weekly earnings of full-time workers

	Manual	Non-manual
Men	£111	£141
Women	68	83

SOURCE: *Women's Right To Work*
National Joint Committee of Working Women's Organisations, Table III.

and found ways to preserve their financial supremacy. The Act is now powerless to advance the cause of women's wage equality – and the fact that it cannot even protect women from being systematically outstripped in the wages market has led to a growing disgust and disillusion. The Equal Opportunities Commission has criticized the operation of the Equal Pay Act:

> *which insists on the existence of definite male comparison, does not allow comparison of equal value in the absence of job evaluation schemes*
> *does not provide for women segregated in jobs traditionally performed by women and where there are no men engaged on like work and does not recognise the concept of indirect discrimination.*

The Equal Pay Act is in fact full of weaknesses and loopholes. It is the only piece of employment legislation which puts the burden of proof upon the applicant and not upon the employer – this places the employer (almost invariably male) at an advantage over the female complainant. Connie, in charge of an assembly line of female employees in a plastics factory, sought parity with a man performing virtually the same job – only the components produced by the two sections were different. At the tribunal she was the only female present out of nineteen people, the majority of whom were there to testify against her. 'I lost my case as soon as I looked round the room and saw all those men', she confessed. 'It was like an army against me.'

'The same or broadly similar'

Connie's case highlights the Act's greatest single weakness – it requires a *direct* comparison of a man working in an equivalent job for equal pay to be obtained, and can thus only cope with unproblematic cases. Megan, literally working side-by-side with a male supervisor in a factory, he in charge of 'the lads' and she 'the girls' and both doing the same work, had little difficulty with her case at the Industrial Tribunal (although she still had to take her case to adjudication before the management would even concede that she had a point).

But such straightforward examples are rare – and before the Act even became law, ingenious managements were at work regrading and reclassifying occupations to evade the effects of the legislation. Often a simple change of title would suffice – many a lucky man found to his surprise that he had been dignified with a fancy handle to distinguish his work from that of a female colleague, and so justify the continuance of the wage differential between them. In addition, the Equal Pay Act totally fails to take account of the simple fact that 78% of all women workers are employed in the three service industries:

professional and scientific   *(Teachers and typists, eg)*
distributive trades   *(shop assistants, etc)*
personal services   *(hairdressing, catering)*

Not one of these industries employs more than 10% of men. How then in shops, clerical work, the catering trade, nursing and light industry can the direct male equivalent be found? The Act has no machinery to recognize the discrimination *by segregation* of women into these ghettoes, nor to raise the level of their wages or status – in 1981 the average catering employee earned less than £1·50 per hour, gross.

And who enacts the Act?

Guess who! All these shortcomings and weaknesses of the legislation are hardly improved by the hamfisted and myopic handling which it has received from the men entrusted with its operations. Difficulties which might have been overcome by committed and imaginative handling have been exacerbated by the fact that the Act is administered by a male-dominated and unashamedly sexist legal profession. The legalistic tribunal format, with its excessive weighting of males, has successfully deterred many potential applicants, and individual tribunals have concurred in interpreting the 'broadly similar' clause in such a narrow way as to be actively discriminatory.

In structure and in administration, the whole system is loaded against the women who need it most – of the 72 chairs on the Industrial Tribunals, *only two* are filled by women. Small wonder then that women are making their disgust with this spurious piece of supposed equality legislation felt. The number of applications under the Equal Pay Act is falling drastically each year – from 1742 in 1976, to less than 400 in 1978. Since *under* 5% of all equal pay claims have been upheld by Industrial Tribunals, women are showing their recognition of the declaration by the Equal Opportunities Commission that however much work the Equal Pay Act provides for men, it fails utterly to provide for the women for whom it was supposedly designed. Sylvia Greenwood, a factory convenor has established herself in the North as an energetic campaigner for women's

31

rights, and is one of the few women who are connected with an Industrial Tribunal. But as she reports, 'In the four years I've been on, we've never yet had an equal pay case, and there's only been one maternity leave case in the whole of Sheffield.'

The longest journey

Recent legislation like the Equal Pay Act, and the equally toothless Sex Discrimination Act of 1975 have tended to suggest that women's efforts to obtain their work rights are a modern phenomenon. Kath's experience of this struggle goes back to 1934, when the Managing Director of the motor car factory where she worked decided to introduce a conveyor system on the lines where women worked as car seat machinists. As the women would no longer have to fetch the work, he proposed to cut their rates. The women, banding together, achieved such solidarity of opposition that they not only resisted this move, but forced an increase in their low rate of pay. This local but crucial triumph launched Kath upon a career in Trade Unionism for which she has just been honoured by a gold medal from the TGWU and the TUC. She looks back over many years of the equal pay battle:

> *The first equal pay struggle I was involved in started around 1949. I was invited to a meeting with other women from many different work places, teachers, local government workers. In fact, I was the only industrial worker there. I was secretary of the campaign for two years, but eventually it fizzled out for lack of support.*

The battle sites

With the passage of time, it is becoming more and more clear that women are not simply contending with the lack of support and a general inertia. The active and positive aspects of oppression and repression are emerging, as women call them into question and direct the searchlight of critical scrutiny upon habits and practices which were previously taken for granted. Sometimes these are simply the stubborn attachment of habit to outworn conventions, the inability to rethink old stereotypes.

Beginning with a friend and £1000, Barbara built up a fast-food chain which now sells over a million take-away meals a year. But although she is the director of a business with a half-a-million pound annual turnover, men still insist on the phone that she should put them through to the boss: 'People often assume that I'm the secretary because I'm a woman. I now understand why so many successful businesswomen are described as aggressive: it's the result of constantly meeting this kind of attitude.'

Sometimes women suffer this kind of repressive pigeon-holing through misplaced and patronizing paternalism. Margaret qualified as a forensic scientist, but it was seven years before she was allowed to follow her cases through to completion by giving evidence in court. It only took a year for the male graduates to get into court, but women were supposed to break down, weep, or faint under questioning.

Attitudes run deep . . .

and they are fed by subterranean springs. Some of the manifestations of masculine dominance can be traced to the operations of the capitalist patriarchy which so disadvantages women. It will obviously be a long task to undermine and overthrow the many processes of discrimination against women which for hundreds of years have not only been legal, but actively encouraged by Church and State in the name of the sanctity of womanhood, family life, or some such convenient and restrictive notion. Undoubtedly, though, some of the springs of the desire to dominate and degrade women are to be found deep in the morasses of the male psyche – a survey of the range of pornography makes this quite clear. 'Soft porn' uses females as decorative objects in a

33

leisure setting – the lovely creature languidly caressing her nipples or displaying her rump while draped across a sofa in a luxury flat is ostensibly awaiting a man's return from work, where her unproblematic availability rewards his labours. The fatuous title of the playboy's 'playmate' reveals the off-duty fantasy world which this pornography inhabits.

The hard core

Specialist pornography, however, draws on different obsessions and associations, and frequently locates the site of the fantasy sex in the work place. In both written and pictorial pornography, attention is given to making the setting as realistic as possible. Scenarios vary – in one large shop, all the female sales assistants are in fact the objects on sale. A male 'purchaser' moves among them, while a male floorwalker requires the girls to display their wares for the customer's benefit and he freely handles and assesses the 'goods'. Another places the girls as captives in a factory setting, each one chained to her machine half-naked, and either fondled approvingly by the supervising man if she is producing her quota, or released for disciplining and punishment in the sight of all the other girls if she is failing. Yet another employs a quasi-technical background, in which the 'scientist' first hypnotises his female assistant, binds her, and then proceeds to burn her clothes off piece by piece with his 'laser'. The culmination of this high-technology strip-tease occurs when the scientist finally uses the laser to penetrate the girl, and she writhes in agony or ecstasy. One thing unites these productions – no matter how laughable or contrived the 'storyline', the pornographers always take care to make the situation as recognizable as any shop, factory or engineering works in real life.

Take a letter, Miss Jones

One of the commonest settings for work-place

pornography is the office. The frequency of its appearance as a setting indicates its importance for the consumers of porn. In solid office scenes with desks, chairs, typewriters, even bulging in-trays, girls are shown studiously taking dictation in owlish glasses and severe hairstyles, quite unconscious that their neat white blouse is completely open down the front, and the boss is absently playing with their breasts. Office girls cannot open a filing cabinet without revealing that they have nothing on under their respectable grey skirts – nor can they go shopping in their lunch-hour without feeling compelled to model the see-through bra, suspender belt and black stockings for the boss in the afternoon.

Office pornography also often includes discipline or punishment elements. The penalty for getting a letter wrong is having to bend over the boss's desk (the offending typist is seen shivering as she contemplates the choice she is given, between six of the best on her bare bottom, or twice the number if she insists on remaining clothed). Other peccadilloes are punished on an ascending scale of severity, and the most serious infractions merit a lengthy, detailed and ritual stripping and spanking by the boss in the presence of all the senior management.

To make a dream come true

This puerile and impoverished invention could be dismissed as harmless if the 'office encounter' remained in the realm of fantasy. Many men, however, are compelled to try to enact some of these scenarios for themselves. Patricia, who runs what she describes as a 'Sexual Services Salon' in Birmingham reports that her office setting is easily the most popular of all her speciality rooms, easily outstripping her schoolroom and medieval torture chamber. Even in this controlled situation, the office fantasy is far from harmless. Magda, one of Patricia's 'business girls', described the behaviour of one office sex punter:

35

I sat at the desk, started taking dictation, and he started messing me around. When he got going on the business he wanted, he suddenly put his hand on my neck and started to squeeze, not hard, but hard enough to make me panic. I told him to stop it, he just kept squeezing harder. I tried to get him off, but he'd got me across the desk, it was impossible. By this time I was choking violently and going dizzy. Just as I was about to black out he suddenly let me go, and said, 'That'll teach you to answer the phone politely to our clients.' I ask you! What do you make of that?

In real life . . .

most secretaries do not end up strangled or choked to death. But few office workers who are women get through their working lives without some experience of the masculine domination of their world, and a reminder of their subjection as women within it, in the form of sexual harassment. Whether this is expressed as jokes, innuendoes, gross personal obscene remarks, or physical advances, it is often so totally the norm that protests are received with bewilderment and incomprehension. For Andrea, it began at the interview, where her putative boss kept asking, 'Are you a fun girl? A party girl? Do you know how to give a man a good time?' Avis met it head on when the group of men she joined on her first day all rose to their feet and assaulted her with piercing wolf-whistles, which they kept up despite all her attempts to talk to them. Heather gave in her notice and sought another job when her boss made it plain that her continued refusal to accompany him on business trips as his 'assistant' would block her promotion in the firm – Jane, in a very similar situation, gave in through the fear of losing her job, but was shortly afterwards dispensed with during a 'rationalisation programme' anyway. From the other side of the desk, a London businessman running a very busy office complained, 'I don't know why we can't keep girls. We run a happy office, lots of jokes, lots of sex jokes, lots of fun – what's wrong with them?'

What's wrong with them . . .

is that they've put up with all this for far too long. The chains of social, cultural and economic subordination are hard to recognize, and harder still to strike off. But discrimination against women can no longer be passed off as a reflection of 'the nature of things', 'the way things are'. The way things are is the way men have arranged them to be, and the time has come for women to begin on the task of dismantling some of these assumptions and structures which hamper them so much. Work is a critical site of women's struggle for independence and self-expression, since it is the nexus where personal and social conjoin. This book provides the background information on the danger from men at work, and the ammunition for women to do something about it. Starting from a lower base position than working men, women have much farther to go, and much more to gain by self-assertion and activity. So what are you waiting for?

2

Into the Jungle

Women constitute half *the world's population,*
perform nearly two-thirds *of its work hours,*
receive one tenth *of the world's income and own*
less than one hundredth *of the world's property*
— United Nations Report, 1980.

The first job of your working life is to wise up on the
work jungle *as it is for women*. Almost everything that is
written or said about work comes from a masculine
standpoint, and has little or no relevance to the experiences of our sex. Here it is, then, straight from the
shoulder — when you enter the world of work you will
encounter

blatant discrimination
structured inequality
sexual harassment
rank exploitation

   plus

**entrenched resistance to changing any of it*.

'Change is a very difficult matter', explained a leading
Midlands industrialist who declined to be named, 'you
can hurt people's feelings. My impression is that most
people are happy as they are.' Roger, a TGWU official,
was franker: 'What, change things to benefit women,
you mean? You've got to be joking! My men are interes-

ted in benefiting themselves, they like women the way they are. There are worse things in life for you girls than working under men, you know.'

Working under men . . .

is one of the first realities of your work scene. Your immediate supervisor or superior may be female, but the one who bosses her at the end of the day will be a man. You're most likely to be appointed by men, promoted or disciplined by men according to their view of your work, rewarded or sacked by men. Iris (38) is a well-qualified data processor in the regional head-quarters of a multi-national car corporation. 'They've never had a woman up top here', she commented. 'And they never will. They say it's bad for morale.' Whose?

A woman's place . . .

is under a man – at least so far as men are concerned. Yet it is definitely in the work force, and no longer simply in the home. Statistics from all round the world demonstrate the steady rise of female participation in the labour market. In the last seventy years, the number of working women in this country has *doubled*:

Numbers of working women

1911	–	5,424,000
1921	–	5,701,000
1931	–	6,265,000
1951	–	7,419,000
1961	–	8,407,000
1971	–	8,708,000
1975	–	9,506,000
1977	–	9,815,000
1979	–	10,054,000

SOURCE: Reid and Wormald (1982)

This picture holds good throughout the rest of Europe. EEC reports of 1975, 1979, 1980 and 1982 draw attention to the rapidly increasing numbers of women working not only in the Commission itself, but in the Community as a whole. Regional variations between Germany and France, for instance, and the existence of employment black spots for women like Italy and Ireland, do nothing to affect this basic trend, which is affecting women of all ages and educational backgrounds. Nicole Guilbert, a full-time home-maker of Arras, France, with three children of her own, regularly cares for Guillaume and Matthieu while their mothers work. 'Everything's changing for women', she says. 'They all seem to work these days. I think I'm a dying breed.'

The American experience

dramatically confirms the importance of women's contribution to the national work force:

US Labour Force Participation Rates, by Sex, 1947-78

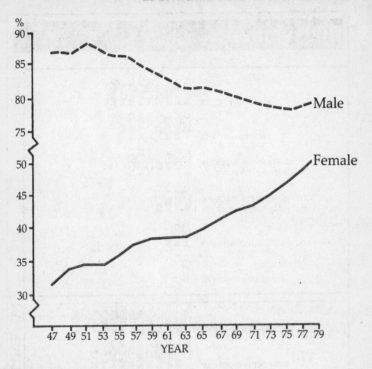

SOURCE: *US Dept. of Labor,*
Employment and Training Report of the Preside

Translated, these figures and graphs mean *millions* of women all round the world; literally millions of women 'hold up half the sky', as the Chinese proverb expresses it, and do a day's job of work as well. You don't have to be John Maynard Keynes to grasp what this means to the economy as a whole – they can't do without us.

But what do they do with us? . . .

First, they shunt us into the traditional female jobs which all too often means the jobs that they are not

41

prepared to do themselves. Consider this picture of the *distribution* of women in the work force:

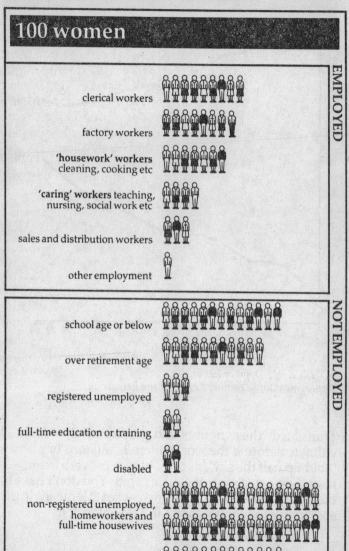

100 women

EMPLOYED

clerical workers

factory workers

'housework' workers cleaning, cooking etc

'caring' workers teaching, nursing, social work etc

sales and distribution workers

other employment

NOT EMPLOYED

school age or below

over retirement age

registered unemployed

full-time education or training

disabled

non-registered unemployed, homeworkers and full-time housewives

SOURCE: Huws (1982)

This means that for every hundred of us, the vast majority will end up doing clerical or factory work, the 'caring' work of society in its hospitals and schools, or worst of all, cooking for and cleaning up after the army of *male* workers – no matter what hopes and ambitions girls start out with. Ivy works as a night cleaner in a large office block in Birmingham. '*Want* to do this?' she snorted, 'Who'd want to do *this*? Fat choice I got, didn't I?' Marianne Herzog completed an apprenticeship as a bookseller in Germany. When she wanted a job, there were long waiting lists for such posts. As she grimly outlined her situation: 'I had to earn money immediately.

'The second possibility was to take unskilled work, and I wanted to try a factory. I did not want to be an unskilled child-minder, an unskilled salesgirl in a department store or an unskilled orderly in a hospital. I didn't want to be a waitress or a cleaner. There just isn't much else.'

There isn't much of anything for women at the bottom of the heap, as Marianne soon discovered even in Munich, capital of south-west Germany: 'There are no vacancies for women advertised in the papers. I go to the Labour Exchange, look at the list for industrial women workers and find just three vacancies.'

It is a tribute to the buoyant economy of the DDR that even three of these jobs were available. Many British women are denied even this limited option.

*

'Choice is a luxury. Most men haven't got it. What are you bleating about? It isn't a thing women can expect – not in work, not anywhere' – Maurice (36), Midlands businessman and Rotarian.

*

Describing the *status quo* as it exists in the main does not mean that you have to take the situation in the traditional female way, lying down. Be determined to develop your awareness of the limitation on women's options, and build up your knowledge of where change has to come.

Think big

Recognize first of all that this is a global situation, and not something that is just happening to you. An EEC survey of 1975 asked men and women of all the countries of the Community if they thought that women were worse off than men. Interestingly, even countries with the lowest level of economic development and a catholic tradition combining to limit perception of women's disadvantages agree that women are worse off than men in these ways:

The main areas of agreed discrimination against women, in order of importance, country by country

France		Germany	
1. Wages	77%	1. Wages	75%
2. Opportunities	64%	2. Promotion	64%
3. Promotion	62%	3. Opportunities	52%
4. Work conditions	59%	4. Job security	50%
5. Job security	52%	5. Work conditions	43%
6. Training	38%	6. Training	30%
7. Study	·2%	7. Study	12%

Ireland		Denmark	
1. Wages	78%	1. Promotion	53%
2. Promotion	67%	2. Wages	52%
3. Job security	48%	3. Opportunities	38%
4. Opportunities	45%	4. Work conditions	35%
5. Work conditions	24%	5. Job security	34%
6. Training	19%	6. Training	23%
7. Study	11%	7. Study	14%

44

Belgium		Italy	
1. Wages	51%	1. Wages	41%
2. Promotion	44%	2. Job security	37%
3. Job security	40%	3. Opportunities	37%
4. Opportunities	38%	4. Work conditions	36%
5. Work conditions	33%	5. Promotion	34%
6. Training	18%	6. Training	25%
7. Study	12%	7. Study	11%

Netherlands		United Kingdom	
1. Promotion	49%	1. Promotion	49%
2. Wages	45%	2. Wages	48%
3. Job security	36%	3. Opportunities	38%
4. Opportunities	34%	4. Job security	38%
5. Work conditions	27%	5. Training	16%
6. Training	17%	6. Work conditions	15%
7. Study	10%	7. Study	10%

Luxembourg	
1. Wages	40%
2. Job security	35%
3. Promotion	34%
4. Work conditions	24%
5. Opportunities	24%
7. Training	20%
7. Study	12%

SOURCE: *European Men and Women, official report of EEC survey to mark International Women's Year, 1975. Items underlined are those most often referred to throughout the Community as a whole.*

There are some fascinating national variations here – agreement about discrimination against women at work in wages and job prospects is highest both in the two *strongest* countries of the European Community, *and* the smallest and weakest. Great Britain has, comparatively, a lower level of *awareness* of women's disadvantages in their work lives – but *not* a lower level of difficulty for its working women. As the report warned:

Statistical evidence . . . amply demonstrates *that discrimination against women exists in this country on a wide scale at all levels of employment.*

Wherever you are, whatever your job or job ambition –
this means *you*.

Where does it come from?

Discriminatory and oppressive behaviour has a long
and ignoble history in all communities. But discrimination on the grounds of sex is the primal act of discrimination from which all others derive the basic technique of
classification which then works to the detriment of the
less powerful group. Our 'advanced' society has built on
this by employing a mish-mash of pseudo-physiology,
misplaced paternalism and brutal self-interest to justify
and reinforce male supremacy. Men have erected a
series of barriers against women's full participation in
the world of work, of differing degrees of ludicrousness.
Women were originally excluded from Medical School
on the grounds that their frailty meant that they would
be distressed

> *if they had to work alongside and consort with
> male students*

> *if they had to dissect or even see an 'unclothed'
> male body*

Judith is a final-year medical student at Birmingham
University who agreed that these aspects remain among
the hazardous and disagreeable aspects of the job: 'Well
yes, male med. students are a highly specialized species
of nasty beastie. They're fixated on sex, for one thing –
that's why they want to become doctors in the first
place. As to the "unclothed male body", they spend
enough time and energy trying to get you to look at
theirs! Ask any of the nurses. That's all a joke now, but
you're still having to fight it as a woman. Now, it's not
the weakness of your nerves but the strength of your
brain that's called in question – I had to get three A's at
A-level to be sure of getting in.'

The medical profession is renowned for its conserv-

MEDICAL OPINION
BY BETTY PENSON WARD

Newspaper Columnist, Twin Falls, Idaho

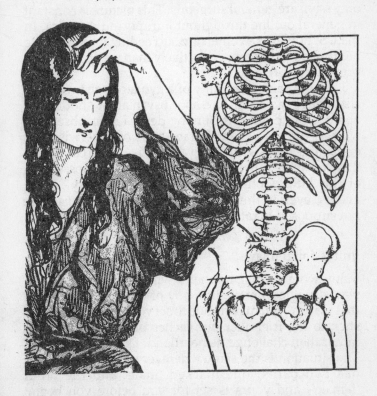

As a longtime newspaperwoman in our capital city, I was invited to be a Rotary Club speaker. In deference to their ultraconservatism I gave such a mild talk on the women's movement that I was almost ashamed of it. Yet the emcee, a middle-aged gynecologist, concluded the program with, "Betty, any psychiatrist would sum up that speech in two words: penis envy."

My publisher, who was in the audience, refused to let me write about it, even in my signed column, because "it would damage the doctor's professional image."

SAVVY, November 1981

ative (read 'reactionary') attitude to the recruitment and deployment of women. Although numbers of girls entering medical school has risen, women still comprise only 17% of GPs and 20% of hospital doctors. Females who reach the higher echelons and become consultants are bunched together in anaesthetics and pathology; only *seven* are general surgeons. This picture is constant in general outline throughout Europe and America. In the US, however, women are succeeding in rattling the medical dovecots more effectively than we are here (see previous page).

The admirable versatility of a gynaecologist who can also double as an on-the-spot psychiatrist should not obscure the point. As Simone de Beauvoir observed, women have no grounds (aesthetic or otherwise) for envying a penis – the envy if any is quite reasonably directed at the power and prestige which the possession of this little doohickey confers in our society. At all events, even in the capital of the US, those *without* are not supposed to rattle the composure of those *with*!

Professional image

Many women imagine that it will be an uphill-all-the-way struggle to make it in any of the professions. For that reason, you may decide to set your sights lower and stick to the friendlier outreaches of the work jungle, rather than challenge its heartland. Don't kid yourself. The situation is the same wherever you go. The jungle has two paths, one marked 'male' and the other 'female', and yours is set for you before you begin. Consider this profile of occupation in local government, an area which many girls are attracted to for a number of good reasons (see opposite).

As this shows, you don't have to set your sights high to stumble over this ever-present problem. It raises its head at every single employment level, from the highest to the most casual. The British Universities North America Club exists to foster links between students in this country and the Land of the Free. Its Hon President

Who Does What in Local Authorities

% of total employees	MANUAL		NON-MANUAL	
	Male e.g. Refuse collectors, road men, parks staff, caretakers	*Female* e.g. School meals assistants, school cleaners, home helps, domestic assistants in residential homes	*Male* e.g. Administrators, architects, solicitors, surveyors, accountants, planners	*Female* e.g. Clerks, typists, social workers, teachers, librarians

Full time female   Full time male   Part time female   Part time male

Each figure represents 1% of work force

SOURCE: Local Government Training Board Survey, 1972

is the Rt Hon Lord Harlech, PC, KCMG; its Hon Vice-President is the Rt Hon John Freeman, MBE. Do these honourable men know that letters like this one are going out in response to students' application for BUNAC work programmes?

> *Dear Caroline,*
> *It has come to my attention that you are interested in participating in the Tobacco Picking programme in Ontario this summer.*
> *The brochure will not be ready for distribution for another three weeks which is why I am taking*

*this opportunity to write to you now. Unfor-
tunately, the programme is open to males only at
the request of the tobacco farmers who are unable to
arrange accommodation for women.*

*I am sorry to disappoint you, but there is plenty
of time to apply for one of the other programmes we
operate . . .*

*Good luck with whichever programme you do
apply for. We look forward to hearing from you
soon.*
Yours sincerely,
Amy Tolmach

Good old Amy. Notice how smoothly she pulls the
familiar 'It's-not-me-it's-them' routine. With hench-
women like these, men don't need to do their own
discriminating. And 'Good luck', Caroline – as long as
you stick to the females-only path.

The exclusion of girls . . .

because they are girls was pronounced illegal in this and
other contries years ago. Yet it continues to be practised
so widely that no one notices it, in a variety of ways and
in every kind of occupation, from the highest to the
lowest. This table clearly shows the deeply divided
nature of the British work force, with male and female
territories marked out:

British Employees by Sex, 1977

	% men	% women
Mining and quarrying	96	4
Shipbuilding and marine engineering	93	7
Construction	93	7
Metal manufacture	89	11
Vehicles	89	11
Mechanical engineering	85	15

	% men	% women
Agriculture, forestry, fishing	84	16
Coal and petroleum products	84	16
Transport and communication	82	18
Gas, electricity and water	80	20
Timber, furniture, etc.	80	20
Bricks, pottery, glass, cement, etc.	75	25
Chemicals and allied industries	74	26
Metal goods not elsewhere specified	73	27
Paper, printing and publishing	70	30
Instrument engineering	67	33
Other manufacturing industries	66	34
Electrical engineering	64	36
Public administration	62	38
Food, drink and tobacco	60	40
Leather, leather goods and fur	59	41
Textiles	57	43
Insurance, banking, finance and business services	50	50
Distributive trades	47	53
Miscellaneous services	46	54
Professional and scientific services	32	68
Clothing and footwear	26	74

SOURCE: *Department of Employment Part E, Table 135 (1% sample). Crown copyright.*

The first hurdle, then, is the structured inequality of the labour market. You passed your test first time, you're really into cars and would like a job capitalizing on that interest? Have a look at 'Vehicles' above. Cars, like most machines (other than domestic appliances), are a masculine preserve. You think you'll go for banking and finance with its reassuring 50/50? The Banking and Finance Union has recently asked itself 'Is there Equality in the Finance Industry?' and come up with this reply:

> *In theory, yes – equal pay existed in our industry well before the legislation of recent years.* In practice, however, there is not equality. *The majority of female employees are in Grades 1 and 2, but there are very few in higher grades.*

To confirm this, the Union produced figures from the National Westminster Bank of the female percentage of their employees at the different grades:

Grade 1 – 73% women
Grade 2 – 75% women
Grade 3 – 53% women
Grade 4 – 22% women

Above the level of Grade 4, the percentage of female staff is acknowledged to be 'minimal'.

There's no escaping the conclusion

As a female you are being disadvantaged and deprived both in your original *choice* of job, and in your prospects *within* the job. It almost goes without saying that you'll also be deprived where it hurts most, in the money department. Men consistently make more money than women, for two simple reasons. The first is that they are paid more. The government's New Earnings Survey for 1980 showed that women's hourly earnings were *only 73·5% of those of men*. Of the low paid workers identified by the Low Pay Unit, nearly 57% were women. There must be some value in that little doohickey of theirs, when it consistently makes them *worth 25% more than women* in every type of job. Now if they could market it, I hear you say – but isn't that what they are doing?

*

> '*I do the same work as the men, but they always get more in their pay packets*' – *female road sweeper at a discussion about discrimination quoted by the NCCL.*

*

And this masculine magic is international, of course. EEC figures show similar patterns for all the European member states, except that this country is significantly the worst in the Community, as EEC statistics show:

Female Earnings as a Percentage of Male Earnings

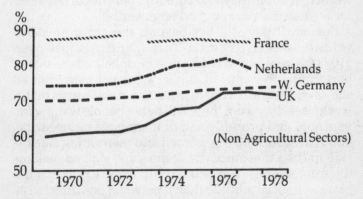

SOURCE: ILO Bulletin of Labour Statistics Q1 1979

Even with the general reluctance of the member states to implement the EEC directive on equal pay rights, the differential between male and female wages is less marked in any country than in the United Kingdom. With the greatest number of women in the work force of any EEC country, Britain is doing the worst by them – and getting away with it. A second point of interest is that after a sharp rise produced by the Equal Pay legislation of 1975, the gap between male and female earnings is *widening* again. Not only have we failed to catch them up, we're failing even to hold the ground we've won. And they're getting away with that, too. It *must* be magic!

It works in America, too

Karen Nussbaum, executive director of 9 to 5, the National Association of Working Women, has attacked the 'extremely low' wages earned by full-time women clerical workers. Their pay averages just over $11,000 a year, as compared with male clericals, who earn over $17,000. 'We feel that if we could just get equal pay within our job classification, we would be doing well', she says. In fact she is doing well for women – to date 9 to 5 has won by legal action over $3 million back pay for women in publishing and banking, plus major pay rises for women in insurance and engineering.

But equal pay still lies beyond the grasp of many women workers. Pamela Yore (28) earns just over $10,000 a year in a small Boston Hospital, where males performing the same or similar work get more. But as she says, 'You learn not to make too many waves in the workplace. If you do, there will be ten people waiting for your job, and probably half of them have more education than you. You see women and men sitting side by side in the same office doing the same job and making different salaries, and you have to tell yourself that it's more of a social attitude than a personal one directed at you. *But it is hard when you are not making as much as you could or should'*.

*

I had made my living by cadging odd jobs . . . I need not, I am afraid, describe in any detail the

54

hardness of the work, for you know perhaps women who have done it; nor the difficulty of living on the money when it was earned, for you may have tried. But what still remains with me as a worse infliction than either was the poison of fear and bitterness which those days bred in me – Virginia Woolf

*

Reaganomics is the name of the game

As in this country, the US pattern is of a rapidly rising female work force with a consistent discriminatory wage differential (see page 56).

How else do they do it?

Men start off by earning so much more than women do, across the board. The other way that they earn more is by collaring the high-earning posts that are going, and keeping women in the support roles. Simple, isn't it? Consider the structure of the supposedly 'female' teaching profession. At the primary level, women make up 77% of the teachers, but only 43% of the *head* teachers – the rest of them are clustered down at the bottom on Scale 1 (90%). And primary level is at least where women are in with a chance – in secondary education women comprise a paltry 16% of head teachers. The experience of Mrs Gates, a Merseyside teacher, may indicate why. Mrs Gates had been a Deputy Head at a Merseyside school, moving from there to take up a headship at Newcastle-upon-Tyne. When the headship of the Merseyside school fell vacant, Mrs Gates applied for it as she wished to return to the area where her husband and family were still living; they had maintained the family home in Wirral from which Mrs Gates had only departed in obedience to the imperative of the teaching profession, which decrees that promotion will only come with willingness to move around.

Number of women in the labor force, in millions

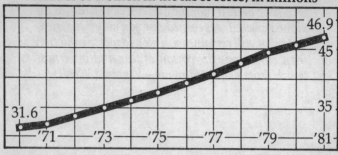

46.9
45
35
31.6

'71   '73   '75   '77   '79   '81

Earnings by occupation, 1981 weekly medians	Women's Pay	Men's Pay
Clerical workers	$ 220	328
Computer specialists	355	488
Editors, reporters	324	382
Engineers	371	547
Lawyers	407	574
Nurses	326	344
Physicians	401	495
Sales workers	190	366
Teachers (elementary)	311	379
Waiters	144	200

SOURCE: Time, July 12 1982

At the interview Mrs Gates was questioned extensively about her personal life and family plans. Was she separated from her husband? How did she get on with him? She lost the post to a man with fewer qualifications and years' experience than she had had. She took her case to an Industrial Tribunal which found in her favour clear evidence of illegal discriminatory behaviour by the interviewers, who concluded that it was wrong for her to have been harassed in this way. But the Tribunal upheld the appointment of the male candidate over Mrs Gates on the grounds that his performance had been better than hers at the interview. *Is it any wonder?*

*

I permit no women to have authority over a man —
St Paul

*

Equal pay within a profession means nothing when the male members are so consistently privileged and advanced over the females. There is no job, occupation, trade or industry in which this does not apply. The latter-day St Pauls are alive and well and flourishing throughout the world. A favoured stronghold of theirs is the British Civil Service (see page 58).

There they all are again, the trusty supportive women propping up the rest of the pyramid from the bottom – 'clerical assistants' this time. But whatever the officialese, it means women – just as surely as 'Permanent Secretary', in every one of its 41 instances, means a man. It is often argued, from examples like this, that men get more money because they are doing more difficult and more important jobs than women. That's another myth that the mighty male members like to

Women as a percentage of all home Civil Servants, by grades

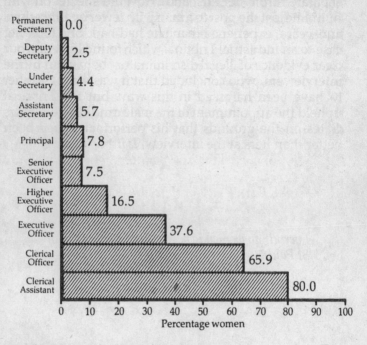

Grade	Percentage women
Permanent Secretary	0.0
Deputy Secretary	2.5
Under Secretary	4.4
Assistant Secretary	5.7
Principal	7.8
Senior Executive Officer	7.5
Higher Executive Officer	16.5
Executive Officer	37.6
Clerical Officer	65.9
Clerical Assistant	80.0

SOURCE: Civil Service Department, Civil Service Statistics 1980. Table 4

cherish as a means of protecting their advantages. But the detailed research of Canadian economist Sylva Gelber has exploded this claim. Where men and women are doing the same jobs – and even when men are doing the 'less difficult and less important "female" jobs' – *their earnings are still greater than women's.* Gelber found that the average employment earnings of male librarians exceeded those of the females by almost one fifth, while male dieticians and nutritionists have average employment earnings almost a quarter higher than those of female workers. Perhaps her most amusing finding was that male *babysitters* earned more than *twice* what female babysitters got for the same work. It's that old magic again. In Britain Megan, a Cardiff businesswoman, did not want to leave her 12-year-old son alone during the holidays, but felt that she could not 'insult' him by employing the woman who had looked after him when he was younger. So she hired a 17-year-old boy, and felt that she could not insult *him* by offering him the rate that she had paid the women. So she paid him twice as much per hour, and any insults to a tender 12-year-old and 17-year-old male ego were avoided at the cost of double the money and an insult to a mature female. How *do* they do it? More importantly, how do they get *us* to do it?

> *We were told of different pay rates for men and women . . . The reasons for the differences were hard to find. We were at a loss to understand, for example, why an experienced* female *fish-worker would receive $2·15 an hour, while an experienced* male *fish-worker received $2·83. We were even more mystified when we were told that an* inexperienced *male fish-worker was receiving $2·37 an hour* – Royal Commission on the Status of Women in Canada *(1978).*

Wake up to the practices that are holding you back

Consider all the stages and degrees of discrimination which are working together to keep these things the way they are. In such cases as the example above, where it's better to be a know-nothing male fish-worker, than a woman who's been doing it for years, the legislation exists to right the women at a stroke. It's not usually as simple as this. An EEC working party on equal treatment for male and female members of staff made the following discoveries of the subtle and interlocking ways that women are disadvantaged, at every stage of the job process:

1 Recruitment

Competition procedures are heavily weighted in favour

59

of men, with a 15-20% proportion of women candidates being the norm across all stages, a figure which the report comments 'seems extremely low'.

Advertising of posts in effect denied women equal access, for the location of adverts in given periodicals and newspapers proved on examination not to provide an adequate balance of male and female interests.

Appointment boards are normally a male preserve and as such unlikely to guarantee equality at the moment of selection.

2 Training

*No training programmes exist to enable workers carrying out boring repetitive tasks – telephonists and data punchers, for example – to change direction. As the report, *Courier du Personnel* (July 1982) admits: *Since the administration knows that by definition, these tasks are not of a kind that can constitute a lifelong activity, it would avoid certain problems if it provided training which allowed these officials a real mobility in their working lives.*

*Training given is proved useless when the employees are returned to the same work that they were doing before: It appears that secretaries who have attended advanced vocational training seminars are subsequently disappointed to find that opportunities for using this training are rare.

*Training takes place outside normal working hours, so discriminating against women who continue to bear the traditional domestic workload which must be performed outside work hours.

3 Promotion

*The imposition of age limits for posts (official or unofficial) discriminates against women who reach career stages later than men, and also reduces the number of female candidates.

*The higher the level, the more males are selecting males – women remain blocked and unconsidered at the lower career levels.

*

No insurance against discrimination

The Commercial Union insurance group is failing to carry out its own policy of equal opportunity employment, according to a confidential report commissioned by the company from The Tavistock Institute of Human Relations. The Tavistock found that the group perceived women as a short-term investment, ignoring the fact that an increasing number wanted to return to work after having children. Women were channelled into separate areas of work – personal insurance rather than property or commercial, life assurance rather than pensions. The Guardian, 21 July 1982.

*

Recognise any of this?

The EEC report clearly shows the policies and practices which continue to hold women back, even where the employing body is constitutionally committed to an Equal Opportunities programme as the Commission is. The experience of other groups tells the same story. Males are policing all the avenues of the work jungle, from the ways in, to the tracks to the top. This exists even in the companies nominally on the women's side in the fight for a fair deal at work. What happens when they're not?

They don't see it as a problem

Simplistically, of course, they're right – it's not their problem but the problem of all the women losing out because of them. The sheer ignorance, brute stupidity and complacency of many employers is illustrated by this bigoted and contradictory statement by the boss of a large private manufacturing company in the Black Country:

'There's no room for women in my company. Secretarial? Well, of course they have to – you have to have them for typing and all that. In fact, 50% of my workforce is female, the unskilled and typing types. But the company is better off with a male sales manager. Men wouldn't take anything from a female supervisor on the floor, they won't let women overlord them.

'No, I've never tried it and I never would.

'Women have got it over men in some ways. They're more in tune, they can see trouble brewing and avert it. But the average man is still very prejudiced. I'm not, of course, but I can see their point. There's still so many things girls just can't do. Operating power presses, setting tools, things like that. Men have just got it on the engineering side of the brain.

'You have to use women for the jobs they can do. How do you mean, *my* Miss ——? You don't want to believe everything you hear round the factory, you know. She's my Personal Assistant. She's been to college. She's very good at her job.'

Whichever side of the brain employers have got it on, they are fertile in finding reasons for discriminating against women, on a personal and on a general basis.

Other excuses from a ripe crop collected in the course of this survey include:

*'We're only a small company, not big enough to make any difference' – this poor-little-us whinge was offered by firms whose workforce ranged from 14 to 425.

*I would if I could – 'I like women. If I had a personnel manager, I'd have a woman.' 'Some jobs are for women, some for men. Mine are men's jobs.'

*Enough is more than enough. 'You can have too much of women, you know.' 'It's easy to get too many women around the place.' 'One woman is enough – me-the boss' – female managing director.

*Where are they all ? The problem of the invisible women. 'They don't apply.' 'I advertised for a woman, and no women applied.' 'You can't get them when you want them.'

All these employers, from across the British Isles, have uncritically swallowed and then regurgitated the myths about women workers which maintain women's disadvantage and inferiority in the workforce. By acting on the basis of these nit-brained notions, they then confirm them.

For women, it's a vicious circle

The American economists Lloyd and Niemi sum it up like this:

1) employers often justify discriminatory behaviour on the basis of women's higher turnover rates and therefore secondary status – claims which are 'documented' not just by women's lower labour force

participation rates, but by their lower wages and higher unemployment rates as well

2) the design of government policy makes implicit assumptions about the role of women in the economics of the family and the proper occupational division of labour between the sexes.

'The first phenomenon is what economists call "statistical discrimination" and results from the tendency on the part of employers who lack full information [that's the kind way of putting it] to assign characteristics to an individual without taking account of individual differences.

'The second phenomenon sets up incentives in such a way as to slow the inevitable process of change, by rewarding those men and women who conform to traditional stereotypes.'

What this means in the first instance is that being a woman will ensure that you are treated as such first and foremost, without due regard to anything you have achieved. Anne Oakley reports a case which has become famous, of the Cable and Wireless Company Limited. The company advertised for school-leavers to join the telecommunications engineering side – required qualifications were five O-levels, with preference given to holders of two A-levels. One female applicant who held twelve O-levels and was about to take three A-levels was rejected. As Oakley drily observes:

One of the reasons she was turned down was that there were no separate lavatories at the residential training centre. The cleaners, presumably women, no doubt waited until they got home. The fact that the girl was obviously far brighter than the average recruit was in no way allowed to offset the central objection that she was a woman.

What do you want a career for? – question asked by male interviewer at job interview, reported by nearly 200 women in a recent survey.

*

When even 100% is not enough

Many women job applicants find that not just one company, but the laws of their country are against them. One woman in Dallas, USA, took the federal Air Traffic Control exams, and passed out top with 100%. She was rewarded for this success by being placed *147th* on the Federal Jobs Register – preference is automatically given to military veterans under US law. A 'veteran', in case you're wondering, is *any* man who began his military service before 1976, so there are some pretty young oldsters pushing American women out of the jobs they are entitled to. These men get a *lifetime* preference of five extra points added to their ranking for federal jobs. In many cases these preferences apply to promotions and seniority too. So:

  * *While 'veterans' comprise only 25% of the US work force, they make up 48% of the 2·8m federal jobs, and 65% of the executive level appointments.*

  * *Of all those who pass the college-level test of the US Civil Service, 53% are women but only 31% of them ever get hired.*

  * *The 'feeder pool' – from which all higher level civil servants are drawn – is 65% veteran, 94% male.*

Great, isn't it. That's what Uncle Sam can do for you – as long as you're male, of course.

Just an accident?

It could be claimed that this legislation was not deliberately designed to hit at women – even though it has had this effect. The same cannot be said of the rednecks whose response to women at work recalls Max Miller's dilemma on encountering a girl on a one-way mountain track.[1] Baroness Seear made a study of the position of women in industry for the Government in 1968, and reported that when senior managers of companies were asked what jobs they thought were unsuitable for women, they produced 'a fairly lengthy list'. But on closer inspection it was found that 'in nearly every case, a job mentioned as unsuitable for a woman in one company was *in fact being done elsewhere by a woman!'* This, of course, does nothing to shake the conviction, which is rooted too deeply to allow the access of reason. A more recent British survey of managers' attitudes discovered that men came out on top in virtually every quality rated as important: education, personality, even salary required. 'The lesson to be learned here,' the report concludes, 'is that a majority of the people [i.e. *male* people] who are responsible for the engagement of employees start off with the belief that a woman is likely to be inferior to a man as an employee' (Hunt, 1975).

Many working women are unfortunate enough to encounter the expression of this attitude face to face. Beverley Bruges began as a school-leaver in the electronics industry, and soon developed an ambition to train as a manager. When she raised this with her boss, 'he nearly died of shock,' she recalls. 'He had to pick himself up off the floor. He was one of the school that believes women can't do anything but filing.' The only centre at which Beverley could study for the necessary qualifications was on the other side of Birmingham from where she was living. She was denied day release (which was granted to any male who wished to do it)

1. The exact phrasing of the immortal Max's joke is not included here as it is unsuitable for the delicate susceptibilities of any men who might be reading this book. But if any women who do not know it write to me c/o my publisher, it will be a pleasure to share it with you.

and told that she had to do it in her own time, *and* make sure that it did not interfere with her work. 'It's difficult to work all day and study all night', was her restrained understatement. At the point at which she obtained her qualifications, she was made redundant. 'The boss being what he was, I had no chance of progressing in that department anyway.'

Everyone isn't equal

It's just that women are more unequal than men. Eighty women bank employees in America filed a suit against their employer because after 15 years in banking they were only making $600 a month, while newly employed males began at $700 a month and were trained by women earning as little as $400. When the US Equal Employment Opportunities Commission cautiously found that there was 'reasonable cause to believe' that the women were being exploited, the President of the Bank defended his all-American outfit in these terms:

'Everyone *isn't* equal – you have the President and officers [read guess what?] and you have the employees [read guess who?] down there . . . This isn't a fight over unions – these girls are being exploited by the National Organisation of Women. My wife's a lady. She wants the door held open for her. She's no women's libber.'

Perish the thought!

What would the world come to if women were allowed to interfere with employers' natural rights of selection in the work force? As one Manchester industrialist explained it: 'The restrictive legislation is stupid. If you want an assembler, you want a woman, not a man. Women have nimble fingers. So you advertise for an assembler – then tell all the men who apply that the job is filled. Employers will *always* take what they want and lie to the others. It's stupid, and it's a waste of time and money. You're not allowed to say 'youth' or 'girl', but you know what you want.'

What employers want is a docile, un-unionized work force that despite the possession of 'nimble fingers' (a necessary requirement for the job) can still be paid less than a man would take for the work. This, of course, only serves to confirm their low status in the eyes of employing men, and to encourage the kind of crude sexism that makes such 'intelligent and efficient' men as this the ornament of the human race.

> *I am prepared to say that the general run of men is more intelligent and efficient that the general run of women . . . It is probable that the best men craftsmen are better than any woman could ever be. We all know that the best men chefs, dress designers, poets, playwrights, musicians, composers, are better than anything women have ever produced or are likely to produce in their departments – Woodrow Wyatt, former Labour MP and employer*

Keep 'em down . . .

is the recurrent motto of employers over the world. Not only do they cash in on the sex stereotyping that ensures that certain jobs remain 'female' – and low paid. They take positive steps to ensure that both women and their wage levels stay pegged down. In Connecticut, USA, it was discovered that local companies were actually co-operating *with their competitors* to keep women's pay down. The Permanent Commission on the Status of Women in that state reported that local businesses and companies in the Hartford Area joined together to fund a common survey of each other's clerical salary levels, agreeing only to pay competitive wage rates if they could not get the type of woman worker they needed on the lower level. This fits in with national practices – the US Labor Department reports that employers generally list a clerical job at a low wage, and only raise it if they are unable to hire anyone at that price.

As this shows, *employers are prepared to spend money to*

get out of having to pay it to their female employees. This fact was highlighted by Marie-Luz Samper, Labor Education Professor of the University of Connecticut, who lashed out at the bread-and-circuses tactics of the US insurance companies determined to keep their women workers as a low-paid under-class: 'The Insurance companies won't be unionised. They are spending a lot of money to keep the unions out. One company, for example, has provided all sorts of things for the women there – a swimming pool, a tennis court, beauty parlour, shopping centre. So the secretaries say, "We have all these things, why do we need a union".'

'Why do we need a union?'

Never mind dear, just you pop off, do your shopping and get your face fixed (all courtesy of your kindly employer) and just don't worry your pretty little head about your pay, and prospects, and your real and long term interests. The US National Council on Working Women has tried to take on the insurance companies. Among other proposals it has suggested that the companies should set up career ladders providing routes for women to move into better jobs within the company – or even to move at all, since so much female work is dead-end. A former Commissioner of the Council commented: 'As far as I know no company has *ever* set up a programme to move women from clerical positions into sales.' But just before you go back to the typewriter, girls – anyone for tennis?

They know what they're doing

Recent research has exposed the extent of employers' conscious and deliberate reliance on discriminatory practices. The US leads the field in unravelling the methods that companies use to depend upon, and even to engineer, both *part-time* and *short-term* working among their women employees; this will

keep costs down (they needn't pay rises or pensions)
ensure a passive and fragmented workforce that won't have the beef to push for either.

One insurance company has openly declared its reliance on 'A and P' (attrition and pregnancy) to keep down the salary levels of its female clerical employees. Women workers were always encouraged to leave rather than to stay on, and the company counted on the exit of women employees after a few years at work, and the entry of new high-school graduates to take their place.

This strategy was pinpointed by US researcher Ivar Berg. One 'highly-placed insurance executive' in a mammoth international company told him that 'tender-minded academics' were 'downright naive' in their concern with worker turnover:

> *If clerical personnel stayed in their jobs, they would become wage problems – we'd have to keep raising them or end up fighting with them; they would form unions and who knows what the hell else!*

> *(Education and Jobs, 1970).*

The same strategy (not exactly brilliant in its complexity) is operated throughout the 'advanced' world, as this open comment of one data processing manager shows:

> *We don't pay enough to hire males, so our programmers are female* Datamation, *(1980).*

So much for your kindly employer

What about your workmates? Well, that all depends. If you are sticking to your distaff, you may avoid the overt signs of hostility and harassment. But never lose sight of the fact that your average male is a territorial animal and will defend what he takes to be his patch, against what he takes to be an invasion. Even a high-level education, even an apparent commitment to women, may only be a glossy veneer – watch out for the dog beneath the skin.

One woman who described herself as 'savaged' by a male colleague was a doctor who joined an all-male group practice in the Cotswolds immediately after qualifying. Her partners had made a point of taking a woman, and the seniors were complacently conscious of their positive contribution to the advancement of women. The only resistance came from the young male partner, who seemed at first 'very hostile' and would try to catch her out over diagnoses, prescriptions and a hundred and one matters of the daily routine of general practice.

In time, however, his manner changed and over a period of months he began to pay her attention, to ask her out, and eventually to court her in the old-fashioned way with hearts and flowers. 'At first I didn't want to know', she said, 'but I was touched by his persistence. And he was intelligent, sensitive – good-looking, my type – in the end I just fell.'

One night she and he were left alone at the end of a long evening surgery. He proposed that they should adjourn to the local pub for a quiet drink – 'everything was lovely, we were so happy. I'd never been in love before, I thought this was it.' Afterwards they returned to the abandoned and darkened surgery to collect their things before going home. There he began, for the first time, to make love to her, gently removing all her clothing on one of the consulting couches, and finally carefully unpinning her long hair which she always wore coiled up in a severe bun. As she lay there he stared at her, and suddenly said in a spasm of hate, 'Now we know what kind of a doctor *you* are, *doctor* – and what kind of a woman! Every patient that comes to consult you, I shall think of this.' Then he went out and left her there.

She has not worked in general practice since this episode. 'And unless I could find an all-woman group,' she says bitterly, 'I don't suppose I ever will again.'

> *Give a woman a job, and she grows balls* – Jack Gelber, *author of* The Connection.

But a man who knows what he's doing can always cut them off. Or he can try. Lots of them will. So it's into the jungle, girls, wide-eyed and wary – to boldly go . . . Good luck – and watch your . . . step.

3

First Steps

It may be that society can justify the striking differences that exist between the subjects studied by boys and girls in secondary schools – but it is more likely that a society which needs to develop to the full the talents and skills of all its people will find the discrepancies disturbing –
Government Education Survey 21, 1975.

Looking for a job?

First take stock of yourself. This is usually an invitation to list all your attributes and assets, anything in fact that will make you attractive to a potential employer – can you take dictation in Arabic, make corn dollies or lavender bags, drive a HGV wagon (legally)? But it is equally realistic to come to terms with the disadvantages that you are labouring under, in order to try to put yourself right as soon as you can. Number one, of course, is the still staggering difference between what's expected of boys, and what's *not* expected of girls, in school, in jobs, in life. As a girl, you will have had in the first place, simply *less* useful education than a boy.

What have you learned?

Well, the one thing they'll have done their best to knuckle into your head, is 'How To Be A Girl'. Ellen Mintz, a psychologist of the City University of New York, ironically offers the following commandments for those involved in the rearing and training of girls:

73

1) Reward her incompetence and dependence by encouraging her to ask for help at every turn and then doing the task for her rather than expecting her to learn. Respond quickly to crying in any stress situation with consolation and affection so that she will learn to become 'emotional' as a way of avoiding or responding to stress rather than expecting to take care of herself.

2) Discourage fighting, arguing, or any form of self-defence by keeping her from confrontation, taking care of the situation yourself, or telling her, 'little girls don't yell or fight. It's not ladylike'. Teach her that she needs protection. Do not request or allow her to make decisions or express opinions – if she offers any, indicate how they are wrong. She will learn not to trust her own decisions. This will effectively reduce her self-confidence.

3) Teach her to love and show affection by showering her with love and affection. This, in combination with criticism, will establish her absolute need for approval.

4) Be concerned about her appearance. Compare her to the other girls in the neighbourhood and tell her over and over how pretty she is. She will learn that her appearance is crucial, and it is important to be pretty. In addition she will learn that she must compete with other females. Change her clothes whenever she gets dirty and send her out with admonitions not to get dirty again. Dress her in clothes that restrict her movements. She will learn to become inactive and concerned with cleanliness.

*

Recently a whole new world opened for us. My wife was an only child and I had just brothers. We had all boys, so experienced boyish loves like cricket and

football. Then we had a granddaughter. She is three now and suddenly we have discovered hair ribbons, dolls and dresses. It's wonderful! –
letter from a Sheffield grandfather in *Woman*.

*

5) Set high expectations for obedience to authority and at the same time minimize her assertiveness by rewarding her with praise for listening when she is told to do something and by telling everyone 'how good she is'.

6) Encourage or reward her for caring for dolls or siblings, growing plants, raising a puppy and the like, in order to develop nurturing qualities of compassion and gentle concern for people. Call her attention to lovely things. She will become aware of and appreciate them. Assign her responsibility for repetitive tedious tasks in order to teach her patience. Reward her with your gratitude.

7) Have low expectations for accomplishment and accept her failures readily. If she does succeed, act surprised, as if it hadn't really been expected from her.

8) Do not accept demonstrations of anger; or teach her not to recognize her own anger with comments such as 'Oh, you're not really angry are you?' or 'She's getting hysterical again!' Ignore or become embrarrassed by her sexuality and reward her modesty. Emphasize how you do or do not trust her with boys. Let her know how much 'trouble' she can get into if she lets boys 'use' her. She will learn that she is not only responsible for inhibiting her own sexuality, but controlling that of males as well.

Any bells ringing?

Among recent examples of this 'Be-good-sweet-maid'

CRY MY
DARLING
IN THE
NAME OF
FEMININITY
AND THE
SANCTITY OF
WOMANHOOD....

brainwashing are the following hot contenders for the 'yuk!' award:

* An independent girl's school in Warwickshire where the girls do no games, but 'Health and Beauty' routines in the school hall. Arm-swinging is accompanied by the rhythmic chant of 'I must! – I must! – I must improve my bust!'

* A comprehensive school in the Black Country where the fifth-form girls become 'Cleanliness monitors' and the boys become 'Discipline monitors' – 'a licence to bully', commented a member of staff bitterly.

* A Liverpool junior school where the girls put on a Fashion Parade, coming to school in their best outfits, and the boys put in their pennies for the girl/ensemble that they liked best – to raise money for the school's charity.

* A state secondary school in Cornwall where lessons in human biology (including reproduction) were given to the girls, but not to the boys. This course, blandly entitled 'hygiene', heavily stressed 'personal daintiness' for girls, by means of free handouts entitled 'Are You A Stinker?' and 'Feet Need Friends'. The menarche was the subject of a film, in glorious technicolour, vistavision and 3-D. Not a word about the onset of puberty in males – girls were left to fathom out unassisted the mystery of the bulging Adam's apple, the switchback voice modulation, the trouser legs ascending to half mast every three months, while the androgens raced around the immature male systems unacknowledged and unsung.

So you've learned how to be a girl

Unfortunately, that in itself is not a very marketable commodity – you have to be a successful business woman as well to trade on that alone. What else have they taught you? *Less of the useful qualifications you will need to get a job than you would have had if you were a boy.* Figures from the Department of Education and Science continue to show that girls throughout the country take *fewer O-levels* than boys do. The girls actually achieve a higher pass rate of those exams that they do take – around 64% in comparison with the boys' 58% – but girls, who are either the more intelligent or the more responsible sex, or both, whichever way you read these figures, are sent out into the world at a primary disadvantage. They are short on the basic qualifications which employers increasingly look for, as some objective indication of industry and ability.

This pattern is not only repeated but intensified at A-level. Boys here outnumber girls three to two, though girls still demonstrate their superiority in the pass rate. A-level success is directly linked to university and college entrance – at this point too the males streak ahead, cornering the lion's share of higher education. They not only get more boys into it, but they also collar the high prestige places, so that boys go to university while girls go to teacher training colleges, so that boys get *degrees* while girls get *certificates* and diplomas. From 3 to 2 against girls at A-level, the figure rises to *2 to 1 against* at university, where males are not only studying their chosen subject with the intelligence and devotion of which we know them to be capable, but forming the contacts and enjoying the experiences which will shape the whole course of their working lives:

Less means worse off

At whatever level girls enter the world of work, they are handicapped in comparison with boys, thus ensuring their unequal competitive or pulling power in getting jobs – those territorial males protecting their jungle again! As a Labour Party White Paper, 'Equality for Women', comments:

These figures illustrate the extent to which

Full time university students at undergraduate level, Great Britain, December 1976.

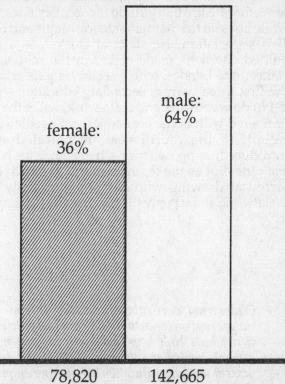

female: 36%

male: 64%

78,820   142,665

SOURCE: Statistics of Education, Vol. 6. 1976, Table 1, HMSO 1978

women receive less education than men during and after school . . . In the 25-34 age group, some of whom towards the end of the century will be assuming many of the most responsible positions in our society, only 2½% of women as against 7½% of men have university degrees or equivalent qualifications – and 59% of women as opposed to 48% of men have no formal qualifications of any kind.

Fobbed off with less

That's the story of girls' education in a nutshell. But that's not all. Girls also are systematically given a *less useful, less marketable education* by the discriminatory patterns that ensure that girls do the 'gentler' Arts subjects, while boys do the 'harder' practical Maths and Sciences. This segregation also starts at O-level, as a result of guided decisions made earlier in the school. For instance, one London school separates girls and boys in the first three years of secondary education – the boys get to do woodwork and metalwork, while the girls are lumbered with home economics and needlework (yippeee!). In the fourth year, technical drawing is introduced, supposedly as a free choice for both boys *and* girls. But as the teachers refuse to let anyone take technical drawing who has not previously studied metalwork, in fact only the boys can do it. Simple, isn't it?

*

> *Widespread curricular differences narrow the range of options open to girls. Premature specilization affects both boys and girls, but the more general curricular differences in the first three years of secondary education too often pre-empt the choice to be made by girls about subjects to pursue in the fourth, fifth and sixth forms, and in post-school education –*

Ernest Armstrong, MP

*

So simple that a clear pattern emerges from the official figures to give the lie to the pious hopes of educators and education officers that their precious commodity is freely available to all. Equality of opportunity is complacently taken a) to have existed all along or b) – in situations where a) is manifestly rubbish – to be on-its-way-very-nicely-now-thank-you. But look at the picture:

GCE 'O' Level Passes (A–C Grades) by sex, 1976, England & Wales

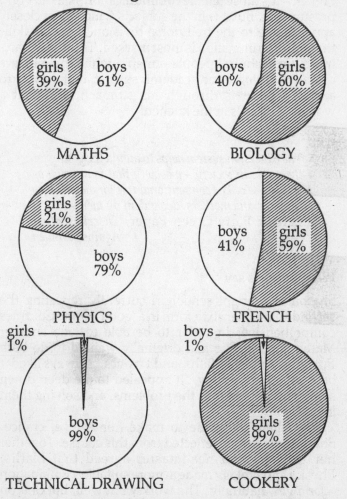

MATHS   BIOLOGY

PHYSICS   FRENCH

TECHNICAL DRAWING   COOKERY

SOURCE: Statistics of Education, Vol.2., Table 26, HMSO 1978

So by the age of 16, young males are establishing maths and sciences as a masculine territory – less than *one-fifth* of girls are allowed to do the 'Macho intellectual subject' physics, as one head teacher described it. Girls have a science, of course – dear old 'Bio', 'the caring subject, science with a human face', according to one female biologist. They're also numerically superior to boys in French – it's those female communication skills at work, presumably. But it is in the subjects which most closely approximate to the traditional division of sexual skills that the discrimination is most marked. Technical drawing is for technical people – men – while the girls are actually *learning*, as an academic subject, that the way to a man's heart is through his stomach, and that a woman's place is in the kitchen!

> *The education system helps to mould the young for their role in society – a society that is unequal as regards sex. The conventional role for women is to be wives and mothers, dependent on men –*
> Labour Party Green Paper, *Discrimination Against Women*

What the girls say

Sharon is a bright schoolgirl currently repeating the second year of her sixth form in a 'good' Home Counties comprehensive, in order to be able to take another Maths A-level. She had originally wanted to do both Pure and Applied Maths, and Physics. 'I always liked it best', she says simply. 'It appealed to me deep down somewhere. I enjoyed the problems, and solving them logically.'

But when she came to make her A-level choice, Sharon was firmly deflected from this course. Together her teachers and headmaster agreed that Maths, Physics and Biology made a 'more suitable' combination – *for a girl*, naturally. The work went well, but Sharon increasingly felt that she was on the wrong track.

This feeling was confirmed when she attended a seminar for young scientists, at a women's college in Oxford which her ability would lead her to try for. There she found that with Physics, the two Maths were much the preferred subjects.

'I've just had to backtrack', she states. 'I'm very lucky that my parents are behind me – that's great, I know I'm lucky. But I feel resentful at the waste of time and effort.'

Sharon is at least fortunate to be able to do the subjects of her choice eventually. Other girls encounter an outright 'No' to any request for schooling that does not conform to the traditional female stereotypes. An EOC report for *Women and Manual Trades in Scotland 1980-81* discovered the following responses:

> **'I wasn't allowed to because I was the only girl who wanted to do it'*
> **'My parents asked the headmaster if I could take technical drawing. He said "no" and wouldn't give a reason'.*

Well he wouldn't, would he?

Other 'reasons' for excluding girls from scientific or technical subjects include that potent weapon, The Timetable – 'it doesn't fit in with the timetable' and 'we'd have to re-jig the entire timetable' are evasions commonly offered. Frequently, though, craft masters disdain to employ any craft, when they can get away with bloody-minded antifeminism. 'Over my dead body!' declared the Head of Technical Studies in a Birmingham ex-technical/grammar school. 'I'll never teach girls. I didn't join this profession to wipe little girls' noses and tie the ribbons in their hair. They can't do it anyway. Their hands aren't big enough. *Nor their brains* – you can put that down.'

Dianne was interested in taking the subjects that would fit her for an engineering apprenticeship. When she mentioned this at school, 'the teachers just laughed at me'. She finished up as a clerk. Another aspiring young female scientist eventually left school in disgust and gave up her hopes of pursuing a career in physiology. She feels strongly about the rigid and unsympathetic thinking that held her back:

'The first thing that a bright girl discovers is that she should have chosen her sex with more care. I'm sick of hearing that it's not right for girls, no prospects, I'd never get into college, all the rest of it. They say to you, if only you were a boy. Well I'm not going to have a sex change operation to please them!'

The bias against girls in science and maths . . .

particularly handicaps you if you're thinking of higher education. The DES figures for A-level candidates show how your options are narrowed by the stress on arts subjects:

*Pupils taking A-level courses in
England and Wales*

Subject	% girls	% boys
English Literature	53	23
French	24	8
Biology	21	16
Maths	15	41
Chemistry	13	30
Physics	9	41
Economics	8	22

SOURCE: DES statistics, Crown Copyright.

This tendency for girls to specialize in arts subjects makes you vulnerable to pressure on places at college or university. Arts courses are generally heavily oversubscribed, while many of the interesting new courses at Polytechnics have a scientific/technological bias. In fur-

84

ther education, about two-thirds of the courses offered require passes in maths and/or physics which girls rarely have. In fact you fail before you've even applied!

It's a self-perpetuating situation

Because so few women get into these subjects *in the first place*, and because women get less education anyway than men, they never make it to the higher reaches to encourage the next generation of girls. Of students on science courses in Polytechnics in 1977, only 275 were female, as against 5,102 males. At university, the discrepancy is even more glaring – 1,657 girls were swamped by no less than 32,086 men (DES Education Statistics). Males are also far more likely than females to be qualifying to practise or teach computing and other advanced technical subjects for which there is a real and increasing demand.

And it's international

Look at this picture from America of the *widening* gap between boys and girls in educational opportunities (see overleaf).

Is this the lesson from the most advanced civilization that the world has yet known, that the Land of Promise is the Home of the Free *white male?* That in an open-opportunity society, your best opportunity is still to be born with the Y-chromosome that entitles you to the magic extra 25% throughout life? And what hope then for the Old World with its old habits and faiths?

In Great Britain female students and employers alike bemoan the denial of opportunity that this blinkered sexism imposes. Beverley Bruges, a buyer who began in the engineering industry, always liked Maths, but attended an all-girls private school in Coventry which had *no* laboratory or science facilities even for O-level study. Later, at technical college following a secretarial/commercial course, she found that Shorthand clashed with Maths on the master-timetable – the assumption

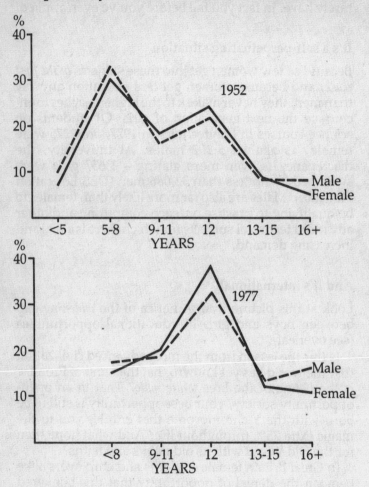

Years of schooling in percentages, completed by US males and females 1952 and 1977

%
40

30 — 1952

20

10 — - - - Male
— Female

<5   5-8   9-11   12   13-15   16+
YEARS

%
40

30 — 1977

20

10 — - - - Male
— Female

<8   9-11   12   13-15   16+
YEARS

SOURCES: 1952: Current Population Reports, Series P-50, no. 49, p. 7. table 1.
1977: U.S. Dept. of Labor. BLS, Special Labor Force Report no. 209. p. A-10 table B.

was that anyone who was doing *one* of these subjects could not possibly be in the intellectual league to be considering the other – by some law of nature! Beverley finally caught up with Maths by her own efforts. 'But

I've been disadvantaged by not doing the sciences', she says. 'I'll always regret that.'

All over Europe . . .

girls and women are deprived in the same way as Beverley – often with even more damaging effects where a rigid orthodoxy and traditional patterns reinforce obsolete conventions of 'suitable' female behaviour. Hilaria had 'the best ladies' education that money can buy' in Milan, where her father is a wealthy industrialist. 'But I'm *useless!*' she laments. 'All I can do is embroider, recite and sing!' Angelika, one of Germany's Catholics, attended a convent school in Munich where she studied 'what will make me a good woman'. Regrettably, female virtue is neither examinable or marketable, as she has since discovered. These are only two of thousands of girls in the same boat – which is sinking under them, as the European Commission recognizes. Their sense of the urgency and importance of this problem is indicated in the fact that change has been called for from the very highest level. Dr Hillery, Vice-President of the EEC, demanded in 1976 'a fundamental reorientation of basic education and vocational training in the Community, to give girls an equal opportunity in competing for future careers.'

EEC reports have steadily tried to highlight this situation: 'The increasing number of young women in Belgium, France and Italy who are unemployed is a result of the bad vocational and educational guidance given to girls, who either come on to the labour market *without qualifications* at the end of compulsory schooling, or *with qualifications which are not easily usable* in the labour market.'

Many factors combine to produce this highly unsatisfactory state of affairs. An EOC survey reported to the House of Commons Select Committee on Education in rousing terms: *'Girls are not inherently less able than boys in science subjects*. But the ethos of the subject within the school, the attitude of the teachers and the influence of the peer group combine, and contribute to the under-achievement of girls in science.' Ruth Low, Head-mistress of St Martin's-in-the-Fields Comprehensive and herself a physicist, has proved that this harmful

LUCKY WOMAN
BY LINN SENNOTT
Associate Professor of Mathematics
Illinois State University
Normal-Bloomington, Ill.

Last year I became the only woman mathematician on a tenure line in the 40-member mathematics department. Last fall I was assigned to teach an overflow section of probability and statistics.

I entered the classroom the first day to be confronted with twelve students – eleven men and one lone woman. The woman, who had no knowledge of me, took one look, let out a big sigh, and exclaimed, "Oh, thank goodness!"

SAVVY, May 1982

trend can be reversed, by her school's success in science teaching. 'Good teaching in the first few years is self-perpetuating', she told Maureen O'Connor of *The Guardian*. 'If you get the science right then, they will want to follow it up later.'

So why not try to perpetuate a process which helps girls, rather than the other way round?

For there's plenty of room for them in the world of science, and employers keen to utilize their skills. Suzanne Hunter, British Oxygen's only woman Branch Manager, was herself at school persuaded by her Headmistress not to apply to Cambridge on the grounds that as a girl she wouldn't stand a chance. She later discovered that she would have been favourably considered, as the University was trying hard to attract women at that time. Now in a position of authority herself, she is actively looking for bright girls to bring on. 'I spend a lot of my time trying to get women in', she says, 'But we're not getting the women we want out of Chemical and Mechanical Engineering. A change of emphasis must come at the school level.'

> *Responsibility for evaluating the curriculum to provide equal access to experience, information and guidance rests with:*
> * *local education authorities*
> * *managers*
> * *governors*
> and most important of all
> * *teachers*
>
> *DES Circular to LEAs on the Sex Discrimination Act, 2/76, 1975.*

And there's the rub

Any attempt to put things right must involve a head-on collision with the pervasive, mindless, unquestioning sexism of the educators. Sometimes this appears in an apparently harmless form – Suzanne Hunter, an attractive and casually smart woman, was told on her arrival at one school to speak to the girls, 'We thought that you'd arrive in your overalls, clanking.' More often it proceeds from a mistaken concept of sex-appropriate values. One woman, attending her daughter's secondary school for the first Parents' evening was sincerely assured by her (male) form teacher, 'You've got nothing to worry about, she's a lovely girl – she'll make somebody a wonderful wife.' As the mother holds five degrees, and has been keenly active in the cause of the education of girls for years, this was hardly what she had come to hear. The interview was slow to recover from this infelicitous kick-off.

All for the best

Equally oppressive is the discrimination which is meant to be kindly – many women of achievement are amused by some hangover of the protective paternalism of the nineteenth century which took as its basis the belief that females were fragile vessels. Outmoded as it is, this too lingers on in the schools. An independent secondary school in the Midlands offered among its post-O-level activities the chance of participating in a Local Authority scheme, Projects in the Environment. This facility was withdrawn when the pupils who signed on for it proved to be girls. A query as to the apparent discrimination against the girls drew the following response from the Headmaster:

> *Earlier in the year you asked me if sexual discrimination in favour of boys had occurred in our dealings with local government officers in the matter of the post 'O' level programme at the end of the summer term. My investigations show that no discrimination of any kind was perpetrated by any such officer, but that fewer pupils than at first*

*thought could participate in the activity, which
happened to be unsuitable for girls. The decision
was taken at the School, and is not therefore one
that can be regarded as within the provision of the
act. In fact it was no different from my excluding
my wife from heaving coal. Your concern, which of
course is welcome, need worry you no further, and
when I have time I will explain this to the parents
of the other girls concerned who complained to you.*

It would take a cerebral double-declutch to shift the
mental gears of such men – 'I happen to think that girls
are *different* from boys', explained the master in charge of
the original decision, earnestly. These attitudes go
deep, and engrained but unconscious sexism can affect
more than students' leisure activities. Recent work in
America has been directed at unravelling the responses
of male lecturers to female students, that they don't
know themselves that they possess. A research project
at De Pauw University, USA, has demonstrated a cause
and effect relationship between the females' figures
(pun) and their grades. It's amazingly simple, and
mathematically pure, confirmed by computer analysis –
the bigger a girl's hip measurement, the higher her grades!
Who'da thought it?

More harmful still . . .

is the blatant sexism which rejoices in its own unbridled
exertion of crude masculine sexuality. At a College of
Education in Birmingham, regular meetings of the staff
were held to assess the students' progress; the marks so
awarded went towards the final degree. One male lecturer in English Literature, a Cambridge graduate, had
his fancies among the girls in every year, and as soon as
a favourite's name came up he would murmur dreamily,
'A-plus for knockers'. The same lecturer was not
amused when a female colleague nicknamed one of the
well-endowed male students 'Ten-inch Terry' and

91

proposed that he should be entered for the Dangling Dong award. But this sharp taste of his own medicine did have the salutary effect of keeping his mind on the students' work in future.

Another girl student suffered directly from the sexual abuse of one of her teachers, and from the sexism of the system that supported him. At a large general hospital in Birmingham, a group of trainee radiographers, all female, enrolled each year. Their first weeks were spent in familiarization, during which they also underwent full medical checks which included tests for eyesight, colour blindness, everything. Each girl was called on a different day, and at different times, in order to avoid disrupting the work of the department by having all the girls involved at one time. Sometimes these appointments were changed if unexpected pressure of work caused the doctors to fall behind. Margaret was therefore not surprised when one of the doctors told her that her medical was due, and that she should go immediately to an examination room and undress.

She did so, and the medical took place. It seemed to her unusually thorough and protracted – she was absent from the ward for over an hour altogether – but not in any other way remarkable. She was however taken completely aback when two days later the sister told her that her medical was due – with another doctor. 'But I've had mine, Sister', she protested. The sister gave her a stunned look, and departed without a word. Later in the day Sister had an interview with Margaret, in which she described the first medical as 'something that shouldn't have happened'. Doctor Blank had been working hard, she said, and 'overdoing things'. Sister had spoken to the consultant in charge, who had instructed her to 'put Margaret in the picture'. 'You're a grown girl', Sister concluded briskly (Margaret was 16, and had just left school). 'You wouldn't want to ruin a doctor's career, would you? It'd finish *you* in medicine if you did – the medical profession hangs together on these things, you know. Anyway, it's all over now. It'll never happen again.'

Margaret later found out that this disgusting phoney 'medical' in fact happened *every* year. And every year the resident pervert was given a restrained wigging, and offered in return his contrite assurance that it would never happen again. Of course it did. And it was allowed to continue. Because you can ruin a young girl's peace of mind – but you don't want to ruin a doctor, do you?

*

A dozen of our classmates walked out in mid-lecture after a professor of surgery pinched the breast prosthesis of a mastectomy patient, and the breast of a woman radiologist, saying 'I'd like to bump into either of you in an elevator, anytime! –

'Sexist Schooling', *Working Woman*, October 1982.

*

Other doctors involved in the training of students develop offensive practices which go unchallenged in the 'boys' own' atmosphere of medical schools. In one London training hospital, despite the presence of women students, one doctor used to take out his penis (which in medicine is worth considerably more than the 25% wage superiority it earns for the possessor in other jobs) and pee down the nearest sink, as a 'practical demonstration' of the sterility of urine. Not a pretty sight, bystanders say – but it obviously gave him a big bang. And the use of this novel teaching aid failed in its effect, as students male and female missed the bang and got the flash, and were so mesmerized that they had to ask afterwards what was the point of the demonstration!

So check out your schooling

You will probably be lucky enough to have escaped the friendly medical sex pervert. But you are unlikely to have come entirely unscathed through a process which wastes so many girls at every stage, preserving the highest reaches for Men Only. Try this quick check list. Did you:

Want to study any subject not taught at your school (e.g. technical drawing, economics etc)

Want to do a subject and be told that 'the time-table' didn't allow it

Find yourself steered away from something considered 'not suitable' for girls

Have aspirations of a certain job, qualification or higher study which you have not realized

Get to a certain level in any job and realize that lack of basic qualifications prevents you from going any further

Look back on your schooldays and regret the waste of time and opportunity – feeling sure that you could have done better

???

All or any of these

That's right – you've got it! Congratulations! *You learned to be a girl!*

I would have liked to have taken technical drawing, but I couldn't fancy being the only girl in a male group. I would have liked to go into engineering as a draughtswoman. You can't go into engineering

without technical drawing, so I gave up the idea –
Sarah

Sidetracked, Yves Benett and Dawn Carter,
December 1981.

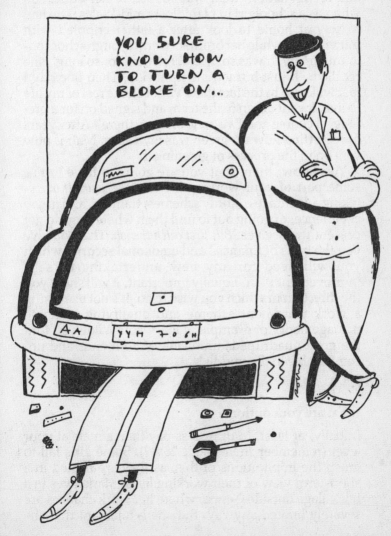

Undirected and understretched

Is this the story of your work life so far? Accept this as something that happened outside your control – school kids can only buck the system at St Trinians and Grange Hill, not in real life – and set about making up for lost time. Don't waste your precious energy in bitterness and recrimination. Mair was robbed of her education when as a schoolgirl in Llanidloes, mid-Wales, she had to stay at home to look after a father crippled with miner's lung while her brothers went through school on-to university. 'I was so mad about that, for so long', she recalled. 'It just burned me up inside. Then one day I just woke up to the fact that I've got all the rest of my life to live. I went down to the tech, and signed on for a pre-O-level course and I've gone on from there.' After years of regretting how un-green was my valley, Mair is now well on in the process of greening it.

You know, then, that you are going to have to use some part of your working life to *make yourself over* – taking advantage of study schemes, training, and in-job experience, or going out to find them where they do not present themselves. *But first catch the job*. This will give you the basis of financial and emotional security which you will need for any new undertaking or self-improvement plan. Equally important, it will show you the direction in which you wish to go. It's not use taking a work placement scheme and qualifying in horse management, for example, if like Oscar Wilde you find the great quadrupeds unreliable at both ends and un-comfortable in the middle!

What are your options?

Initially, at least, to draw less pay than a male at your level (remember their magic 25%?). Some girls fail to grasp the implications of this, as they are fixated in a short-term view of their working lives. Maria lives in a hill village outside Genoa, where her work chances are severely limited anyway. But she is adamant that she would not want to work 'seriously', or for long. 'Work is not the real thing for a girl', she claims. 'I work only until my children come along.' Interestingly, her attitude was challenged by her mother, who was constantly murmuring 'Cretina, cretina!' at Maria's pronouncements. And Mama is right, of course. Across the world women are (literally) paying for their lack of awareness of how they let even much less well-educated men than they are steal a march on them. Look at this diagram from America, plotting the income curves of Americans in relation to their education standard throughout their lives:

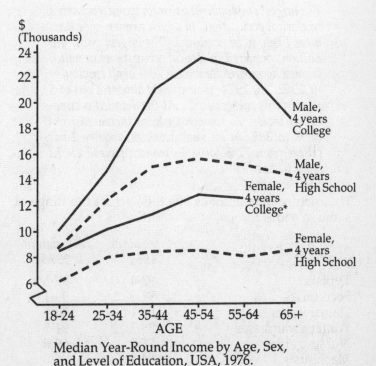

Median Year-Round Income by Age, Sex,
and Level of Education, USA, 1976.

SOURCE: Current Population Reports, Series P-60, no. 114, pp.192-201, table 47.

How can you avoid this?

One way is to avoid like the plague taking any job in one of the female ghettoes where women workers are herded together like sheep and deliberately kept on low wage rates because there are no men doing the same or similar work on which an equal or improved pay claim could be based. *The most obvious tiger trap for women is the clerical/secretarial dead-end.* US trends clearly show that not only are large numbers of women confined in these unhopeful jobs, but that the restriction of women to 'women's occupations' is actually *on the increase.* Stuart H. Garfinkle stressed this factor in the US Department of Labor's *Monthly Labor Review* of November 1975:

> *The largest employment gains for women occurred in clerical occupations in which women have been more likely to be employed. The largest gain, 4·8 million, occurred in clerical occupations in which women accounted for almost 70% of all employees in 1962. By 1974, women held almost 4 out of 5 jobs in this category . . . At the detailed occupational level . . . women cashiers increased from 82% to 88% of all such workers, women bank tellers from 72% to 92%, woman payroll clerks from 62% to 77% . . .*

The picture overall looks like this, across the range of 'women's jobs':

	% female in 1962	% female in 1975
Typists	98·4	98·6
Secretaries	98·5	99·1
Hairdressers	88·1	90·6
Waiters/waitresses	88·1	91·5
Nursing aides	75·2	85·8
Machinists	94·1	95·8

Garfinkle's statistical picture is reproduced across the 'civilized' world – a recent study by Canadian Patricia

Connelly (1978) has independently produced remarkably similar figures of women's confinement in specific low-grade, low-paid jobs: typists 95·6%, secretaries 97·4%, for example. Finally there are the occupations which are and remain solidly female, like nurses, elementary school teachers and telephone operators (97·0, 85·4 and 93·3% respectively of the US workforce in 1975).

*

Secretarial

I type all day
For lousy pay
Because they say
There'll come the day
When I'll be wed –
And then they'll get another fool instead.
Shrew, *Autumn 1976.*

*

Finally, this rising trend will rise yet again. In February of 1976 *15½ million* US women were employed as 'clerical and kindred workers'. This figure is expected to climb to *20 million* by 1985, when it would represent *one fifth* of the total US work force, male and female. Already one out of every 2½ of all US employed women are engaged in this work, according to the US Department of Labor's 1975 *Handbook on Women Workers*.

Compare the US experience with the work situation at home:

Employees by selected occupations, Great Britain, 1977

Occupation	Women	Men	% Women
Catering, cleaning and other personal services	13,692	4,423	75·6
Clerical and related	22,311	8,548	73·3
Professional and related in education, welfare and health	9,843	5,346	64·8
Literary, artistic and sports	252	757	25·0
Professional and related in science, engineering, technology and similar fields	517	6,775	7·1
Processing, making and repairing and related, metal and electrical	1,109	22,041	4·8
Construction, mining and related	13	5,620	0·2

SOURCE: DoE (1977), Part E, Table 135. Crown Copyright.

These are the dead ends . . .

and a dead end kills. This is what a group of women between 16 and 25 had to say about their early job experiences in clerical, secretarial and service jobs:

* 'I worked as a "receptionist" at a vet's. The pay was disgusting and the work was deadly. But their attitude was, there's 50 waiting for this job, if you don't like it, get out.'

* 'Filing in a manufacturing company – it was boring and loathsome! I don't know how I stuck it!'

* I did that pathetic "secretarial" routine till I knew it backwards, it was coming out of my ears. I used to think all the time, Oh God, have I got to be doing this for evermore?'

* 'It was my first job – typing pool – but I soon realised I'd worked myself into a dead end.'

Why do they think we're so stupid we don't notice or care?

This was the recurrent lament of these young women, all of whom had embarked on their work lives with hopes and ambitions of something more than incessant, degrading dogsbodying – and for what dogs! 'You don't keep dogs and bark yourself', said Norton, a Leeds businessman working profitably in a trade heavily dependent on female labour. 'Your mistake is, you think of these silly bitches as women like you. You're wrong – they don't want a proper job, or anything that'll distract them from their boyfriends, knitting patterns, their mums' bunions – it's all rubbish, what they've got between the ears. You wouldn't believe it'. You're right, Norton – *I wouldn't.*

Avoid these ghettoes . . .

where you're not only exploited, you're despised for it too; insult upon injury. Maybe 'secretarial' isn't too attractive – but don't make the mistake of falling for a 'glamour' job in the belief that that will be different. It just smells nicer, that's all. American Louise Kapp Howe has made a pioneering study of 'pink collar workers', women in hairdressers, beauty parlours, retail sales and personal service jobs. Her investigations showed a staggering degree of casual and unchallenged exploitation of women's work, skills, and dedication.

101

The women beauticians were attracted to the attractiveness of that job, and trained long and hard to figure out all the wrinkles. Howe interviewed a union boss of the US Journeymen Barbers, Hairdressers, Cosmetologists and Proprietors' International Union of America – the union that acts for all the women hairdressers and beauticians of the US. The whole set-up is loaded against women from the start – Journey *men* rule, OK? Barbers come before hairdressers – and who ever heard of a union that had the *bosses* ('proprietors') in it??
The interview revealed to Howe the extent to which the barbers had out-sharped the hairdressers:

> *I asked Mr Woods how the wages of the beauticians in the union compared with those of the barbers.*
> *'Barbers probably make about 30% more on the average', he answers, obviously finding nothing strange about that.*
> *'Even though' I ask 'the work that beauticians do is often vastly more complicated than the work barbers do? How does your union justify that kind of disparity?'*
> *A swing to the left, a swing to the right, safe at second base.*
> *'We don't try to justify it, but we do have different contracts for barbers and beauticians, and barbers, yes, are guaranteed more. But they are men, after all . . .*

They are men, after all

Not surprisingly, the union totally failed to protect its women members from such dirty tricks as one uncovered by Howe – the fixing of the wage bill for women employees at no more than 42% of the gross takings in any one week. What this means for the hairdressers is, that in a week when the takings are down for any reason, *the women are sent home from work as soon as things go quiet*. As they are paid by the hour, they not only lose

102

directly. They are also trapped permanently in the position of never knowing from week to week how much money they can rely on. Will the union fight for them? A *boss's* union? Will it hell!

Proceed with caution...

in the work jungle. Remember that for every booby there's a trap, and every dog expects a female body to gofer him. It shouldn't have to be like this for you. Work is supposed to exercise not exploit you, and you are entitled as a right to feel good at work. No less an Institution than the World Health Organisation outlined this right when it summed up occupational health as

> * *the promotion of the highest degree of physical, mental and social well-being for workers in all occupations*

> * *the prevention among workers of departures from health caused by their working conditions*

> * *the protection of workers in their employment from risks resulting from factors adverse to health*

> * *the placing and maintenance of the worker in an occupational environment adapted to his/her physiological and psychological condition.*

Fine and dandy, huh? All good virtuous stuff. Unfortunately in all too many cases, nothing could be farther from the reality of the work situation.

Work is a dangerous place

Watch out! All kinds of jobs pose health hazards for women workers, and can damage you in ways you don't even think of when you begin. This is the voice of painful experience in waitressing, American Joyce Betries:

Most women eventually develop varicose veins, box feet, and uneven shoulders from carrying heavy trays on one arm. I worked in Schraffts chain for a while. We had to carry round heavy trays balanced on one arm, piled with food. It was just too heavy. I had to wear an elastic wrist support, but even that didn't help.
The worst thing was, we had to hold the tray on our arm while we cleared the table, piling it with dirty dishes. We weren't allowed to rest the tray on the table because it 'didn't look nice'. Along with the dishes and the silver, we had to clear off enormous water goblets that were very heavy. Then, when the tray was piled up, we had to remove the dirty table cloth with our free hand (pick up the salt, pepper, ashtray and sugar), tuck the dirty cloth under our arm, and spread a clean cloth, balancing the tray all this time!

And all this in the interests of 'looking nice'. It must look wonderfully nice to see a woman struggling like this. But waitressing anywhere is a painful and stressful occupation. Among other bad things about the job (supposedly easy money, and certainly keenly sought by many women) waitresses isolate these factors:

> * *Bosses always threatening, bullying, hassling you to handle more customers than you humanly can*

> * *Snatched, hurried, inadequate meals – the supposed perk of free grub on the job in fact turns out to be what's left over/unwanted by customers, either bolted down when you're still technically on duty, or delayed until the food is stale and you are past it*

104

The chefs taking out their tension under pressure by shouting and swearing at you – filthy language and hurtful insults, and blaming their mistakes on you

Never getting a proper holiday or break like everyone else, not even Christmas – 'we have to be working so that everyone else can be relaxing.'

*

They also serve who only stand and wait
– John Milton

*

Take a tip – don't wait

But even these painful disabilities pale in comparison with what women can suffer in industry. Marianne Hertzog gave a graphic description of a piece-worker at AEG-Telefunken in Berlin, who had to 'beat her wages out of the machine each day':

Frau Winterfeld sags. She has been sitting on her chair welding without a break for 2½ hours: 14 welding spots a minute, each one requiring a tread on the pedal; each time she contracts her stomach muscles, and each weld produces fumes which she inhales. Her arse hurts, she can't sit on her chair any longer, her calves have stiffened because she can only take her foot away from the pedal every 30 minutes, her left shoulder hurts because she welds with her left hand, she feels as if her spine is broken because she can't lean back.

What was that again from the World Health Organisa
tion about 'the promotion of the highest degree of well-
being among workers . . . '?

Researchers are trying hard . . .

to direct employers' and workers' attention to the desperately dangerous hazards of certain types of industrial
work. The tragedy of asbestosis is now becoming widely
known, but there is still an official reluctance to acknowledge this deadly disease. Turner and Newall, Britain's
largest asbestos company, has recently admitted that it
was 'incorrect' in a 1978 statement that the deaths from
lung cancer of its Rochdale factory personnel did *not*
'differ significantly from the national average'. In fact
*asbestos cancer is 'the granddaddy of the occupational health
killers'*, according to David Gee of the GMWU.

Another old favourite still with us is lead poisoning.
Awareness of this factor had resulted in the agreement
of a new code of industrial practice only just introduced
in Great Britain, which sets lower levels of lead in the
blood for women workers 'of reproductive capacity'
than has previously been tolerated. Very good, you say.
Except that in operation this means that as soon as the
woman's blood lead level rises above the permitted
minimum, *she is laid off*. As the blood level for men is
much higher, *they carry on working*. In order to avoid the
unsettling and damaging effects of this discrimination
(however well-meant) five women from the Cynamid
Company in West Virginia, USA, had themselves
sterilized rather than lose their jobs. They lost them anyway when the plant later closed down.

So you think you might be safer in an office?

Don't you believe it! With typical Teutonic efficiency the
Germans led the way in work study and man/woman
management to fuel their impressive economic recovery
from the ruins of World War 2. They have now made a
study of what results their efforts have produced, and in

a damning Government report show just how bad office work can be for your health, especially in an open-plan office. Nothing apparently is more stressful than beavering away in close proximity with up to fifty or a hundred of your fellow-beavers. It gives you:

irritability   indigestion   fatigue
susceptibility to infection   glandular disorders
sleeplessness   headaches

All this and a full day's load of boring work as well! So strongly do the Germans feel about the badgered office worker that in introducing the report to Parliament, the West German Secretary for Labour recommended that all open-plan offices should be *abolished*.

And it's getting worse

Open-plan offices can be dismissed as an ergonomic bloomer of our benighted forefathers, like tower block housing and comprehensive developments quite out of touch with human needs. But what makes you think that 'they' have changed in their attitude to ordinary workers – especially female? The new technology is hailed as the machinery to 'liberate' people from boring and repetitive tasks. But on inspection, *the people are still serving the machines, rather than the machines the people*:

> *If I had known about it before as I do now, I would advise other people to look for another job. We are on it 6¾ hours a day and we're shattered by home-time. We are all fed up with it but other jobs are not so easy to find at the moment, and as our office has nothing else but computers there is no change during the day to rest your eyes from it – VDU worker talking to Ursula Huws*, Your Job in the Eighties *(1982)*.

107

A particular example is the wonderful word-processor, or any work involving a television-style VDU screen. Focussing on the illuminated screen all day long, even with the prescribed ten-minute break in every hour, places an enormous strain on the eye muscles, and the intense concentration required is highly stressful. In addition, the operator is usually working in a room alongside others similarly occupied and cannot obtain the calm and quiet which would enable her to do the work more easily. And the 'new' technology is always co-existing with the remains of the old, so the word-processor will have to be operated amongst the noise of the typewriters, dictaphones etc, which have yet to be replaced. No special provision is made for the women having to reconcile these contradictions and tensions and little or no sense exists among employers of the alternating boredom and strain to which the women operatives are subjected. At the Whitley Talbot plant outside Coventry all the data punchers are female. Men go straight to data *processing*, as befits the master race, while the *untermenschen* spend their working lives transferring 'hard copy' into the new format. Supervisors display a cheerful disregard of the implications of this for the girls: 'Of course it's an awful job. Nobody could sit at it eight hours a day except those girls. It's not suitable for a man – a man'd go bonkers. It's all right for the girls, they just sit there and think about their love lives.'

But even thinking about your love life cannot protect you from the harmful effects of this – workers in a variety of different situations all report that the new technology has brought for them personally an *increase* in:

Headaches   Eye trouble   Fatigue   Depression
    Back pain   Insomnia   Anxiety

Check out your chances . . .

of getting all or any of these from your work place.

Obviously you can't and shouldn't avoid the new technology like a peasant confronted with a threshing machine – see Chapter 4 for how to make friends with it. But you need to be wary of its potential for harm as well as for good, and ready to educate your employers and supervisors in the *correct* use of machines which they all too often embrace quite indiscriminately and mindlessly as The Thing which is going to 'put the company on the map', 'help us ride out the recession', etc. Similar high claims have been made for *all* technological advances in their time. The telephone, the telegraph, the advent of 'the wireless' – all were once going to bring in the New Dawn. This is only more of the same, so don't let it get on top of you with its ambitious pretensions!

Another way to stay healthy . . .

is to avoid, if and where humanly possible, any experience of shift work. Medical experts in Great Britain, Europe and America agree that the disturbance in life patterns which shiftwork produces has harmful effect upon eating, sleeping, concentration, enjoyment of life, and all bodily and mental functions to some degree. Particularly stressful is the rotation or switching of shifts. This is because your body never gets a chance to settle down into one regular set of bio-rhythms. As one authority explains, 'Your body clock is the key to the most harmful effects of shift work. It is set to a certain programme when you are a child and you cannot reset it completely unless you change to a different living/ sleeping routine and *stick to it!'*

> *I feel squeamish all the time. There's a break at about midnight, and I eat for nourishment, but I'm not hungry.*

> *It upsets your sex life. You get back in the morning and you just don't feel like it. I was on the pill for a while and I found that it was upsetting me because*

I was taking it at such odd times.

*Two women shiftworkers interviewed by Jean
Coussins for the NCCL*, The Shift Work
Swindle *(1979).*

Why work antisocial hours at all?

Europe leads the way. In Belgium, Norway and Sweden
night work is banned, except where special exemptions
have been negotiated between unions and employers in
areas where it is unavoidable, such as hospitals. In
Britain, women and children are 'protected' (forbidden)
from working between 8 pm and 7 am by legislation as
recent as the Factories Act of 1961! Yet such is the cynical
exploitation of women workers that this patronizing
piece of paternalistic discrimination (excluding women
from the more highly-paid overtime rates, and also from
hours that may suit them better than daytime working)
is happily subverted when employers cannot get
enough *men* to do the jobs. Currently around *200,000
women* working in factories are 'covered by exemptions'
which allow their work time to be extended into the
forbidden hours. Over 300,000 women are specifically
excluded from the protection against night work. The
law applies only to women working in *factories*. So you
can't work nights because it's bad for you – unless it
happens to be good for the employers!

*For working the antisocial 'housewives' shift',
6-10 pm, I received exactly half the pay of full-time
male workers. Men working shift work in most
industries are compensated by receiving more than
day shift. It was an accepted fact that the really
hard work was done on the housewives' shift
because the lorries had to be loaded and ready for
early morning delivery at grocery stores –
Elizabeth Beckley, one-time ham packer at Wall's
Meat Co., Cheshire.*

110

Good for the employers . . .

is a reserve pool of cheap labour willing to work anti-social hours. Unsurprisingly, bodies like the CBI are pressing to have the protective legislation repealed, in the name of sexual equality (not a cause they are conspicuously fighting for elsewhere). Again, enlightened European thought runs counter to such British practices – Sweden, in 1967, so far from withdrawing the protection from women, *extended it to men*. No one should do night work, male or female, since their researchers had conclusively established its deleterious effects on health (physical and mental), social welfare and family life. In fact, it's so bad for you that British employers cannot wait to *extend its benefits to women*, to further our march towards equal opportunity!

Equal protection from shift work . . .

remains the European aim. The EEC has been giving consideration to the possibility of legislation to regulate antisocial working along these lines:

> *the amount of shift work performed
> *the right of shift workers to return to day work
> *early retirement of shift workers
> *a reduction in weekly hours of shift work
> *longer holidays for shift workers
> *the establishment of minimum rest periods
>   between shifts

Good ideas? The employers didn't think so. Entrenched resistance came specially from Great Britain, where employers are attempting to move in quite the opposite direction. *These proposals have now been shelved.*

Linked with shift work is part-time work . . .

as something to be avoided at all costs – especially your

own. Part-time work is often immediately attractive, since it seems to offer a flexibility that you may need. *But it always costs you more in the end than you should pay.* It benefits countless thousands of employers every year, by depriving women of nearly all their work benefits. In this country, that is – the part-timer gets more protection in every other member state of the EEC. As a British part-timer, you don't *ever*:

>*build up seniority, even if you work for 40 years*
>*get considered for promotion*
>*receive holiday allowance*
>*become eligible for sick pay*
>*enjoy the full range of insurance benefits*
>*get a pension*

Not only do you lose all these basic work rights – you stand to *lose the job itself* at the drop of a hat. Bosses and managers have cold-bloodedly taken advantage of women's need for short-term or flexible working patterns, using part-timers whenever they need to extend the scale of production, only to dismiss them without a backward glance when orders fall again.

Part-time work . . .

puts paid to any real work prospects for women. But it's not even worth it on a short-term basis. A 1978 survey by the Low Pay Unit showed that ¾ of part-time women workers in Great Britain earned *less than £1·20* per hour – that is, below the supplementary benefit level for a full-time employee. These women were not only deprived of the normal social security benefits – 40% of them were not even allowed to have any meal or tea breaks during their work hours! These are the experiences of some of the women in this position:

Mandy works four hours a night as a barmaid in a plush

and popular country pub outside Banbury. For ministering non-stop to the sports car/chinless wonder/ flannelled fools brigade, she gets *86p an hour*. 'I'm allowed to let the customers buy me a drink,' she says, 'provided it's non-alcoholic, and provided I don't stop work to drink it.' She's learned how to keep serving drinks with her other hand – and to slip down her Cokes when her mouth is not otherwise engaged in returning the punters' inane banter.

Mel works six hours every night, including Saturdays, in a Coventry chip shop. She is paid *£1 an hour*, and gets no breaks, nothing to eat and drink, and no chance to sit down. 'There wouldn't be time, anyway,' she said. 'We're just too busy.'

Ellen is a domestic in a private Old People's Home in Eastbourne, working every morning for four hours. She receives *£1·26 an hour*, and is paid for four hours, although her 'morning' invariably extends for at least another half hour when she has 'finished', as she is expected to help out with the 'care assistants' who serve the old people's lunches. When she raised this with the Head of the Home, he told her that if she didn't like it she could 'do the other thing'. 'I've got hundreds of girls on my books that'd jump at the chance you've got,' he boasted.

> *Despite having made a valuable contribution to industry, we part-time workers are still treated as though we are some form of industrial leper, often poorly paid and always expendable in a redundancy situation – letter from a part-time worker to the NCCL.*

A bad British habit

The exploitation of part-time workers on a large and systematic scale is a peculiar British phenomenon. This is not to say that it is unknown abroad, where part-timers enjoy no higher status than they do here – one French survey reported in the *Nouvel Economiste* of 30 April 1979 referred to them with typical Gallic charm as the 'hole-fillers' in production. But in Great Britain *over 40%* of employed women work part-time, as opposed to 5% of employed men. This puts our sceptred isle at the very top of the league for employing women part-timers: in the UK, roughly *1 in 5* workers is now a part-timer, compared with 1 in 10 in Germany, 1 in 14 in France, and 1 in 20 in Italy. But although the proportion of women working part-time in this country has increased so substantially, and although the British economy is vitally dependent on their efforts, 'women still, by and large, do those jobs with which they have traditionally been associated, semi- and unskilled manual and clerical work', according to economists Peter Manley and Derek Sawbridge in *Lloyd's Bank Review* of January 1980. They add that it is 'unlikely' that there has been any change from a 1974 research finding that *'most part-time work is still undemanding, ill-paid, and of low status, with no prospects of advancement'*.

You have been warned!

Unless you're careful you, too, could be

The Boss's Darling

Now come along girls to the
                    factory,
The production line is
                    turning,
If you work all day for the
                    minimum pay
God knows what you'll be
                    earning.

Get stuck in when you
                    arrive,
To keep your family alive,
At the end of the week,
                    you'll just survive,
To be the boss's darling.

The boss he loves you well,
you bet,
He knows that you'll be
loyal,
You're a breeding ground for
the working man,
And a resting place from toil.
You have no time for the
union,
You leave that kind of thing
to men,
You're a second class
worker, and a mother hen,
That's why you're the boss's
darling.

Your patience and dexterity
He's endlessly adoring,
He says you're suited to the
job,
Which means the job is
boring.
You think you're earning
equal pay
But he has found a million
ways
To keep you bottom of the
heap, OK?
'Cos you're the boss's
darling.

We'll come along down to
the factory,
We'll keep you on your
toeses,
There's lots of
unemployment now,
So don't look down your
noses.

There's shi(f)t work here and
shi(f)t work there,
What you do with your
family's your affair,
'Cos if you don't like it
there's plenty more
To be the boss's darling.

These days we're getting organised
This time we won't be beaten,
It's 'You lend me a hand with the frying pan,
I'm off to a union meeting.'
You men who cross our picket line,
Remember you'll get yours in time –
The enemy's the same, it's yours and mine –
The scab is the boss's darling.

Jean Hart, Women's Theatre Group,
'Work to Role'.

The job, and how to get it

The simplest way to find out what you want is by looking. This may sound dead obvious, but it's amazing how
many job-hunters don't research the field properly. If
you're after a job you should be looking all the time,

everywhere, until you come up with it. This means covering every outlet in local or national papers, everything from the card in your post-office window or Job Centre to high-level specialist publications in your area of interest. Enlist friends and relatives on your side, especially if they live outside your particular patch. It's a boring, time-consuming and often discouraging task, as you plough through lists of jobs thinking, 'All these vacancies and not one that I can do, or want to.' But it is the only way that you will catch your job – and it's better than resigning yourself to living on the unparalleled luxury of Supplementary Benefit, or rusting away in inaction without ever discovering what you can do. And it really is surprising how many girls, when asked, 'How did you get the job?' reply, 'I saw it in the local paper.'

Don't be put off

You'll feel like screaming if anyone tells you again that there's a recession on, so I won't. And even in a recession, work goes on, jobs are going, and someone has to get them – let's make sure it's you. Don't cast around wildly, firing off letters and applications at anything that moves on the job horizon – the buckshot principle is all right for some things, but in the job hunt you only need to bring one quarry down.

Establish one general area that you would be prepared to work in, and then remain as flexible and adventurous as you can within that. So you want to be a buyer, and working in a sex shop isn't your mother's idea of a nice job? Our mothers had different battles to fight, and mostly they ducked out of them – if they hadn't, we wouldn't be in the mess we are today. You can gain experience of the retail trade just as well there as anywhere else, and study there, too, for the Business Education Council exams that you will need as your next step. And when you move on, you will have had a unique training in the mysteries of buying and selling to offer to your next employer. 'It's all retail, darling, knives, knobs, knickers or knockers, as my old boss

116

used to say. Somebody, somewhere wants to buy 'em, and you've just got to give it to 'em' – woman buyer in Oxford Street department store.

Have a go

Don't hang back. You and your hesitation are your two worst enemies. 'Get to the phone box, and *phone up*,' advises Suzanne Hunter. 'There are ways you can do it. Boys are from the beginning used to going off and doing it, getting a job for money, from their first paper round. But girls can do it. You've just got to batter a few doors down.' And don't give up on yourself. Blow your own trumpet – if you don't, nobody else will, they don't know the right tunes!

*

> *Woman's development, her freedom, her independence, must come from and through herself –*
> *Emma Goldman*

*

Among girls who successfully tried this tack was Lucia. Looking desperately for a job, she told everybody (*everybody*) she met that she was in the employment market. She was at last lucky enough to get an interview with a politician who was looking for a research assistant. Through inexperience and nerves, she made a mess of the crucial interview. 'I realized later that I just didn't tell him about *any* of the qualities I have that might have been of use,' she admitted. But instead of going away and fruitlessly blaming herself, Lucia sat down and wrote him a follow-up letter, in which she described herself, her experience and her enthusiasms. She also

117

asked her referees to send him her references. When she judged that he had had time to absorb all this, she followed up again with a telephone call, refusing to be fobbed off by his secretary. When he finally spoke to her, it was to offer her the job. In her follow-up tactics she had displayed the tenacity and commitment which she had not revealed at first, and which were qualities that he was keen to seize on.

*

> *Our doubts are traitors,*
> *And make us lose the good we oft might win*
> *By fearing to attempt – William Shakespeare*

*

Nice work if you can get it

Not everyone has Lucia's combination of gumption and good luck in landing a job. Mostly, you'll be looking at the adverts in which *they* are looking for you. *So what are they looking for?* Whatever they say, they may well be looking for a *man* to fill a post you've got your eye on. Overt discrimination by sex difference in advertising is now forbidden by the law. Employers may no longer demand as they used to (honestly!) 'Bright Young Man to take charge of Women'. This legal requirement has also succeeded in weeding out some of the more idiotically jokey ways of demanding female labour like 'Help! Are You A Girl Friday?'

Yet job adverts continue to indicate *indirectly* a preference for male or female candidates. The assumption is still entrenched in the bone brains of employers that men take charge, women service and support. Consider these examples:

*'*You will be responsible for organising and motivating a team which will formulate, develop and produce our output . . . we want people who are excited by a tough challenge . . .'*

*'*An interesting and exciting job for an electronics enthusiast with sound theoretical knowledge and practical experience in building electronics circuits . . .'*

*'*Duties include controlling all administrative functions and secretarial work of the section . . .'*
[Man wanted to take charge of women, no?]

*'*The successful applicant will have the opportunity of a highly lucrative and progressive future . . . a high earning potential for an industrious and ambitious person.'*

*'*Can you handle the action?'*

*'*Candidates must have an exciting track record in sales management . . .'*

All this potential, excitement and success! Is this what some men do instead of sex, do you think?

Bright young things

Women also suffer from employers' insistence upon specified age bands as appropriate for certain jobs. Again and again advertisers state that 'the successful candidate *will be* between 25 and 35'. This is by far the most popular age band sought by employers, although some declare 'we are looking for a degree of mature self-sufficiency that indicates the 30-40 age group'. This common requirement has the effect of discriminating against women in two ways:

119

1) It reflects the rooted habit of regarding women as less mature, experienced or grown-up as a man of the same age; in fact, as 'children of larger growth', as Lord Chesterfield put it – so that at twenty-four a male can take charge of an office full of women, while a female much older will be expected to defer to him. Consider any hair salon with a male manager, happily if inexpertly bossing women with twice his age and experience – who have to call him 'Mr Paul' and see to it that he gets all the best customers.

This habit of calling females by their first names, while the male is accorded the honorarium of 'Mr', also perpetuates the juvenile and inferior status of women in comparison with the mighty male. At a recent Midlands trade fair, stand after stand was occupied with packs of males standing round trying to impress one another, while their female colleagues were hustling like mad to push the goods, even picking up customers in an unguarded moment at the bar or on the way to the loo.

The women were also pulling their weight in another traditional way, too, being all tarted up to the nines and massively underdressed for a wet Wednesday in Warwickshire, with acres of obliging pink flesh to act as bait for the business clientele. Yet all the men were entitled on their lapel badges, '*Mr* Harris, *Mr* Jackson', while the women rejoiced in the familiar 'Mary, Sue, Jan'. A boy becomes a man as soon as he gets his first management position, even if he's only 'managing' one hapless typist. A woman, by contrast, remains a 'girl' until she's forty – at which point she is promoted straight to silly old moo, junked as a geriatric without ever having achieved the maturity that goes with manhood.

2) For many women these years of 25-35 will be years of home-building or child-rearing. Her own work life and career prospects will, willy-nilly, take second place to the imperatives of creating and servicing a home base for a male who will expect this support as a natural right, and who will be too busy chasing the 'bright young man' chimera to give much help if any with the domestic work

120

load. The establishing of an upper age limit for a post has now been ruled *illegal* discrimination against women, after the case of Belinda Price against the Civil Service. She found that applications to the Civil Service Executive Grade were not admitted after the age of 28. She took them to law, and won. Now that the principle is established in law, it is even more important that covert and unacknowledged forms of keeping all the boss jobs for men should be exposed and challenged.

What's left for women . . .

after all the Johnny Brightsparkses have been catered for? Women's jobs are very clearly signalled in the ad phrasing by employers, who know just what they want. The key concepts are of loyalty, support, uncritical acceptance:

> *'Secretarial skills and organising ability are essential, but a genuine commitment to the aims of the company is also required . . .'*

> *'First and foremost you must be an experienced and well-trained secretarial all-rounder, with neat hand-writing and an eye for detail . . .'*

> *'Patient, unflappable and conscientious person, with the ability to get on with difficult, sometimes impossible Company Directors (an ability to drive would be an advantage) . . .'* [this means you can drive them to meetings and they can drive you nuts]

> *'Can you retain your sense of balance and humour, to keep people happy at all levels?'*

> *'Candidates must be personable, of smart appearance, with a ready smile . . .'*

121

OK all you Girl Fridays, smarten up, smile, and get ready to put up with the worst that a bad-tempered boss can throw at you, while still serving the company faithfully with dog-like devotion and your best hand-writing – *hand-writing*, for God's sake, in this day and age!

At the interview

Make allowances for some of the really dense men that you will meet on these unsocial occasions. Beverley Bruges recalls with amusement entering one interview in the engineering industry, to see four male jaws dropping in unison. 'But you're a – a – woman!' one of them goggled at length. They all had before them copies of her application form on which she was five times referred to as '*Miss*' Bruges, and which she had signed with the all-time butch name of Beverley! Other girls report sticky and unproductive interviews in industry. This was Dianne's experience, when she lost an engineering apprenticeship to a boy whose educational standard was much lower than her own:

'He asked how I would cope if I rose to the top of the firm, or if I would be satisfied with a lower job . . . he made it clear that he didn't think I would get the job and that he didn't want me to get it. He said, "We have never had a girl here yet." The atmosphere was very tense. He asked how I would feel working with men, he went on a lot about this. He kept plugging leadership potential.'

But even in a so-called 'woman's job', a woman is still likely to be asked patronizing and discriminatory questions. Olwen Marmion, a capable and experienced teacher applying for a headship, recalls being asked, 'As a mere woman, how will you manage discipline – don't you think that men are better disciplinarians than women?' Even more wide of the mark was the question, 'As a woman, you can't don football boots – don't you think that in a junior school, the boys will think you're a bit soft?' As it happens, this teacher is keenly interested in football, and has supported Liverpool Football Club for years. She now actually takes the football in the junior school where she won her headship, since of her two available male teachers, one is 59 and can't make it, the other is 29 but doesn't want to know.

'As a woman, do you want a career, or just a job?'

'You're very quietly spoken, I don't suppose you could possibly get angry.'

'You've had several jobs in the last ten years, is your husband likely to stay in this area?'

'Don't you agree that women are never really committed to a job?'

'Are you one of these women's libbers or something, what are you trying to compensate for?'

Questions asked of women candidates for a variety of posts up and down the country

Don't be hassled

If faced with these inane and provocative approaches, let it wash over you and calmly re-state your own case – your serious interest for the post, and what you think to be your qualification for it. But *don't submit to harassing and possibly even illegal questioning*. This particularly refers to the apparently inescapable moment when employers are compelled to start plumbing the depths of your personal life/reproductive capacity/plans to exercise that natural function which alone can accurately be called 'women's work' since men can't do it, child bearing. Almost every girl reports a fascination by interviewers with this issue, even for relatively junior or unimportant posts. One woman described an interview for a trainee management scheme, conducted by four executives of the company, all male:

Qu: I see you're not wearing an engagement ring.

A: I'm single.

Qu: Well, we all know what that means these days. Are
    you thinking of getting married or . . . (pause)
    anything . . . and if so, when?

A: I'm not thinking of getting married – *or anything*.

Qu: Yes well, you're a very attractive young lady, you
    must be likely to . . . well, something. What will
    you do? Will you leave?

A: You wouldn't ask this of a man.

Qu: Well, we don't want someone who'll leave after a
    few months.

A: You can't guarantee that a man will stay.

Qu: You seem a bit aggressive. Can you cope with other
    women? How would you cope on the shop floor?
    Do you have problems?

This interview ended with one of the men demanding, 'Why industry? Surely you'd rather do something
else till the children come along?' Another saw her out
with the cheerful remark, 'I'm all against employing
women anyway, they get so catty when they're together.' Men, of course, are always such regular chaps.

124

The patter of tiny feet . . .

seem to echo and re-echo inside employers' skulls. One London recruitment consultancy freely confessed to grilling women candidates in detail about marital status and what they euphemistically call 'Future Plans'. 'Well, you have to, don't you? But we're careful to do it nicely, of course,' said the old-Harrovian managing director virtuously. Pressed for examples of 'how to do it nicely', he came up with the following:

*'*How's your love life?'*

*'*What about the old man, then?'*

*'*When's Prince Charming going to come along, then?'*

*'*Now looking to the future – any plans for the deployment of the old multiplication machinery, eh?'*

At best these baby questions are grossly intrusive – at worst, *coarse, inappropriate, and painful.* One woman candidate for a post at Birmingham University was only applying in order to get back to the Midlands where her married lover had promised to leave his wife and set up home with her if she could get employment in this region – he could not leave his job, and two salaries would be needed in order to start afresh and keep the wife and family. Children were quite out of the question as neither wanted them, and she would have to work anyway. She travelled down from Edinburgh the day before, to spend the night with her lover, who told her that he had changed his mind, it was all off, and he was going back to his wife. The night was spent in an agony of rows, recriminations, remorse, and bouts of frenzied last-time love-making. Next day at the interview, which she still had to attend as she would be unable to explain to her referees and colleagues why she had dropped out, she was asked in detail about her 'personal situation'. A panel of distinguished dons, including one very famous name, asked her if she was 'thinking of being married'. 'There must be someone in *your* life,' said one admiringly. She could hardly reply – 'Not since this morning, no.'

> *Discrimination against women does not mean dislike of women. Discriminatory behaviour is behaviour, possibly unintentional, that puts them at a disadvantage. Can you be sure that no-one in your authority makes remarks such as:*
>   *'I expect she will be leaving soon to have a baby.'*
>   *'She is likely to take time off because she has young children.'*
>   *'She has the qualifications but women are not very good at delegating'?*
> *If views such as these influence decisions about recruitment, training or promotion,* they amount to illegal discrimination under the Sex Discrimination Act 1975.
>
> 'Women In Local Government, The Neglected
> Resource', (1982).

Don't put up with it

It's irritating, it's irrelevant, and it's *illegal*. If you are harassed with these questions, have a reply ready up your sleeve. Try something like this:

* It's kind of you to be so interested, but I think you can safely leave it to me to sort this thing out *when or if* the time comes.

* I don't think you need raise this at a *professional* level.

* I appreciate your concern, but hadn't we better get off this? We don't want to fall foul of the *Sex Discrimination Act*, do we?

Or more tersely:

* This is highly personal, and *my business*.

* Do you realize that this is *illegal*?

* Can I be assured that you are asking all the *male* candidates these questions?

Or if you want to be outrageous, use the line of a now well-known media star applying for her first job in television: 'Look, buster, let's do a deal – I won't ask you about your reproduction kit if you don't ask me about mine, OK?' *She got the job.*[1]

Now do you have any questions?

There's always a point in an interview when they ask you this – and all too often women say, 'I couldn't think of a thing!' You must learn to use this moment to your own advantage – an interview is a two-way process, and this is your chance to interview *them*. This is not purely selfish. It creates a good impression if potential employers see you sizing up realistically to the task in hand, trying the job for size, so to speak. But the main purpose is to protect yourself from undertaking through ignorance something for which you are not suited. Be sure to ask in detail what the work entails.

[1] What she actually said was a good deal more crudely functional than this. But as this book is meant to be a good read for all the family, I leave it to you to fill in the Anglo-Saxon.

Establish the job description

Ask for this verbally, and then see how much of it you can get written down. Not to do so lets you in for – well, the sky's the limit. Rosemary was keen to get out of teaching, which she had chosen under parental pressure, and soon hated to distraction. So she did not look too carefully at a promising job with a travel firm specializing in exotic holidays. She thought that she would find her business feet more easily in a 'small informal outfit', as it was described to her by one of the two bosses who ran it jointly. She was to be the Chief Administrative Assistant, and it sounded good.

But from her first day it became clear that the firm was run largely as a toy by these two wealthy playboys. The spacious and impressive offices had ten telephones, but only one telephonist, and one typist in the way of staff. Rosemary had, in short, to run the whole shoot. On her first morning she arrived to find twenty messages on the answerphone from all over Europe – the ten phones rang incessantly, and she spent most of the morning trying to handle an enraged foreign tax expert, whose services the firm had used, but not remunerated. He spoke in French, a language she had abandoned after O-level. The bosses took it in turn to look in at lunchtime each day on their way to the club. Rosemary had to handle the advertising, bookings, legal business, staff management and recruitment, working every day except Sunday from before 9 am, to at least 7 pm. At the age of 25, as an Arts graduate, for this invaluable experience she is paid £5,000 p.a.

Ask too about job prospects

'If I got this job, what would you see me doing in two/five years' time?' is a perfectly reasonable question. It not only should help you to sort out what your future could be – it lets them know, clearly and from the outset that you are not content to mark time and let all the men whizz past you in the promotion stakes, but are looking already for *your* chance on the inside track. Ask them how promotion is won, and who decides on it. Ask about the work structure, and who you would be responsible to. What are the welfare benefit arrangements, holiday, sickness, pension schemes? You may think you are too young and healthy to worry about the last two, but both youth and health wear away in time – and anyway, *you should never enter a situation in which you sign away your natural rights*. You never know when you will need them.

Jackie Marlowe qualified at 18 as an Assistant Instructor in Riding and Horse Management, after passing the extremely difficult and very highly regarded exams of the British Horse Society. The numbers of keen young girls dying to work with horses makes it difficult even for qualified people to gain employment, so Jackie was delighted to win a post in a livery yard specializing in the breaking and training of young horses, which was her special interest. The woman boss offered her a month's trial, after which her employment would be confirmed if both were agreeable. Pay was to be £5 per week, and keep.

During the four-week trial Jackie did not ask for money as she believed that she would get her wages in a lump sum as soon as her position was fixed. But the four weeks turned into six, then eight, and still no mention had been made of regularizing her position, nor of giving her any wages. She was provided with lodgings and full board, but no money. Her inexperienced hints and efforts to raise the topic were brushed aside and soon forgotten in the non-stop hurly-burly of a busy stable yard.

But in the tenth week of work, Jackie had a serious accident when a pony she was trying to school, bolted, reared and fell on top of her in a concrete yard. She broke her collar bone, and damaged her shoulder blade, ribs and back. She was also shocked and seriously concussed. After discharge from hospital she was 'signed off' work for six weeks. Within ten days she was back at work, having yielded to pressure on the lines of 'I may not be able to keep you on if you can't work'. By now any questions about her situation or salary were deferred until it could be seen if she would recover or not. Some weeks later still, she left in disgust, having received neither wages, nor sick pay, nor compensation for her injuries, which could have serious consequences for her professional future – you are not allowed to progress to the higher levels of the British Horse Society exams, unless you can sit straight in the saddle. Jackie's shoulder has not so far returned to its normal angle, and may never.

On entering work

1) *Get a contract of employment that covers all the points of your natural rights.*

2) *Be especially alert when taking employment with a small firm not big enough to have a personnel manager.*

3) *Watch out for men who don't know what do to with their staff, especially female staff –*

advice from a highly placed judge experienced in employment legislation.

Don't let them put you down

You have your rights, and as Jackie's case showed, you never know when you are going to need them. This advice is number one priority and applies *in all situations*.

Next, don't put *yourself* down. Wendy Curme, who has just opened her own successful consultancy firm in London, advises, 'Most women just downgrade themselves in interview. You're asked what salary you want, and you say, Oh God, I don't know. A man would say straightaway, £13,000. A woman would *think* thirteen, and *ask* ten. You haven't got the guts to put a proper price on your head.' It pays to work out what you're worth to yourself in other ways too. Be prepared to adjust your expectations, not only when getting started, but at any point in your work life – many women have found that what can look like a sideways or even backwards step can be a move in a hitherto unthought-of direction. But don't accept a job or a move if it's really and clearly below your hopes and ideas of yourself. Look how many girls joined the BBC as secretaries in the hopes of greater things, and spend their working lives typing out other people's greater things!

Chance your arm

The final thing to remember at interviews is to be bold and resolute. Don't miss a chance through failure of nerve at the critical moment. Persuade them that the best man for the job may be a woman, and that woman may be you – then grab it, with both hands. Fay is now a successful sales manager controlling the whole of the South of England for her firm. But her first break in selling came quite unexpectedly when she was being interviewed for a post as a personal assistant to a sales manager. He was impressed by her experience, her references and her outgoing personality. As it happened, the firm had that morning interviewed for a junior salesman and had decided not to appoint any candidates as they were not of the required calibre. The sales manager quizzed Fay about her interest in sales, and then asked, 'I don't suppose you can drive, can you?' She had got as far as taking out a provisional licence, but had had no lessons. Crossing her fingers under the desk, she said, 'Yes.'

*

You can't win the raffle if you don't buy a ticket –
Joe Mercer, football manager

*

By the end of the afternoon, a Friday, she had been appointed to the sales force, and told to pick up 'her' car the following Monday. She rushed home and threw herself on the mercy of her sister, who on the Saturday drove her into the country until they found a large flat field. Under her sister's tuition Fay drove figures of eight around sticks her sister fixed up, and having done the same again on Sunday, Fay felt fairly confident when she went to pick up her car on the Monday. But when she was taken to it, parked facing a wall behind the works, she realized in a blinding flash of horror that her driving lessons had not proceeded as far as reverse. She could only drive *forwards*, not back. But her wits came to her aid again. Turning to the man who had showed her the car she said, 'I'm not too familiar with the reverse on these cars, I don't suppose you could get it out for me?' He obliged without question, and Fay triumphantly wobbled off, safely through the gates and out down the road to a success story that has currently culminated in a TR7. 'Which I can drive. Legally,' she says with satisfaction.

It's up to you

You have to make what you can of your work life. You won't have the leg-up that society gives to its male children in getting going – this is acknowledged at the highest level. An EEC report, *Equality of Treatment Between Men and Women Workers* (1975) summed this up:

'The concentration of women in certain types of activity, the limited training opportunities open to them, and the actual or potential disruption of their careers exert, albeit in different measures in the various Member States, an inhibiting effect on their working careers . . . Unimaginative guidance at home and at school frequently leads young women to opt for so-called "Women's training courses", often without any professional future. In some countries there is also the segregation between boys and girls in the general education systems, and even at the point of vocational training. This produces a demarcation in the labour market which no longer corresponds to the jobs which are actually available . . .

'A women still tends to be regarded on the labour market, because she is a woman, with an element of suspicion. When she presents herself for an interview or a promotion, the fact that she is a woman tends to weigh more heavily than her other attributes.'

But as the report makes plain, '*A growing number of women are aware of this situation. They actively resent the discrimination which they suffer, and their confinement to a ghetto of women jobs. They demand a substantial change towards a greater equality of treatment*'.

Right on, EEC, right on. That's how it is, and that's how we feel about it. If knowledge is power, men have still got more than we have – but we've got much more than we used to have, and are on our way to getting our full share. So off you go – walk, ride, hitch your way into the jungle, finding new paths or making your own. Just make a start, in the comforting thought that when you start right at the bottom – *the only way is up!*

4

Moving Up

You're on your way

So you've landed the job – good. But don't let your relief or delight blind you to what lies ahead. Keep the euphoria in check, and above all restrain yourself from telling everyone how pleased you are to have got this one. It doesn't do to look unduly grateful – it makes employers suspect that they have lumbered themselves with some dud that no one else would take on.

'I couldn't stop thanking my boss for appointing me,' said Nancy Macdonald, a Scots trainee executive. 'In the end he narrowed his eyes at me doubtfully and asked, "Why, shouldn't I have?"' *This excessive gratitude derives from women's insecurity about being in the workforce in the first place* – a man would not think that they'd done him such a big favour – and can lead to a build-up debt that you won't want to pay. 'Immediately after I was appointed by a panel of five men', recalls Rosemary, a Polytechnic lecturer, 'John approached me and told me that it was his casting vote that had secured it for me. I didn't like his approach – he described his summary on me as "I'll go for the blonde", and I had *four degrees* at the time. And later, when he was fighting for his life against redundancy, he tried to call in "what I owed him". I was supposed to go and try my "feminine charm" on the Director. I told him it was out of my hands and refused. But that shows you how he worked.' So tread very carefully in your early stages at work. A certain amount of mutual back-slapping is called for, of course, and you don't want to look superior – even if, as is likely, *you are*. But in general, use the honeymoon period in a new job to assess:

*your situation as a whole
*your position in it

Things are looking up

Paradoxically, in spite of the recession, your work chances are better now in general than ever before. This is not to minimize the very real difficulties which women still face. But things are changing as our male-dominated society is beginning, however grudgingly, to accept the disadvantages that women have suffered, and to commit itself to righting them. The impetus for this is coming down from some of the highest echelons, as policies and principles are formulated in our favour, at last:

> *Discrimination against women, to the extent that it denies or restricts equal rights between men and women, is fundamentally unjust and constitutes an attack on human dignity –*

Article 1 of the Declaration on the Abolition of Discrimination Against Women, United Nations General Assembly, 7 November 1967.

At the same time, the wind of change is blowing up the trouserlegs of the male power-holders from the very bottom, as females are steadily working their way into what had previously been 'men only' domains. In reply to the question 'Do you have any women in jobs traditionally done by men?', companies in Yorkshire and Humberside recorded over 70 'yes' examples in a 1980 survey for the CBI, including the following rare and exotic specimens:

Fine wire annealing	Wolkmann twisting	Dyer
Workshop soldering	Dyestuffs technician	Chief Accountant
Coremaking	Lathe operator	Crane driver

| Fettling | Meter inspector | Safety officer |
| Spindle drilling | Work study engineer | Artist |

'CBI Asks Yorkshire Companies About Women At Work', 28 July 1980.

Women move in

As this shows, even the old-style 'masculine industries' are yielding to the advent of women. The construction business is thought of as a man's world par excellence – yet women are making their way in Taylor Woodrow, the world-wide engineering, construction and property group. Two factors help here, as reported by Alan Jenkins in *Built On Teamwork* (1980). First, the company has never evolved a practice of institutionalized discrimination, as so many others have. There is no difference between men's and women's earnings as such; there is no 'rate for the job' at Taylor Woodrow, since you are paid what management thinks you are worth. 'The Taylor Woodrow Policy' stated one executive when asked about this, 'does not discriminate between men and women.'

Another factor has been the appointment of Cynthia Taylor to the parent and subsidiary boards of the company. Her influence has resulted not only in the appointment of more women, but also in their greater involvement in all aspects of company work. Women now in all levels at Taylor Woodrow are encouraged to visit sites, wade through the mud in wellingtons, and get to know people so that they are not merely voices on the telephone.

What the bosses say

In the CBI survey, an encouraging 48% of the Yorkshire and Humberside companies reported progress for women into male areas. A general spread of positive attitudes was also recorded:

'We are fully aware of the under-use of women in

the workplace, and intend to develop this potential'
                        – manufacturing company

'Women are more adult in attitude and performance usually. [They've noticed!] Would opt for 100 per cent female strength if opportunity arose'
                        – Hull manufacturing company

'We modestly claim to be forerunners of equal opportunities with three female associate directors. We regard female staff at all levels as a very valuable part of our organisation'
                        – manufacturing company

'We would welcome women in more senior positions'   – engineering firm

'Positive attitude to developing role and promotion of women'
                        – mechanical and electrical engineers

All good stuff, no?

And it's worldwide

The women's breakthrough has been particularly visible in America, where they are at least free of the centuries of repressive conditioning towards *Kinder*, *Kuche*, *Kirche* [children, kitchen, church] that cripples the women of the Old World. US psychologists Dr Helen S. Farmer and Dr Thomas E. Backer of the Human Interaction Research Institute of Los Angeles draw attention to the *steady trend of increasing career options for women*. In their research and counselling publications they show doors now opening into areas which had previously been closed to women – or, at best, sparsely populated by the sex which is, after all, over half (53%) of the

137

American people. Women are now getting their chances in:

Crafts

Over the last twenty years, women have been employed as

Bakers	Bookbinders	Decorators
Furriers	Opticians	Tailors
Lens grinders	Mechanics	Carpenters
Aircraft workers	Electricians	Telephone installers

As Farmer and Backer note: 'It used to be that employers said women as a group don't have the natural skill or the physical strength to do most of these jobs. *Experience has shown that just isn't true* . . . Women today are realising that a person employed in a skilled trade may be more independent, can be outdoors more of the time, and earn more than those who hold traditional "women's jobs" like secretary.' Any of those reasons appeal to you?

Management

A growth area for women, because it is a growth area in itself, growing at the same time as we are. Almost one-fifth of US business executives today are women. Women are doing especially well in the management branch of government and politics. In 1974, eighteen women were elected to the US House of Representatives, a record for any one election. Women have become governors (Connecticut), mayors (San Jose, California), chief justices and lieutenant governors (New York) and secretaries of state (California). On an individual level, women are claiming and receiving their management rights in a variety of occupations. 'I suddenly wised up to the fact that I was training men who then went on to manage *me*,' said Betsy Benham Angelico, Minnesota banker. 'So I told them the next whizz-kid I wanted to boost on up the ladder was *me*. And it worked!'

In the coming decade, many new positions will open up for American women in management. Partly because of some new US Federal laws, companies are eager to get women into management trainee programmes, and even into upper-level jobs – if only to ward off the possibility of any Equal Employment Opportunities legislation against them!

Professions

New laws have made it easier for US women to gain

access to the vital training programmes for entry to numbers of the professions. There is a continuing shortage of qualified workers in many other fields, and new opportunities are emerging every day. Farmer and Backer predict fresh openings for women in all these fields in the decade ahead:

Accountant	Mathematician	Rehabilitation counselor
Architect	Librarian	Social worker
Chemist	Physician	Speech pathologist
Dentist	Dietician	Veterinarian
Economist	Psychologist	Electrical engineer

So what are we waiting for?

Europe changes too

Habits, rhythms and styles are different on the other side of the pond. But throughout Europe, both in EEC and non-member states, women are making their presence in the workforce felt. Their welcome may be due not so much to egalitarian idealism, as to hard economic necessity. But the net result for women will be the same. As a report of the European Trades Union Confederation noted:

> The need for female labour is however gradually altering such attitudes, and new outlets for skilled work are being offered to women. Thus, there are more women becoming managers of service stations, hairdressers for men, traffic and auxiliary police constables, stewardesses and naval officers.

> ETUC White Paper on Women In Europe, *Women At Work* (1976).

These may not sound to you like the most exciting jobs you'd ever hope to hold down. But coming from countries where in the past the nearest women ever got to equality of opportunity with men, was to be an assistant in an inter-sex *lavabo*, you have to admit that it's a start!

Individual countries also report specific advances for women in their policies, or practices, or both.

Austria
now has a law in force which encourages any initiative in job creation, training or readaptation courses, to foster the full integration of women into the working life of the state.

Germany
reports *de jure* and *de facto* equality of training for boys and girls on the key schemes for entry into industry and commerce.

Luxembourg
has 3,900 women in managerial positions in the different economic sectors. Their statistics show that the percentage of women filling executive and managerial posts is 32%, while the percentage of working women in the country is only 23%!

Nathalie is a junior director of a printing firm in Brittany. 'It's pretty backward here in some respects, in my opinion', she said. 'But my boss is building up the business in other areas of France, and hoping to go out into the other EEC member states too. He wants to look *avancé*, and not be caught *en arrière* (left behind). So here I am. I may be only bait for the customers. But I've been given a job to do, and I'm doing it!'

That's the way

Hold on to the optimism and determination that you've shown so far. Too much concentration on the gloom and doom of the recession is self-defeating. Focus instead on all the *job opportunities* open to you now that we can get into previous no-go, men-only areas, and don't need to be held back by worn-out clichés of men's work and women's work. A glance at the US picture will show you that there's plenty of room for us to move out, across and up in the world of work, and how far we still can go.

Women's representation in the US Labor force as skilled and managerial workers

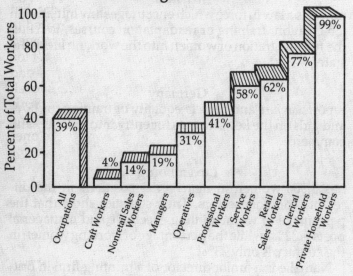

SOURCE: *Prepared by the Women's Bureau, Employment Standards Administration, from data published by the Bureau of Labor Statistics, US Department of Labor*

So where do you start?

Start on your own organization. Take a good long look at your industry, your firm, your boss – and at yourself within all this. Whether it's retail, manufacturing, local government, distribution, computers or whatever, some sectors of the economy are more buoyant than others. *Make sure you're on a winning not a losing streak.* You don't have to be a rat to desert a sinking ship that single-handed you'd be unable to bring to shore anyway. As the great Karl taught us, it is in the nature of capital enterprises to break up and re-form. Don't be smashed in some break-up, when you could be borne up by a re-grouping. 'Ours was a ramshackle group of companies', recalls Lynette, now Group Personnel Director on the parent board. 'We'd diversified in the sixties and seventies, and couldn't hold all the frontiers. The empire was bound to crack up, and everyone knew that the telecommunications sector was failing, through wrong and over-investment, and bad management. But I was the only one of the women who was prepared to join the men in the mad scramble for the exit. I managed a lateral move, had to go down a grade, and wasn't too pleased. But the others were all made redundant – and though I had to work my way back to my previous level, then mark time for three and a half years, *I stayed in work, and I got there.*' Try to apply this kind of survival thinking to your own situation at large. 'They' may be the ones taking all the decisions – but *you* are the one to know about and act upon what you know about your work area.

How big is your outfit?

Another critical point in your assessment of your work position, both for your early adjustment, and for your future progress. It may look as if there is nothing in common between a packer in a bacon factory employing 1,200 people, a typist in a pool of thirty, and the lone girl slogging it out as the solitary equine in some one-horse outfit. But apart from the privileged few self-employed women churning out hand-knits from the splendour of their front room, or potting serenely in a shed in the back garden, *everybody works for somebody*. Sociologists of 'small group theory' have stressed how instinctively human beings band together and structure themselves into small manageable units. This derives ultimately from the family, and operates just as much at work as in our so-called private lives. So who are the members of your work 'family'? Remember that you aren't going to like and understand all of them, any more than you do your own biological kin!

People forge family-type relationships on the job because of proximity, and common interest –
Denise Fortino, *Working Woman*, April 1982.

Get to know your boss

Concentrate first on the person you're immediately answerable to. You can make your work easier and more efficient if you take the trouble to familiarize yourself with their ways and habits. One particular boss of a Midlands social worker was the grizzliest of sore-headed bears until about 11 am every day. She observed that others simply pitied him for his inefficient physiology, and avoided him till he'd come round. Failure to do so ensured the rough edge of his tongue, which one stubborn clerical assistant persisted in drawing on herself by continuing to approach him in his off-hours. You can minimize your period of adjustment by watching how those around you respond to the boss – they've been there longer, after all, and have had time to learn the ropes.

The power structure

Get to know your boss, and then find out who they are answerable to. It's worth sorting out the chain of command, as you may need to avail yourself of any link in it for your own purpose. Una, a college lecturer, applied for leave of absence to travel to America on a study programme. This was turned down by her Head of Section, then by the Head of her Department. She applied directly to the Principal, who was so tickled by receiving a personal application of the sort normally handled by his juniors that he not only granted the leave as requested, but even dug some cash out of a hitherto unknown travel fund, and paid for her trip!

Moral: *Don't take no for an answer*

Go to the top

144

Knock on every door

You never know your luck

*

Big fleas
Have little fleas
Upon their backs
To bite 'em.
And little fleas
Have littler fleas
And so
Ad infinitum

*

Where the power lies

No matter how many women you work for or with, don't be fooled – in the last analysis, as Marx said, the real power lies with men. 68% of teachers may be women but 68% of *Head* teachers aren't. The post of Chief Nursing Officer of the Royal College of Nurses has been held by a man. So if men are dominating the management of the traditionally 'female' professions like teaching and nursing, what chance has your line of work got? *Check out the men* in the upper reaches where you work – how many there are, how old, what qualifications, how long with the firm, and so on. Many men are highly competitive, but competitiveness can easily outrun ability as they are compelled to keep reaching for things which they cannot acknowledge are outside their grasp. In the words of Peter's Principle, *men get promoted beyond their competence.* In two recent appointments, it may have been luck, but it wasn't good judgement that made a man the Head of English in a Business Studies School, when his only qualification was a third-class degree *in Russian* – or placed a man in charge of 350 female lingerie workers when he had previously been employed as a football coach!

145

Make a map . . .

of your work situation. This is not as complicated as it
sounds, since all organizations are remarkably hierarch-
ical in structure, and remarkably similar to one another.
Trace your accountability from where you are to the top,
carefully marking in all the members of your work
'family' and their relation to you, whether higher or
lower. It could look something like this:

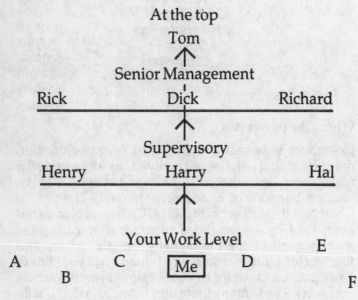

Remember too to plot in any other relevant departments:

Personnel   Finance   Planning

Flesh out this skeleton with the dimensions peculiar to
your organization – for instance, many top bosses have
an 'inner cabinet' among senior management who exert
a special influence – who are they? And the people on
your own level need to be very carefully plotted, so that
you can be sure where you stand in relation to them. You
will need this information in case of a variety of work
eventualities – training, promotion, transfer, welfare,
travel – but the time to assemble it is *before you need it*, not

when you are suddenly placed in a situation where you are at a loss without it!

Study the form

The important thing is to sort out precisely the size, specificity and working of your particular organization. One essential question to ask concerns the *number and location of the other women employees*. Even in firms where many women are employed, they tend to be clustered into certain restricted areas. Making a 'gender map' of Where the Girls Are will clearly show you what are your prospects (or lack of them) within the work situation. One female journalist on the *Leicester Mercury* did not even know, when asked, how many women journalists beside herself the paper employed, and her guesses ranged from four to fourteen. And this in a job where, as one senior woman provincial journalist stated, 'You have to be clear, from the very start, that you aren't going to be sidetracked into "soft news", the W.I., lost dogs and teddies, etc, time-honoured women's stuff, while the men enjoy all the fireworks.'

Whatever the form, remember that you are the prime runner in this race. *Study yourself*, not simply as you are now, but in terms of your long-term career hopes and prospects. Make the effort to set down what you have, and what you hope for, and then see how many of those goals you can achieve. Jan Dunlap, Director of the Self-Management Institute in California, recommends drawing up a *Life Plan Chart*, as soon as you have any life to chart. It looks like this:

Year	Age	Education	Occupation
1982	20	A-level	Salesgirl

Experience	Income	Marital Status	Children
Retail	£60 p.w.	Single	Not yet!

This was the entry of Tracey, a Coventry girl, who then went on to try to project what she might be doing in

1992, 2002, and so on. From this simple experiment alone Tracey realized how little thought she had given to her own future. She was in no rush to get married, and certainly was not going to build her life round having children. 'But I don't want to be selling shoes all my life either', she sighed. 'I'm going to have to think hard what I *do* want to do.'

So think!

Otherwise the absence of any forward planning will leave you at a total disadvantage. American sociologist and journalist Cynthia Fuchs Epstein has pinpointed the difficulties many girls experience in getting themselves together in the early stages:

> *It is not easy to isolate all the contradictory messages intelligent young women get from their environment about expectations for their future . . . They have no future image of themselves as working women. They also reject the image of home-maker . . . Their rejection of both alternatives indicates that they have no clear visualization of the future, and thus* do not prepare themselves for what is to come. *The talents of these girls die on the vine, since reality-orientation seems to be absent . . .*
>
> *Woman's Place – Options and Limits in Professional Careers* (1973).

A down-to-earth 'reality-orientation' is vital for you

And needs to be undertaken not once, but on a regular basis – initially, much oftener than Dunlap's every ten years. Whatever your hopes for your personal situation (someday my prince will come), try to think of your work life *as a whole*. For statistical patterns show that the majority of women now, married, unmarried, divorced, multi-cohabiting or lesbian, *will work for all or most of their lives.* Professor Alice Yohalem analysed the work patterns of American women in 1963 and again in 1975, and drew out the following picture of results:

US Women's Labour Force Participation Patterns,
up to 1963 and 1975

Pattern	% of women to 1963	% of women to 1975
Continuous	36	53
Minor breaks	13	11
Intermittent	13	12
Periodic	13	8
Terminated	13	1
Minimal or no work	12	15

SOURCE: *The Careers of Professional Women: Commitment and Conflict.*
(1979)

As this shows, even in the palmy 1960s, 36% of these women worked all their lives – and by 1975, the figure had increased by almost another 20%. A small proportion – only 15% – had enjoyed the luxury of being a kept woman all their lives, and not working at all. If, as seems statistically likely, you are in the other massive 85%, the sooner you latch on to that, the better. Otherwise, you may find yourself in the same position as Doris, a waitress in a Frankfurt restaurant. She came to work there 'purely on a temporary basis' and intending only to stay until she decided what she really wanted to do/found her prince/travelled abroad/took up her studies again. That was twenty-seven years ago! 'Young girls should take themselves seriously', she says, 'then they won't just dribble their lives away like me.'

In order to take advantage of equal opportunity,
women must believe they are, and in fact must be,
as competent as their male counterparts –

Dr Margaret Hennig and Dr Anne Jardim,
The Managerial Woman. (1978).

Take yourself seriously

Thinking about your work life as a whole should make you more aware of some questions which otherwise you might not ask. Are you getting parity with male workers, for instance:

* *of pay*
* *of status*
* *of training*
* *of prospects*

If you think of yourself as someone who's not staying, just passing through, these matters will hold little or no importance for you. But think of yourself ten years on, ten years older, and *still* behind the rising young sparks who, like the police, get younger all the time. One US woman computer department auditor commented bitterly to Jean Tepperman on what is all too common a situation:

> *To be an insurance broker, a woman will have to have a BA. And let's say she's got six years of experience. Here comes some guy, straight out of high school, maybe a year or two of college. They tell her, 'Well, Mrs X, you train Willy here.' She trains Willy, but when there's a management position open,* Willy gets it.
>
> *In my department there's a girl—she's been there seven years, longer than anybody else. One guy came to our department. She trained him, and after she trained him (they're doing the same work, she's been there longer),* his job grade was higher and his pay was higher *and he's the guy that's supposed to be the supervisor now . . .*
>
> *You can always tell who's who, just by the sex . . .*
> 'When a Man does Woman's Work', *Not Servants, Not Machines* (1976).

150

Don't let men get past you . . .

without putting up a fight. Make it clear that *you* have a job route in mind for yourself, and are not content to spend your formative work years setting little masculine feet toddling along the road. See job segregation as a process at work in your world, and resolve not to be a victim of this time-dishonoured form of occupational apartheid. You have three possible work routes open to you:

> * *along and up*
> * *just along*
> * *along and down*

*

Capacities clamor to be used, and cease their clamor only when they are well used. That is, capacities are also needs. *Not only is it fun to use our capacities, but it is also necessary. The unused capacity or organ can become a disease center, or else atrophy, thus diminishing the person –*

Henry Legler, *How to Make the Rest of Your Life the Best of Your Life*, 1967.

*

Do yourself a favour. Go all out for the first of these options. Failure to do so condemns you to a work life of increasing boredom, repetition, fragmentation and frustration. You have been warned!

It won't be easy

Working, struggling, changing, growing never is. And

don't expect men to like it. For centuries they have depended on the labour and support of working women working *for them*. Now that women are beginning to move for themselves, men face both the loss of that support, plus the addition of a large number of extra competitors for the work that they see as 'theirs'. As Ross Wetzsteon explosively put it, *'Goddamit yes, men do have one helluva lot to lose to feminism, and the fact that we're only losing what we should – power, privilege, artificial roles – doesn't make it any easier.'* Even a partially sympathetic man can only go so far. US politician Bella Abzug wrote in the *New York Times* of March 31, 1976: 'Our struggle today is not to get an Einstein appointed as assistant professor. It is for a woman schlemiel to get as quickly promoted as a male schlemiel.'

How far we are from any such situation is indicated by the statement of one male manager in an Equal Employment Opportunities company in America, interviewed by Hennig and Jardim:

> *I've thought about this over and over. I'll tell you where I come out. I believe that there are lots of good women in this company. They should be higher than they are. I've decided that I can live with losing out to a gal who is really good – at least as competent for a job as I think I am. But, honestly, I don't think I'm going to be able to cope with a less competent and experienced woman having it ahead of me. And to tell you the truth, that's what I think is going to happen. And if it does, I'll fight it.*

Losing out to a lesser person is presented as the ultimate trauma to masculine pride and professionalism – it is, of course, exactly what women have been putting up with from time immemorial. *But not any more.* Get out there and get stuck in – your choice is movement or stagnation. Choose movement, and move for yourself!

It can be done – do it. There are many satisfactions.
It is considerably more acceptable to pursue such a
plan now than it was 30 years ago. For me and for
those women who think and feel as I do, it is the
only way to remain a human person –

US Professor of Anatomy talking to Professor
Alice Yohalem

Shape up for your career

Accept first that you will inevitably have to change and
develop as you go along – as you learn how to do it.
Change brings conflict, and many women feel uncertain
about committing themselves wholeheartedly to their
work, for fear that it will make them less 'feminine'.
Wendy Curme, a most attractive and well-groomed
woman, said, 'I feel ambivalent about this. I can't help
noticing that it's a whole lot less challenging for some
men to talk with other women than with me – lighter
women are more relaxing to men. I ask myself, am I
getting boring, am I losing my femininity?' Suzanne
Hunter in a similar vein described herself as having 'a
masculine view of things'. Yet why should we be
suckered into accepting any definition of 'femininity'
that depends upon our being passive, ornamental,
brainless and *dull*? There's nothing too feminine about
not working, being stuck in a kitchen on your own,
having neither the means nor the incentive to make
yourself look good, feel good, and enjoy your life!

There are grounds, too, for thinking that this debilitat-
ing conflict is a peculiarly Anglo-American hang-up.
Geneviève, an attractive and successful *chef de bureau* in
Lyons, declares with a laugh, 'European women are
more secure in their womanhood. Your cold and stiff-
necked men, they don't know how to give a woman . . .
the sense of her sex. They want to look at you, even to
have *des rapports sexuels* with you – but to give you the
honour of your sex – no, no, they prefer each other!'
Among the most brilliantly successful women in Europe

153

is France's Maître Blum, the Duchess of Windsor's lawyer. Always described in the press as 'formidable', this woman has masculine kneecaps rattling like castanets throughout the world when she wants to – but no one suggests that *she's* unfeminine.

US counsellor Jan Dunlap trenchantly attacks the disabling effect that such thinking can have:

> *The career-minded woman must experience a frank shift of emphasis to herself. She must do her own thing and be proud of doing it.* She must further experience near discontent in the limited role that has come to be associated with 'femininity'. *I shall never forget my own shock in discovering how thoroughly we Americans have come to accept this false measure of what constitutes 'femininity'.*
>
> *Through a Danish organisation whose purpose it is to foster international understanding and friendship, I met a woman who was the very essence of charm and femininity. She was a Belgian lawyer, presently completing a year of additional study at Harvard. She could not understand why we had so few female lawyers – and I found myself embarrassed to explain that one reason was fear of losing their 'femininity'.*

Personal and Professional Success for Women
(1972).

*

I'm a girl and by me that's only great,
I am proud that my silhouette is curvy,
That I walk with a sweet and girlish gait,
With my hips kinda swively and servy –

Flower Drum Song, Rogers and Hammerstein

*

Don't fall for this pathetic, tit-and-bum, Barbie-doll definition of your womanhood. This is the kind of 'femininity' that every girl can afford to lose – and fast!

Build up your edge

Work on making yourself more effective in your situation. The first task may be to make yourself *visible* as a colleague among sex-obsessed males at all! Women in a variety of occupations, all over the world, report the blasting annihilation of encounters with men who

* *refuse to see them as colleagues*
* *refuse to treat them as such when they are put right*

Katharine was, at twenty-six, the youngest person ever to be awarded a PhD at the college in England where she was employed. She was sitting alone with her boss in the deserted common room, when a male from another department entered. The boss remarked, 'I'd like you to meet my Doctor Jones.' Looking straight over Katharine's head and glancing around, the man replied, 'Where?'

The put-down . . .

won't always be as simple-minded as this. It takes many forms, and you must learn to recognize it, see it coming, and evolve a few strategies to cope with it when it comes your way. You can be badgered, bothered and bewildered, so the technique is *not just to put up with it and suffer in silence, but indicate plainly that you don't accept this view of yourself and you do not expect to hear it repeated.*

Example 1

Fiona, in common with the other customers of her bank,

WHO IS THAT LADY?
BY DEE YEATER
Occupational Health Nurse, Consultant, Chicago, Ill.

While performing plant audits for an international corporation, I often traveled with industrial hygienists, almost all of whom are male. On a trip to Washington, D.C., we left the cab, and I stood by the trunk while the driver removed our luggage. My male co-worker waited on the curb as I paid the driver. After thanking me for the tip, the cabbie turned to my associate and said with a smile, "It sure must be nice being married to a rich woman!"

THE WHOLE TRUTH
BY MERRILL CHERLIN
Journalist, Baltimore, Md.

It was on a business trip to Ireland. American business writers were being informed of incentives the Irish government had set up to encourage American businesses to expand operations into Ireland. All the other journalists on the trip were men.

At a cocktail party the first evening, a senior editor of a conservative business magazine rapidly became quite tipsy. Leaning over me with a suggestive leer, he asked, "Tell me, why are you *really* here?"

SOURCE: Savvy, May 1982

had received a lot of encouraging material concerning the possibility of loans. At the age of thirty-three she decided to open her own PR/consultancy business, and approached the bank for backing, offering her London house as security. There she found that Head Office thinking had not quite filtered down to her man in the High Street. He did not expect her to know anything about money, and was plainly disconcerted when she tried to discuss with him investment, profit and growth. He twice stated his view that women did not understand figures, and had a congenital disability in handling money, finally asking her who she was planning to have as her 'financial manager'. Fiona's solution was to point quietly but firmly to her impeccable track record in business, in house and car purchase, hire purchase, etc, and to assert that if she had so little faith in her money sense as to need a man manager, then she had no business setting up on her own at all. She then said that she would give him a few days to think it over and return for his decision. When she did, she had not only won her loan but re-educated a bank manager.

Example 2

Linda was in her first month of board meetings at the company where she was the only woman at that level. In general her reception was good, though she could have done without the Chairman's elephantine welcome when she began, dwelling on the 'charm and grace' that she would bring to their deliberations. But one board member repeatedly hassled her – whenever she said anything, he would make some crack about 'feminine logic' instead of answering the point that she had made. Ignoring these remarks ensured their continuation. Finally he met his Waterloo when he greeted an important report that she had just delivered with 'Do you know, you think just like my wife.' With a charming and graceful smile she assured him warmly, 'Married to you, John, I'm impressed that she manages to think at all!' No more sexist flak from that quarter.

Don't be pusillanimous

So he didn't like it? So what! Do *you* like being belittled, trivialized and put down? If you do, write to Irma Kurtz or Anna Raeburn, i.e. one of the modern agony aunts that understands these things. If you don't, *fight this routine daily denial of women's rights to existence in the world of work*. It won't always be a you-Tarzan/him-Jane direct confrontation of female and male. Very often the strategies are subtler, so subtle that you are probably unaware of what they're doing to you. An incontrovertible mass of modern psychological and linguistic research has established conclusively that men expect to dominate even in simple conversations, and will systematically sabotage a woman's attempts to make herself heard. As Dale Spender reports:

> *My own research efforts for my book* Man Made Language *(Routledge and Kegan Paul) were severely hampered, for although I had many tapes of mixed sex conversations, so infrequently did women speak that there was insufficient data for analysis. I found that not only do men do most of the talking – they do almost all the interrupting, taking over the topic of conversation and cutting off the previous speaker.*
>
> *My own research findings revealed that 98% of the interruptions came from men: in the United States it was 99%, and in Sweden, the paradise of sexual equality, it was 100% . . . it is a safe bet to assume that when women start to talk to men, they are fairly soon stopped.*

Spender's research findings are supported by other studies, in situations ranging from the most public to the most private. Psychologists Barbara and Gene Eakins recorded university faculty meetings for a whole year in 1978, during which they established that the average *longest* female comment was, at ten seconds, still shorter than the average *shortest* male speech (10·66 seconds). They further isolated a male technique which they called the 'overlap', i.e., when the speaker interrupts at the end and terminates another's speech, rather than interrupting in the middle. In the Eakins study, *men performed 96% of interruptions, and 100% of overlaps.*

Zimmerman and West took this further with the revelation that males have a three-pronged device for reducing women's speech – first comes an interruption, then an overlap, and finally a silence, in which the male did not respond at all to the woman. Again and again it was observed that this strategy was remarkably effective in undermining women and shutting them up. As Pamela Fishman demonstrated in her 1977 article, 'Interactional Shitwork', women perform all the hard work of interaction – asking questions, 'being interested', listening supportively – yet males were consistently successful in initiating the interactions *they* wanted, and blocking those they didn't. Apparently this holds true of men and women even in 'the most intimate setting', i.e. in bed! Think of that next time you're interrupted by a man!

Makes you speechless?

So don't let it. Practise interrupting and see how they like it. Programme yourself out of asking questions all the time – 'I'll just get those letters off then, *shall I?*' – when you already know you're going to do it. It's only a way of seeking reassurance and approval – you don't need that, or rather, the only validation you need deep down is your own. Fight the prevailing conditioning/ temptation to be what one American woman comic has called a 'man-junkie', needing regular shots of men, and male approval. You're a big girl now – stand on your own two feet and don't keep looking, either consciously or unconsciously for a man to lean on, to direct or carry you, or just to keep you afloat with regular injections of praise and flattery. It's no one's job to make you feel good but your own.

*Women tend to experience themselves as passive,
as objects of other people's experiences rather than
subjects of their own –*
Ann Oakley, Subject Women. (1981)

Kick the 'little-woman' routine

What you may think is a winsome display of endearing
female frailty, boosting the male ego with its implied
compliment to their strength, indispensability etc., is
probably triggering in them feelings akin to the Ancient
Mariner about the Albatross (rather have to hump it
then have to hump it around). Many women workers
cannot resist the temptation to play the feeble female
with their boss, in an inane parody of what they take to
be the traditional male/female roles, and men often find
this a trial. John manages the jewellery department in a
large Manhattan store:

> *'You want me to be honest? The more women in my
> department, the more work for me. They all act like
> they're helpless – will you get that for me? Can you
> reach that box over there? Can you fix the strap on
> this watch? It's funny, here they can't even reach
> the third shelf, but at home they won't let you lift a
> finger, they take over the whole show.*

In a similar vein a Birmingham barrister and Head of
Chambers, after courteously detailing and repeating his
instructions to a succession of secretaries, relieves his
feelings by muttering *'Stupid bitches!'* several times with
great venom before reverting to his normal professional
demeanour.

Misogyny like this needs no reinforcement

You need to be aware that anything you do may be used
as evidence against you. Be careful too that you are not
creating a highly-charged sexual atmosphere at work.

'Just look at that one', grumbled Sidonie, a supervisor in a Brussels store, 'Just out of the convent and she thinks she's just invented sex.' She indicated one of the sales-girls, who was in animated conversation with a male manager. 'It creates an atmosphere – unsettles the men. It doesn't do to put temptation in the way of the weak.' A Midlands plastics boss with a largely female work-force was more explicit. He complained that employing women was nothing but a headache:

> Women are obsessed with their appearance, and often see sex when it isn't there. They can be to blame for raising the whole thing in the first place. I've heard secretaries say to male bosses, 'You only want me to get that file out so that you can try to look up my skirt'. All that. They're to blame for slapping it on the agenda all the time.

It's up to you

'Go for PMA not PMT', advises Joan, a Northern saleswoman, 'Positive Mental Attitude, not pre-menstrual tension. In business you can't say, "My sales figures are down because it's time for my period." You can't burst into tears when a boss shouts at you. Allowances won't be made – you'll get far less leeway than men give themselves! You must learn, stretch yourself – and be prepared to make the journey.

'And be prepared to take what they throw at you', she continued. 'The strong woman is the abnormality. They don't know how to handle it. They'll call you a tyrant, a bitch, a dyke – they automatically assume that you don't want a husband or children, or that there must be some-thing wrong with your sex life. "99% of your sort are lesbians anyway", one of my bosses said to me.'

> A woman must be able to say with confidence that she wants a career, and that she is willing to con-

161

front the problems she will inevitably encounter. She must be willing to be far more specific in her planning than the men around her, and even more alert at anticipating situations which might accentutate the pressure she will feel or expose the vulnerabilities she will continue to sense. She must in other words be clear on the need to manage her environment and herself concurrently –

Hennig and Jardim, *The Managerial Woman.*

The hassles, and how to handle them

Many of the pitfalls open up at your feet simply because the road has never before been travelled by women – quite literally, in the case of women 'on the road' as sales representatives, a category of female employment that is not so much expanding as exploding. Figures from America show that between 1970 and 1980 the number of female sales reps in the US rocketed from

* *33,000 to 97,000 in the wholesale trade – an increase of 194%*

* *27,000 to 81,000 in the manufacturing industries – an increase of 200%*

These are pioneer women just as much as their grandmothers, labouring to open up masculine minds and limited horizons just as earlier women had to open up the West. Travelling saleswoman Rose Mary Reed talked about some of the problems and her ways of dealing with them:

1) Travelling with male colleagues

At the end of a day's work on their first trip, Reed's boss told her that normally he would ask his 'junior man' to join him in his motel room for a snifter before dinner.

'However', he went on, 'I'm not sure if I should ask *you*, I'm not sure if you're supposed to say "yes", and if you do I'm not sure if I should let you.' Reed firmly brushed aside the hodge-podge of half-baked sexist notions underlying all this. *'Whatever you normally do, let's do it'*, she said. A couple of martinis later, Reed was steering her mildly tipsy boss into dinner, just as the 'junior man' would have done.

Solution: Find the normal standard procedure, and follow that. You don't have to make it *all* up for yourself as you go.

2) Customer resistance

One of the sales men in Reed's company, Dick Hughes, noticed that women would be 'tested' in ways that men were not. 'A customer would ask for some outrageous service, follow-up calls', he recollected. 'Or nit-pick. It's almost like college hazing' [initiation ceremonies of varying degrees of brutality at American universities]. This experience was echoed by Georgia Hayes, who sells for an industrial company in North Carolina. She found that a saleswoman had to go to extraordinary lengths to establish her credibility: 'One customer told me that he didn't like me, didn't like my company, didn't like women, and didn't ever want to see me again!'

Both Hayes and Reed stress the importance of being undeterred by this kind of crude prejudice. *Treat it as part of the job and press on regardless.* All salespeople have to be able to handle rejection. In the last case, Hayes continued to call on or call up her woman-hater every single month when she returned to his location on her rounds. Finally, armed with a tip that she had picked up about trouble he was having with a competitor's product, she phoned to tell him that she could provide a product which would solve his difficulty. Over a barrel, he agreed to try. 'Today that man is one of my best accounts', she says.

Where no woman has gone before

Very special difficulties can attend a woman whose company branches out into the new and lucrative markets of the Arab countries or the East. Edith Lowy, managing director of an electrical firm, once *led* a trade delegation to the East, and found herself the only person excluded from the ceremonial dinner given by the hosts to mark the occasion. Deciding to retire gracefully, she had just tucked herself up in bed, when the phone rang. The president himself had instructed that she should be invited to attend – so it was speedy transformation time with a vengeance.

Not all women's overseas adventures end as harmoniously as this. Brandy Lawrence, aluminium dealer, was to be entertained for the evening with her male colleagues on a trade mission to Germany. The 'entertainment' turned out to be a sleazy strip show. 'I don't think they could think of anything else to do with a party of visiting "businessmen"', she commented. 'But can you imagine it? It was like watching somebody wash up!'

Worse still were the recent experiences of a British woman banker, who on a visit to Japan was expected to join the men in the bath-house, since the Japanese all took it for granted that she could only be the male banker's travelling geisha/crumpet – and an American woman leading a bid for a big order for her advertising firm from a Chinese company in Hong Kong, who was immediately treated as a sexual object by the customer, on the good old Chinese principle that any woman doing that sort of thing must be a tramp anyway.

Moral: That's one thing that isn't mysterious about the East. If your good luck and brilliant career take you there, *be prepared*.

Don't overdo it

There are very important considerations for you in

pacing your progress. You should expect a lot of yourself, but don't pay too highly for your successes. *Don't give up on your womanhood*, for instance – no need to ape a masculine style with severe suiting and sensible shoes. As one senior woman told researchers Fogarty, Allen, Allen and Walters, 'I'm wearing a red dress today – and I usually wear bright colours. It's so miserable looking at all those grey suits in the dining-room . . . And it means that I'm noticed, which I wouldn't be if I were wearing a grey suit too' (*Women In Top Jobs*, 1971). Brilliant plumage may not be your style – but whatever you wear it should be something that you feel comfortable in, and not what you think you ought to be wearing.

Woman-Style has other benefits too.

Just because you're trying to get into what they call a 'man's world' doesn't mean that you have to repeat all their mistakes. Men are deeply wedded to the effort/ success dynamic, and will romanticize their often boring or sordid work capers in order to jack up their image or self-esteem. Fogarty and Co collected some typically self-glorifying comments from male seniors in two large companies:

* 'A manager in line management must be an entrepreneur . . . I look for individuals. The men working for me are all very marked individuals' [Marked with what?]

* 'I reckon business is authoritarian . . . A man goes into a meeting determined to get something out of it. If I go into a meeting, something has got to happen at the end. Women can give nice little presentations, but they don't turn the knife . . .' [What is it, *The Texas Chainsaw Massacre?*]

* 'Our life is very demanding. It's very dif-

ficult to combine marriage and the kind of work I'm doing, for example. How can you knock off at five and go home? I don't, and very few of my managers do' [Especially not the married ones!]

Who are they fooling?

Individually, women have little difficulty in seeing through the I'm-so-important, busy-bee routine that men work so hard to create, as these remarks of senior women in business, the civil service, and the media demonstrate:

* 'I'm angry if someone rings me up on my days off. I think the organization ought to be able to get someone else to take decisions on my days off'

* 'I think men like to feel important. I just don't think it's worth being such an eager beaver'

* 'They really get so emotionally attached to their work – so dependent on it – it's very bad'

* 'Women have less time for the kind of protocol that men build up around themselves. I think women are more realistic – they look twice at protocol and see whether it's worth bothering about'

Yet on a wider scale, there is some evidence that women are falling into the very traps that men make for themselves, and *succumbing to the work pressures which give men ulcers, heart attacks, and other stress-related*

166

diseases. Cary Cooper, Professor of Management Science at the University of Manchester Institute of Science and Technology, has just completed a study of the working lives of women managers, *High Pressure*. His work holds some Awful Warnings for women on the move, either in management or elsewhere.

Women under pressure

Cooper documents the stresses which these women are under through no fault of their own. 'They're having to manage in companies which have not even begun to adjust to having women around', he says. Most companies do not realize that now *nearly half* of the output of Management Schools consists of women. 'I'm the head of the largest university Management Department in Europe', he told Frances Cairncross. 'Six, seven years ago, 9% of our intake were women. This year it's 42%. And that's happening everywhere. The women get jobs – they get them as easily as the men, maybe more so. Companies like to have a few women around. It makes them look good. But what they haven't realised yet is that the girls stay. *And the companies have no career plans for them*'.

As the women move up, the trouble begins – neither their bosses nor their subordinates have any clear idea of how to treat them, and what to expect. The women suffer conflict, insecurity and wavering purpose: 'Men are called leaders, and women are called bossy,' said one woman executive, 'I have always felt that if a woman wants something done, she is nagging. If a man wants something done, then he is being constructive and showing initiative.' Not surprisingly, women responded to these pressures by working extra hard, failing to delegate, and being over-dedicated to the job. And even less surprisingly, *they are showing an alarming rise in the hitherto 'masculine' stress symptoms:*

   * *drinking too much*

167

* *smoking* (not *'too much'*, any *smoking is too much*)
* *experiencing marital disharmony and break-down*
* *having heart attacks*
* *suffering depression and anxiety*

Take care of yourself

It is vital both to present well-being and to future prospects to *keep well*. Alcoholism, cancer, coronaries, distress of mind and body are all opportunities which we must refuse to share in equal proportion with men. *Pace yourself* – keep a careful watch on your rate of change, since even a welcome change (eg. to a job you've longed for) is now known to be stressful. Don't be hustled into going too fast for *yourself* in the belief that you are doing the right thing for your *career* – the human mind and body are not infinitely elastic and adaptable. It's hard for women on the move to know where to draw the line between reluctance to move about as they are happy where they are, and a willingness to be relocated that may mean their being bounced all over the court. Betty Lehan Harragan, author of *Games Mother Never Taught You* (1980), advises on 'corporate gamesmanship for women' in situations such as this:

> *Dear Betty Harragan:*
> *I work for a retail jewelry chain and have done well during the past four years, getting promoted steadily. It is understood in this field that promotion depends heavily on a manager's willingness to relocate, an event that, in my company, occurs an average of three or four times a year. There is a big turn-over in managers as a result, but since I'm single and unencumbered I've been able to move whenever necessary. In the past year alone I've been transferred twice to different states and now my boss has ordered another move. I just*

*got settled in my present community, have joined
some good business and sports clubs, and I hate to
uproot myself so soon. My boss is pure Theory X –
he issues orders and expects them to be obeyed
without question if you want to get ahead here
(which I do). His explanation for the latest transfer
is, "We need you there." My question is: What
effect does relocation have on one's future advancement? If I object to this move, will I have cut off
chances for continued progress? I have a degree in
business administration and don't want to muff
any opportunities early in my career.*

Cooperative

SOURCE: *Savvy*, May 1982

Harragan's advice was detailed and thoughtful – she did
not for a moment accept the right either of the company,
or of the boss, to 'play musical chairs with employees for
no discernible reason'. Her final suggestion of a course
of action was based on a careful analysis of this situation,
with a reminder to the questioner that *her final responsibility was to herself and her full career development – not
necessarily within that organization.*

This is a dilemma that upward-moving women often
face – to go or not to go – and it's worth insisting that you
can only take as much movement as you're comfortable
with. 'I rushed on, rather far, rather fast', said Jill, a
producer in a television company. 'Got swept upwards
on the dolly-bird thing in its last moments. I suddenly
realized that I'd got out of my depth, and was thrown
into a flat panic in case "They" found me out. With a
mixture of luck and desperation I busked it, and slowly
started to grow into the job. But then I was offered
another big leap up, and I *was* tempted – more cash, more
status, more fun – but more demands, too, many more.
Fortunately I had the sense to stay put for a time –
otherwise I'd be in the bin by now!'

Be where you want to be

In the long and the short run, this promotes your personal health *and* your career hopes better than anything else. That goes without saying. It also goes without saying that especially as girls so often leave school poorly qualified and inadequately equipped for their work life, *very few women feel that they are where they want to be*. Whizz-kid rapid rises are all very well, and do in fact happen to some girls. But the majority of us have to reckon on the long-haul bootstraps job to get us anywhere near our work goals.

Study, train, re-train . . .

are the order of the day. And on top of working, too, I hear you say. 'Fraid so. In fact your real education for work only *begins* when you leave school. There are three major avenues for learning available after school and/or in the world of work:

* *study*
* *training, pre- or in-employment*
* *learning through experience*

Of these *studying* is the most straightforward and open-ended proposition. Look at your qualifications, and decide to fill in the blanks. There are over 600 colleges of Further Education in Great Britain where you can take everything from O-level maths to ONC courses, from technical education to pre-nursing to the A-levels you need for the next step. *It may seem a long haul, but don't be daunted*. Maureen Glover, an attractive girl whose natural brightness had been eclipsed by her mother's determination to make her a model girl, joined her local College of Further Education to take O-level English. Despite having done no studying for years, she enjoyed it, and did well. Encouraged, she pressed on to take a couple of A-levels, and on the strength of these won a place in a College of Education to train as a teacher. She is now a headmistress. None of this happened over-night, but as a result of sustained application over a number of years. 'Was it *worth* it?' she asks in-credulously. 'Well, it taught me all the things I wanted to know, and it got me where I am now – *what do you think?*'

Studying does not have to be geared to an immediate job aim. Many women find deep fulfilment in a long-term study programme like a degree at a Polytechnic or University, or an even longer Open University course. Again, even with the current climate of cut-backs, opportunities have never been so diverse, with the Polytechnics in particular leading the way with new courses and individual arrangements for mature students or 'special cases', i.e. those without the normal entry qualifications. Donna had always liked languages, but dropped out of school because she could not face the idea of going on to university to do a traditional literature-based course – 'three years of ploughing through Goethe or Flaubert, ugh!' Later she discovered a degree course at the Coventry Polytechnic which is directed towards the acquisition of *contemporary* lan-guage skills, applicable to trade, industry, business or commerce. After completing the degree, she won a job in a publishing house in Bonn, Germany. 'I used to be bitterly angry with myself for flunking out of my degree chance the first time round', she said, 'but if I'd done that, I would never have got on to this – and this is where I want to be.'

What about languages, then?

You don't need to have a degree, but only a working knowledge of one European language to consider a job in the EEC – yet many girls don't even entertain this attractive and lucrative opportunity. Over the Channel other member states of the EEC are not suffering the effects of the world-wide recession as badly as we are. They can offer, too, wages and conditions of work that make British jobs look paltry – plus other work-related benefits, and the chance to live another cultural experience which differs from ours in some fundamentally exciting ways. Yet many girls, even with appropriate qualifications, shrink in fear and trembling from seizing their chances, chances of the sort that women have never had before, and that many would have given their eye teeth for. Twenty-six female language graduates recently completed an advanced secretarial course in Bristol which was especially geared to working with foreign companies. Yet of these only *one*, Maxine Long, was planning to go abroad to work after finishing. Maxine is now established both professionally and socially in Heidelberg, while many of her contemporaries are still without jobs in Britain. So brush up on your O-level French and German, *wake up to the EEC* and get out there!

Use:

* *your local education authority (in your Council House or Town Hall) for details of* further *and* higher *education in your area* – plus *the grant possibilities to assist you with whatever you wish to do*
* *your local library for careers information and guides to specific occupations; and for* Which Degree *and the* Polytechnic Handbook *if you're thinking of an academic qualification*

Training

differs from study in that it is directed towards equipping you for a particular job or function, rather than simply giving you ideas, information and a knowledge base of a general nature. You may be trained *either* before taking up a job, *or* by your employer as part of your job. Either way, seek out and take the chances provided by

* *the Business Education Council*
* *the Technical Education Council*

These courses are for you either at your point of entry

172

into the job market, or on a re-entry after a fallow phase or dead end. They are both vocationally oriented and wide-ranging, with a number of interesting elements and components. Investigate these and others at your local College of Further Education, and ensure that if this is the route for you, you take it with the determination that it will lead you out of the low-key, low-pay, low-status rut that so many working girls get stuck in at the very start of their working lives.

In-service training . . .

is something that you should expect, even press for if it's not forthcoming. No matter how well qualified you are when you start, you cannot be expected to master all the potential implications of your firm/business/industry without any direction, let alone keep abreast of any new developments relevant to your work area. Be ready to encounter the apathy or even the hostility of male managers to this perfectly reasonable request. A *Cosmopolitan* survey of October 1981, 'Are You Being Served?', elicited these complaints from respondents:

* 'Ideally I would like to train further as I returned to work three years ago and appreciate how technology has changed offices. Yet few employers in my area offer training to use word-processors, etc.'

* 'My boss has stated that he doesn't see any need to train women staff. He calls them a "bloody nuisance" '

Reporting on the survey results, Patrick Hare and Frances Hatton comment: 'Overall, the replies to the questionnaire strongly suggest that women do *not* turn down training opportunities for "family reasons" – *it's just that employers do not offer them the same chances as men.'*

Learning through experience

This again is an area where women tend easily and quickly to fall behind men through the deadly old system of sex-typing and job segregation which is at work in every organization where men and women work together. Janet and John both joined a major Northern industrial firm as statisticians, the only difference between them being that she had a first-class honours degree, and he had a lower second. Both were moved around the firm in accordance with company policy to familiarize them with the different operations, and to assess their management potential. Yet in several departments Janet was denied entry, or unable to participate in the work. In one work area where lead was employed, necessitating strict precautions because of its toxicity, Janet was excluded on the grounds that no safety equipment was available in her size (although at 5' 7" she is only *one inch* shorter than John) and also that there were no toilet facilities suitable for a female. So in defence of the myth of the mighty male, and the myth that female anatomy requires extra-specially different plumbing, Janet is being held back from gaining the invaluable work experience which will in the fullness of time make John a manager while she is trapped on a secondary, outside track, in some 'supervisory' capacity. Alternative versions of this device operate at all levels, in a thousand different ways, in innumerable work situations. 'They' will insist that it isn't deliberate. Maybe not – if we're being charitable. *But if you suspect that anything like this is happening to you, and once you've drawn 'their' attention to it, then if it continues*

IT IS CONSCIOUS
AND DELIBERATE
AND ILLEGAL!

Men like to dismiss our appeal for equal treatment as a monstrous female joke. But we really mean business –
Jeanne Charetier, MLF (France's Women's Movement).

*

You're the TOPS . . .

if you want to be . . . One way to fight creeping male sexism openly and up front is to make your way into a non-traditional job for women. The government's TOPS scheme could set you on your way – it is offered to anyone over the age of nineteen who has been out of full-time education for at least three years, and would like to learn a trade or skill. On this scheme you are eligible for a grant while you train in the area of your choice – either find a course that appeals to you and try for a grant, or consider the range of courses available at Government Skill Centres which already have TOPS support and investigate any that sound like you. TOPS details are available from your local Employment Exchange or Job Centre – this could be your passport to the 'man's world' of interesting, varied skilled work, *which pays far better than any kind of work you'd be doing as an unskilled female.* So if you'd rather be a carpenter than a lady, in the words of the old song (or a plumber, or a welder, or an HGV driver, or a picture restorer) check out what the Training Opportunities Scheme holds for you. More and more women are discovering the rewards to be gained from this type of training and work:

Eighteen months ago when I was unemployed and wondering which TOPS course to apply for – I was determined it should be something physical and useful – a building collective was started in Nottingham where I live . . . For fifteen months now I have been working with the collective as a trainee plumber . . .

For me it was a new experience to 'learn by doing', rather than suss things out from books and theoretically first. I still feel it is positive for me to be doing this . . .

It is becoming more and more satisfying as I contribute more, to be part of creating something –

Mary, Workcon Building Collective, *Women and Manual Trades, Spring 1982.*

More ways than one

Failing TOPS, if the course you want is over-subscribed, or you don't qualify for a grant for some reason, consider a City and Guilds course. These courses were the way into practical work before TOPS was invented, and are still alive and well at your local Technical College. You can either attend for one day a week while working, or for a block of intensive teaching over a few weeks, during the three years of training. If you are unemployed you can follow a City and Guilds course without losing benefit, and women who have followed them feel that you can learn more than on a TOPS course, as they take you over a longer period of time. City and Guilds have the added attraction too of being very well known to employers, since they've been around for such a long time. On completion you are recognized without question as a fully qualified worker in your chosen field. And then, who knows? Sally McBroom trained as a painter and decorator through the City and Guilds, where she has successfully taken the advanced level exams. In June 1981 she was the only woman in the British team of building trades specialists at the International Skills

176

Olympics held in Atlanta, Georgia, having beaten 66 male contestants in the British national finals, and she went on to take the silver medal against world class competition in the USA. *And they say women can't do it!*

They do it in Europe, too

Some member states of the EEC are driving ahead with the task of putting women on the work map in places that they've never been before – in 1980, applications to the European Social Fund (a slight misnomer since work is involved) for projects concerning women amounted to *three and a half times the available budget*. 60% of the applications came from Germany, and France and Italy were also in the running with big projects. Nearly 11,300 women have benefitted from ESF-financed schemes, of whom two-thirds were trained for jobs in which women are under-represented like cabinet-making, engineering, and car repairs.

This entry into non-traditional jobs was most marked in women under twenty-five, and again Germany led the way with schemes which included the training of women as turners, mechanics and electricians. The Employers Association of the state of Hesse, for example, conducted a pilot scheme on the industrial training of girls, with the Research Department of the Hesse Industrial Institute. 57 girls were trained in metal-work in their sample – 100 more training places for girls were on offer, and '92% of the girls enjoy their training', *Die Arbeitgeber* (Cologne, 1980) reported firmly. In addition, the parents were coming round to the idea of Rosie-the-Riveter daughters, while an increasing number of firms were actively seeking to engage female trainees in metal-work opportunities: *'There is considerable room for expansion of females in metal trades without restructuring tasks, or job requirements'* Too right there is!

I like welding. There's no comparison between shipyard welding and assembly line, because I'll

> *have a different job every day . . . I think it's a*
> *marvellous opportunity for women. I wish I'd had*
> *the rights, when I was young, that women have*
> *now –*
> Thelma Carthen, US welder, talking to Terry
> Wetherby, *Conversations*, 1977.

The chances now

Foremost among the chances now for women are those
provided by the new technology. You may think that the
'revolution in electronics', 'microcircuitry' and
'semiconductor technology' are boring, baffling and
brain-battering, i.e. not for you. But as the Government's Advisory Council for Applied Research and
Development has stressed, *this is the most influential
development of the twentieth century because:*

* *it extends or displaces virtually the entire range
  of intellectual skills*
* *it is all-pervasive*
* *it is advancing with tremendous rapidity*
* *it is very cheap and getting cheaper*
* *it is international*
* *it has exceptional reliability*

In your work place, in the form of word processors or
mini-computers, it will change the face of work as we
have known it. What steam, steel, coal and electricity
were to the nineteenth century, information management, storage and retrieval will be in the second half of
ours.

What this will mean . . .

is an enormous impact on every form of employment.
The attraction for employers is the increase in productivity that the new technology can make possible – the pay-

off for workers is presented as the chance to move on to the newest, most sophisticated machines yet devised. *But it's not all good news*. Behind employers' smooth talk of 'rationalization', 'regrouping', 'streamlining', and so on, lurks the ever-present spectre of unemployment. Consider first the irresistible rise of the installation of word processors in the United Kingdom alone:

Installed Base of Word Processors in the UK

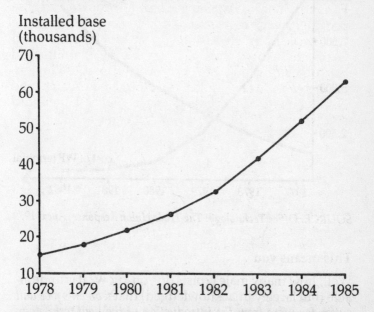

Installed base
(thousands)

SOURCE: Information Technology in the Office: the Impact on Women's Jobs, EOC, September 1980

This invasion of the word processors can only accelerate as the cost of systems continues to fall. Bosses are already weighing up quite cold-bloodedly the price of a typist against that of a WP machine. *The typist is losing hands down*, particularly if she works in Central London, or any big city where wages and overheads are so much higher. By contrast a WP machine once installed will pay for itself inside a couple of years – additionally, it may be shared with another user to maximize its capacity, and it will never need holidays, time off, or luncheon vouchers!

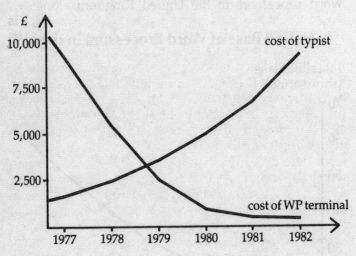

Annual cost of a typist set against cost of a WP terminal

SOURCE: *Office Technology: The Trade Union Response, Apex, 1979*

This means you

Well, how many male typists do you know? It is undeniable (but largely unacknowledged) that *women's jobs will suffer far more from the introduction of the new technology than men's*. In a 1980 survey of 40 workplaces in West Yorkshire, Ursula Huws found that in *only 17%* of cases were men's jobs affected adversely, although men were far superior to women numerically in the work force. This is because where men tend to be scattered throughout a number of different jobs, women are occupationally segregated into just those very areas which the new technology can most easily clean up. In one mail-order office, for example, the female clerical staff was reduced from 1,000 to 550 at a stroke of the computer. Another 1980 survey, for the Equal Opportunities

Commission, *Information Technology in the Office: the Impact on Women's Jobs*, had this to say: 'By 1985 we expect 21,000 typing and secretarial jobs to have been displaced by the introduction of word processing technology . . . The maximum displacement which we would expect by 1990 is 170,000, or 17% of all typing and secretarial jobs . . .'

For the less skilled clerical workers, the market is shrinking even more rapidly as the routine filing jobs disappear, and the ever-advancing technology calls for higher educational and professional qualifications. These trends are echoed with remarkable consistency in reports from other European countries. A study by the firm Siemens in Germany has suggested that by 1990, 40% of present office work could be carried out by automated equipment – this would produce an estimated two million unemployed German women who had formerly been clerks and typists. From France, a report on the financial sector suggests that a cut in office (i.e. women's) jobs of 30% could be achieved in the next ten years. These figures make the UK prediction of 17% job loss for women through micro-technology displacement look modest by comparison!

Whose jobs are safe?

Traditionally, women's jobs, however low-status and low-paid, were at least safe for women for the simple reason that men wouldn't do them. The AEG-Telefunken tube factory in Berlin employs over 2000 female piece workers. For two years the management tried to train first German males, then the foreign male workers (*Gastarbeiter*) to do this work. Failing to do so, they had to employ women. Now, a study from the Science Policy Research Unit at Sussex University describes the efforts of a sweets manufacturer to perfect a robot capable of packing chocolates as precisely as women do. It further reports that in engineering, the number of women manufacturing telephone equipment has been halved by the introduction of the new technology.

So women watch out – *there's a micro-chip about!*

All loss for women?

There are still some positive features for women implicit in the new developments – these, maximized, could if not turn the tide, at least stem the flow. 'It's a radical new system, and as such calls for a radical new approach', explained Rees, a word processor salesman for a US company. 'The chance is there for a whole reappraisal of the work to be done. The worst is when it's done piecemeal, a WP slotted into an old typing pool right next to a typist on a conventional typewriter. At best, there's a rational re-design of procedures and practices, and *a reorganization of jobs based on the primacy of the worker*. After all, if your WP operator is costing you twice as much a year as her machine, it's in your own interests to look after her!'

> Moral: *If the new technology is the catalyst for change, it could be exploited to change things to our advantage.*

Insist on full consultation and proper planning to accompany any move to introduce the new technology into your workplace – remember that it's much easier to influence and change things *before* they are installed than after.

> *There is no sense in turning our backs on the management and technical capabilities of half the population. If we let competitor countries give more opportunities to women than we do, then we are saddling ourselves with a handicap as well as producing a lot of social frustration –*
>
> Lord Weinstock

New jobs, new chances

The mighty microchip does not only wipe out lots of old jobs – it creates new and different ones. At the moment, these opportunities are mostly being snaffled by men, who have been quicker off the starting blocks than we have. As the EOC reports puts it:

> The jobs created will probably not absorb women at an equal rate as they do men. *There are, for example, many more male than female sales representatives for word processing machines, and although customer support staff are predominantly female, approximately* three *sales jobs were created for every* two *in customer support in our data.*
>
> *This shift in the balance of opportunities for men and women, with a decrease in the availability of typing jobs (traditionally held by women) and an increase in sales jobs (predominantly taken by men) is an example of a trend which we expect to become more pronounced in the future, partly because more of the new jobs will be skilled and at present more men than women have the required skills.*

This conclusion was supported by Ursula Huws, who comments, 'In my West Yorkshire Survey, I found that the new jobs were concerned with the design, programming and maintenance of new machines and systems . . . *they were invariably filled by men.*'

The writing's on the wall . . .

for every woman to see. *Don't* go for a typing/clerical post when you *know* that hundreds of thousands of women are due to be shaken out of these jobs in the next decade, as surely as autumn brings the leaves down from the trees. *Do* get into the scientific and technical areas where the men's current superiority means that they are knocking spots off your work chances. *Do* train/ re-train in sales, management and computer-related skills. Susan Harrower, then a Coventry school-leaver, recalls answering an advertisement in the local paper for a computer course:

> *Literally hundreds turned up for the aptitude test, all ages, even graduates. I felt so put off by the strength of the opposition. Lots of people were so discouraged that they decided not to stay. It was an all-day thing, from 9.30 to 3.00. But I persisted.*

Susan was selected for the one-year course and success-fully won her certificate from the National Computing Centre at the end. 'I loved it', she said. 'I had to work hard, but there was nothing I couldn't do.'

You can do it too

And you're going to have to, to make it into the Brave New World of the microelectronic future. But history is on our side, for once. Consider this articulation of na-tional policy from Lord Gowrie, Minister of State for Employment, in 1980:

> *The Government would like to see women making a full contribution to the economy, particularly in the more skilled and technical areas of work, and in industrial management.*
>
> *For too long women have been limited in their job aspirations by outdated ideas of what properly constitutes women's work. And women who have the same potential ability as men to do higher skilled jobs have had to be content with a range of traditional female jobs, many of which are either unskilled or semi-skilled. The challenge of micro-processors offers us all a chance to re-think our concepts of work, and, I believe, a chance to ensure*

184

*that women are given the opportunity to compete
on equal terms for the new jobs.*

So there you are – what are you waiting for?

These are just some of the jobs that you could be looking
for which should last you better into the next couple of
decades than the good old typing/clerical kind of work:

* Word processor operator
* Trainer of WP operators
* WP sales representative
* Systems analyst
* New-tech engineer
* Technician

* Supervisor of WP centre
* WP demonstrator
* Librarian of discs and
  cassettes storing the new
  information
* Computer programmer

Women missed the bus in the Industrial Revolution,
and finished up not only down the mines and at the
mills, but in a position of such wretched subordination
that we are still fighting off its legacy. Let's be sure to
catch this one!

> *The new technology is here to stay and will increasingly enter our lives. Good or bad, we have to
> accept it, learn to live with it, and if possible make
> it work for us –*
>> Women's International Bulletin,
>> *September 1982.*

*

> *In our fight for national regeneration women constitute an important source of expansion in many
> vital technical and vocational areas. Social justice
> therefore coincides with national self-interest –*
>> Baroness Young

Where to begin

First demystify the beast, is the advice of Elisabeth Reinhardt, formerly data processor employed by Siemens of Germany. At the end of the day, they're only machines. There's no reason why technology should remain the province of men – women must smash the myth that the mind-boggling complexity of these things puts them beyond the reach of the tiny female brain, and break the pattern that dictates that men design and create the machines, and women become their unskilled feeders. 'In many ways the computer is simpler than the stereo system', declares Reinhardt firmly. Men foster the mystique that only the initiated few can crack the code:

> The human interface . . . has generally functioned to keep the average person out and the specialist in. We must challenge and change the design of the human interface to make the computer accessible to anybody who needs to use it, without the intervention of experts, or the necessity of years of training . . .
>
> This has served as one of the real challenges for me in working with computers . . . When I worked for Siemens we successfully developed a vocabulary and a procedure by which a lay person could programme a computer. Anyone can learn this method in a matter of days. There is no need for years of math or advanced calculus. All it takes is common sense and clear thinking –

Isis, September 1982.

Women take control

Reinhardt's rules for the new-tech, woman-style:

1) Form networks and communication channels with other women – share information and learning possibilities

2) Work through your union or group of women to curb the power and exploitative activities of the company, ensuring basic standards of health, safety, and an environment conducive to a good work life

3) Make sure that women are *specifically* named and represented in any negotiations – "Workers" will not do

4) Press for men and women to be employed and utilized equally. Don't guard your little-woman's world – there's a fat promotion chance in a hen-house

5) Feed out any information you have to your local press, radio or TV networks, to share your conditions of work, educate the public, raise awareness, and establish links with others similarly placed

6) Work on alternative possibilities or modes of employment, eg. a morning on a word processor and an afternoon on something else

7) Continue to press management for escape routes in the form of re-training or job change for those caught at the bottom end

Each and all of these strategies must be employed if you are to win and hold your place in the bright new tomorrow.

What you stand to win

Informed sources stress the hopeful potential in the rapid advance of information technology. 'Chips with everything' could mean a more skilled, more satisfying, shorter and less routine work life. In particular, the new 'paperless electronic office', the shape of things to come even though it is as yet only a small bump on the American work landscape, could relieve office staff of some of their most tiresome chores. Other possible benefits include:

* Potential career opportunities for women, as males are still trapped in the older industries

* Changes in the work pattern making job-sharing and flexitime widely possible

* Expansion of the market as new products create more jobs

* Elimination of mindless and unpleasant service tasks

There is also an implicit knock-on effect for the rest of your non-work life – for your leisure, for a wide range of facilities, and for a better integration of your home and work life through a built-in computer terminal. Can't be all bad, can it?

Microelectronics offer the opportunity of reuniting the family and making commuting an obsolete and unnecessary activity –
Shirley Williams, *Politics Is For People.*

And all that you can lose . . .

in addition to your job, that is. Pat McDougall, convenor at a vehicle components factory in Calderdale, offered this touching account of the impact of the new technology on her and her women workers:

The effect the new technology had on me initially was one of total panic. Automation and its effects were something I had some awareness of, but here we were, a factory full of semiskilled women workers faced with the ultimate automation. Up till then we had some power, not much but some: as long as the employers needed to buy our labour we had something to bargain with. When they did not need it we were powerless.

We felt helpless in the face of a development which not only would crush us, but also, at the time, seemed to make economic sense. All the arguments were used: 'We must get into the race or we will be losers.' 'You cannot hold back progress.' 'We don't want any latter-day Luddites here.' And that was just from the Union side.

The management played its significance down, and tried to project it as an event which would take place in the far distant future – we shouldn't worry our little heads about it. They used this on the members very successfully.

When you are a woman, working all day, working at home, trying just to keep the family together, smoothing out everyone else's problems, it's difficult to worry about something so far in the future. 'Please God, just let me make it through till bedtime', is about all you can hope for. When a male management comes along and reassures you that everything will be all right, you want to believe it, even though you know deep down it's not so –

Ursula Huws, *Your Job In The Eighties*, (1982).

Don't be conned . . .

and don't con yourself. Women vitally need to master the new technology and the chances it brings because of its invasion of all aspects of our work life and daily existence. Get with it, conquer or make friends with it, to apply it to *your life*, your work, your future. Seize the opportunity of making a positive impact on coming developments, and don't hold back. 'If women grasp their opportunities and get themselves properly trained, whole new areas of employment could be open to them – work that women may compete for on equal terms', the Earl of Gowrie, Minister of State for Employ-

189

ment, told a Women In Management conference in March 1980. If you are a working woman, and on the move, you won't move far, either along or up, before you come across the new technology and its implications for you. You know what to do – so do it!

> *In the next few years, the technical people in government will be making choices about how the new communications technology will be used, who can use it, and under what circumstances.* Women have to be there so we can get our share –
>
> Jan Zimmerman, consultant and technical editor in the telecommunications and aerospace industry

5

Beware Hostile Natives!

The jungle is inhabited

Travelling through the work jungle you cannot fail to make contact on a regular basis with the natives. These, as in all the old movies, are likely to be primitive, ignorant, suspicious, and given to unpredictable outbursts of wild behaviour. Most working women have a low opinion of the men they encounter, with some national differences – European women are more likely to find their male colleagues on the pitiable childlike side, whereas Americans will often display less patience with the stupid savages. Clémence, a fashion buyer for a large Paris store, explained, 'Men are babies at heart. It's important to keep things smooth and easy for them, or they cannot keep up the appearance of being in charge. And as a woman, you can get away with so much by playing up to them, if they're that sort of man. *And most of them are!*' Anita is a US engineer working for an international oil company, and does not see it as part of her work to jack up any male egos around the place. 'It's pathetic really', she says dismissively, 'how many men would rather let a woman handle things than get in there and do it themselves. They'd rather sit around on their fannies and "talk things through". And it's *amazing* how many men protest that they can't possibly let a woman buy their meals, and then they're only too pleased to let you!'

The mighty male ego

As this suggests, masculine egos are very much a force

to be reckoned with at work, and it is a law of the jungle that *they will always feed theirs at the expense of yours.* Virginia was one of four women trainee managers at a world-famous London store – all were graduates of either Oxford or Cambridge, in keeping with the tone and traditions of the joint. The girls had become accustomed to some fairly unorthodox assignments in the course of the ceaseless task of ministering to the world's wealthy. But they deeply resented the occasion on which they had to carry twelve chairs and four tables down from the fifth floor of the building, out of the store, across the road and round the corner to a house where one of the directors was holding a larger than usual reception – and to have to bring them all back the next day. 'I couldn't possibly ask the porters', he explained charmingly, 'as this was a private and personal matter.' 'But he could ask four girls!' Virginia commented bitterly. 'So much for "trainee manager" status.'

They'll demean you . . .

in more ways than this. US economists Lloyd and Niemi draw attention to the fact that even within internal labour markets, job paths may be very different for men and women with similar entry qualifications. *It is not simply a question of slower promotion, but rather of a completely different job tracking*, with men being rewarded by being moved swiftly along the inside track towards management, while women are condemned to lap the circuit uselessly in some supervisory, outside-track position. These differences between men and women in job tracking within internal labour markets have a crucial effect on self-esteem and job performance. And women's natural resentment is then taken to reinforce the view that they weren't fitted for it anyway, as Rosabeth Moss Kanter showed in her 1977 study of men and women in US corporations:

> *The structure of organisations plays a powerful role in creating work behaviour. Women in low-*

mobility organisational situations develop attitudes and orientations that are said to be characteristic of those people as individuals or 'women as a group', but that can more profitably be viewed as a universal human response to blocked opportunities.

They'll deceive you

Even when you think that you are moving on the inside track, you may find that you are deliberately being kept in ignorance of the rules that you are supposed to be playing by. US businesswoman Sara Gray took a big step up with a job as a stock analyst on Wall Street. 'I joined my new employer with the understanding that they work as a team, that I would be well trained, and that their network of inside industry contacts would be shared,' she told Christine Rigby Arrington (*Savvy*, July 1982). But Gray soon found that in this 'team', however dutifully she passed the ball, it never came back to her. Denied this elementary requirement for the type of work she had to do, she failed at the job. She concluded not that she hadn't scored, but that *she hadn't even been allowed to play*. 'I was burned for believing in teamwork', she said angrily. Other women are openly contemptuous of this masculine mythologising of the ball-game, team-spirit, jock-strap factor: says Elaine Franklin, manager of corporate consumer affairs at Pepsico, 'All I learned from lacrosse is not to be afraid of a ball coming directly at my head!' Never forget that most men are operating on the Michael Winner definition of teamwork: 'My idea of a team effort is a lot of people all doing what I say.'

It's everywhere

Don't think that you have to push up to the dizzy heights of Wall Street to unsettle the natives. A group of women working in the building trade shared these experiences:

> Mary: . . . *they were just as knackered at the end of the day as I was. They couldn't lift the stuff that I couldn't lift, they botched jobs that I could botch as well as them!* . . . *The other thing is that anywhere in the building industry some men walk on to a site and say they are carpenters, and they are* not! *That's very commonplace. What I hadn't realised was that men could be totally incompetent at building work.*

Yet even these duds are trying to maintain their 'superiority' over the women:

> Julie: *We are working in teams at the moment and*

*we are supposed to be collaborating. The men tend
to get sulky if you don't want to do it their way – if
it goes wrong your way they are annoyed with you
because they've lost time, but they've got a good
excuse and can blame it all on you. If it goes better
your way, that's even worse, and they're really
sulky then!*

Women across the whole range of employment report
the constant expectation of males that they will receive
preferential treatment, and the failure of bosses and
supervisors to challenge, or even to recognize these
practices. Ruth Hobson worked in a northern biscuit
factory where the 'girls' (i.e. the female workforce) all
wore pink caps. Those in charge of the machines and the
girls all wore caps of the superior masculine colour,
blue, even though they included both men and women.
And even within this primitive sex-coding by colour, the
male 'blue caps' had higher status than the female! Can
women win?

Little Big Man

Arguably the classic example of the exploitation and
downgrading of women in the workforce is the secretary. To be a secretary is not a job standing alone, like
data processor, carpenter or teacher. It is to be a worker
for, and *with*, and on behalf of (usually) *a man*. It's a
complex, multi-skilled and demanding job which may
call for advanced techniques like fast shorthand, audio
or copy typing, WP operation or management, plus tact,
diplomacy and interpersonal sensitivity of a high order.
Yet all this is meant to be as unobtrusive as possible –
and it is all designed as a support system for *his* work,
the super-smooth servicing that implicitly decrees that
his work life is more important than hers.

*. . .He does all the 'difficult', 'responsible'
interesting things like meeting people, making*

decisions, getting projects going or pursuing a specialist activity like law or medicine. She does the follow-up work: typing letters, filing records, making appointments, etc. So there's a horizontal division: he takes the top half, she the bottom –

Clare Cherrington, 'Are You A Typewriter?'
Spare Rib, April 1978.

Secretarial work is a major employer of women, since men abandoned the profession in droves as it began to be polluted by the entry of females. It is the highest aspiration that some girls are ever equipped with in their work lives. It enjoys the dual reputation of being both a good job in itself ('Personal Secretary' to some bigwig if you really make it) *plus* the fact that many very successful women have launched themselves into the stratosphere from this starting-point.

But for every woman who has had lift-off in the media, publishing, business or industry, there are *millions* still pounding a typewriter producing other people's tripe! Weigh up the no-nos to a secretarial career – *now!*

The catches – don't get caught

First and foremost is that in going for a secretarial post, you may be doing yourself out of a job in the very near future – see previous chapter for details of the new-tech revolution that is going to put *hundreds of thousands* of women out of our old-style jobs. But even in the short term, it's not automatically the good job for you that sexist teachers, careers officers, and even parents blithely assume. OK, it's a way out of hairdressing, or off the factory floor. *But it can be a hiding to nothing as far as the rest of your life is concerned:*

Let's face it, after you've been a secretary for more

than two years, you're no good at being anything else. It's a support role, and it breeds a support attitude –

chief personnel officer at the London HQ of a large industrial company, reported by Anna Coote and Laura King

Do you want to be some man's truss for the duration of your work? Look into your other options – before it's too late.

And in the mean time . . .

you can have a *very* mean time. In her famous book *Secretary* (1972) Mary Kathleen Benet gave an exhaustive 'enquiry into the female ghetto', as she dubbed it. Among countless depressing and degrading aspects of secretarial work highlighted by Benet, perhaps the most insulting is the insistence upon secretarial women turning themselves into office geishas, the all-accommodating ideal woman of male fantasy. Here is *How To Be An Effective Secretary* in a publication uncovered by Benet's research:

*Show consideration for others
*Be pleasant
*Be humble
*Be appreciative
*Be attractive

What is this, the acceptable face of Uriah Heepishness? Can you imagine such advice *ever*, in any circumstances, being given to a man? Also, what's attractive? What is the ideal of super-girlhood that you are supposed to be conforming to? Miss World? Brooke Shields? Your boss's first love? How can you know? And what's more

197

to the point, why the hell should you bother! *The whole thing stinks*. Concentrate on looking and being what is right and comfortable *for you*, and not for him.

> *When I asked employers what they would like their secretaries to learn if they sent them on a course, 'How to make the most of their appearance' featured on many lists, and 'To use deodorants' on even more —*

> Dorothy Neville-Rolfe, *The Power Without The Glory* (1970).

For him . . .

you as secretary will have some pretty amazing, ridiculous and disgusting things to perform – all part of the secretarial service. This doesn't mean the kind of work routinely performed by the secretaries of the European Commission for instance, silently correcting their 'Fonctionnaires'' spelling and grammar in any of the seven languages of the Community. 'John doesn't speak any French', explained the wife of one highly-placed British Eurocreep, 'and his secretary is French, so of course that makes things quite difficult for him.' For *him?* Oh, sure. For him.

Most secretaries find that they have to operate not simply on a professional level, but as the 'office wife', in the familiar phrase – even, all too often, as their boss's brain and memory too. Jenny Merriman, 'right-hand lady' to pop producer Mickie Most, reported, 'I have to telephone him at home some mornings to remind him of the day's appointments. I also do silly things for him – like getting his prescriptions, and organising his meat for the weekend.'

Ursula is even clearer about the part she plays in the life of her boss, a leading industrialist of the German Ruhr: 'I take him over where his wife finishes', she says. 'I get him to all his business engagements and dinners.

He could not manage without me to do all this for him. When he is not at home, he is *mein mann'* ['my man' = 'my husband' in German]. *Is half a man better than no bread?* It's better to have your cake, and eat it too – remember that!

This isn't all

Secretaries spend only a quarter of their time in typing – the other three-quarters they spend on 'administrative tasks,' according to a recent NALGO education pack. This bland and abstract phrase covers (up) a whole range of activities and antics that they never taught you about in secretarial college. Among roles forced on them by bosses, secretaries report:

* *ministering angel*
* *big sister*
* *den mother*
* *girl Friday*
* *nurse*
* *housekeeper*
* *hostess*

And that's not the worst! A contest organised by Women Office Workers in 1977 asked applicants to submit the most ridicuous chores demanded of them by bosses. Hot contestants in the final were

* *the secretary whose 'responsibilities' included having to take her boss's toupee to be dry-cleaned and re-styled*

* *the secretary whose daily routine included having to clean her boss's false teeth*

But: overall and hands-down winner of the competition was the poor girl who had to

> * *pluck out her boss's grey hairs to keep him young and lovely, AND had been required by him to shave off his moustache, taking photos of 'before' and 'after'*

Did you ever! In the work jungle, the natives are revolting, n'est-ce pas? Well, *did* you ever? And if so, *never again!*

Danger! Men at Work!

You won't always be able to see the signs of the masculine need to dominate, and to feel his dominance, as easily as this. Men may hold the power, but the more sophisticated especially don't want to be seen wielding it like a blunt instrument, or looking stupid. In the manner of the Victorian *pater familias*, they work through a variety of controlling female figures, and themselves remain benignly in the background. *Watch out for the female 'trusty' in your outfit* – as forewoman, chargehand, section leader or right-hand-woman to the boss, she has bought into the system. Her piece of the bossing action, however petty, puts her on the side of the management. She comes to identify with the bosses, and stops thinking of herself as a worker like the rest of the girls.

Women beware women

In a Midlands clothing factory, one of the women machinists was attempting to start a union. The girls were very poorly paid, and as there were no men employed, they had no chance of an equal pay claim under the law. The managing director wanted to get rid of her, but her blameless ten-year work record prevented a straightforward sacking.

He therefore told the female head of the machine shop

200

to conceal some off-cuts of material in the other woman's bag – and when the machinist came to go home, the police were waiting for her. At her subsequent trial for theft, her defence solicitor successfully undermined her accuser. The other woman revealed that she had acted under the threat of losing her own job, but also because the boss had convinced her that unionization would be the ruin of him, and force the closure of the factory. She was subsequently prosecuted for perjury, and given a suspended prison sentence. But a prosecution against the boss, for conspiracy to pervert the course of justice, failed. Even in her own extremity the head of the machine shop remained loyal to the boss, and would not give evidence against him – 'trusty' to the last.

Deadlier than the male

Some boss-ladies not only stop thinking of themselves as workers, but even as women too. So pervasive, and so 'normal' is the habit of male power, that some women who do succeed in the world do so by becoming thoroughly masculinized – in effect, honorary men. In the old days, the tweed-suited, brogue-shod, gruff-voiced lady doctor wore her masculinity as a necessary and visible badge of her professionalism. Today's high-powered male-identifier looks more feminine, but she wears her masculinity inside. It comes out in her attitudes and behaviour – and *in particular her treatment of female subordinates*.

Shana enjoyed her power as the woman managing editor of the London branch of a top-level US advertising agency. She was famous for her sadistic prodding of the new girl recruits. One was kept in a torture of insecurity for almost a year under threat of termination, when with a husband newly launched on a career at the Bar, her salary was critical to see him through. Although aware of this, the editor was not moved – 'I've discovered through experience that women are motivated best by *fear*', she remarked coldly.

202

Sometimes the identification of such women with the power sex leads them to dissociate themselves entirely from their own. One woman financial journalist, who had herself battled against discouragement and discrimination, finally made it to her own editorship on a national daily. She then gave an interview explaining that she had nothing against women, but that she would never employ one: 'They are so unreliable if their children are ill, and they are never really committed to their work.'

Companions or competitors?

As this shows, women are likely to swallow the harmful stereotypes about women, and use them against their own sex even though their experience has been nothing like this:

> *There is some justification in prejudice against women when it comes to hiring. If I were to choose between two candidates, equal in qualification but one male and one female, I am inclined to choose the male. When one hires a female, one is risking discontinuity and lack of commitment . . . one cannot get the same kind of devotion and commitment from a woman unless she is determined to remain single.*
>
> *In regard to chairmanships or directorships, again I feel that there are good reasons for the prejudice. Having directed a project with two male PhDs under me, I learned my lesson. Men, and even women themselves, don't like working under a female boss. Effectiveness and productivity of work are so reduced by the resentment and tension created by such men that it makes one wonder whether it is worth while to have women head departments or projects unless the nature of the field is such that it has to be or should be a woman (eg. home economics, child rearing).*

The author of this is a highly-placed American woman academic – but she seems short on logic. *Men* create the tension and resentment, so *women* shouldn't be appointed? Women must stay single to get anywhere, but they are still the only sex to know about child care? And women must deny themselves a male partner to be effective, while male academics are allowed the full life of marriage, career and family, not to mention the campus womanizing with which they disport themselves among the groves of academe? Come off it, lady!

Girls against girls

This polarization of women against one another works in all jobs and at all levels. Joyce Betries, New York waitress, reports these experiences:

> *Bosses work hard at keeping their women employees divided, especially the hostesses and the waitresses. Hostesses have a nicer-looking job than waitresses. They're on their feet all day, but they wear street clothes and usually don't have to do the heavy work of carrying loads of food the way we do. Sometimes bosses don't like to be bothered directly supervising the waitresses, so they make the hostesses do it instead. In the last place I worked, we waitresses weren't allowed to eat anything without paying for it. None of us had ever beforehand had a job where we weren't allowed to eat, and we knew how unfair this was. The hostess had to enforce this rule, and if she caught us eating, she would yell at us, and sometimes she told the boss.*
> If the boss caught us, not only our job but the hostess's would be in danger. *The hostesses were also made to enforce the boss's rules on how clean our uniforms and shoes should be, what was the proper length for our skirts, how we should wear our hair and make-up, and how long and how often we should take our breaks. Often she was*

made to check out the bathroom, to see if we were
'hiding' in there. Hostessing isn't an easy job, but
often the hostesses ordered us around as if they
were the boss, when we all know that they were
being used by the boss, just as we were. They
make even less money than we do, but still
forget which side they're on.

It's her fault

Eve was framed – so could you be – US slogan

The female quislings all agree about one thing, that
women are to blame. As a French woman academic
argued:

> While it is quite true that women have been and are
> discriminated against, they have often asked for it.
> While they may well have had to be aggressive and
> suspicious to get anywhere in academic life – or in
> any field of work – once they get there, they do not
> adapt their behaviour. Women have never learned
> that their adamant insistence on being taken
> seriously, on being equal, is what makes them
> uncomfortable in the world, and makes men react
> badly to them.

So now you know. Learn to 'adapt your behaviour',
and you too could become a fifth columnist for male
intelligence – even, in time and if you're good, an NCO
in their army!

Sisterhood is solidarity

As all this shows, it's very dangerous to assume that any
women will be on your side just because she's the same
sex as you are. In the history of the world, *no ruling group
ever gave up its power and privilege without a bitter struggle,*

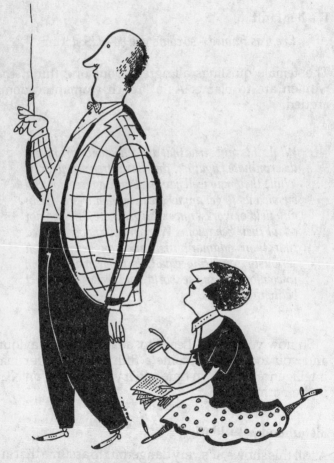

DON'T BE A FIFTH COLUMNIST

and it is in the interests of MCPs in positions of dominance and control to divide and diminish women. But you don't have to join in. *Refuse*. Don't be drawn into management action against another female. Dawn, a London trainee nurse recently resisted pressure to lay the blame for a serious malpractice on another nurse, so that the male consultants and hospital management could evade a costly and damaging action for negligence. Such solitary acts of bravery do not make a revolution – but they are all that stand between powerless women and their random or institutionalized exploitation by the race of men.

Dirty Tricks Inc.

But in the end, your greatest danger in the work jungle will come from men. Males take very seriously women's intrusion into their territory, and have perfected a variety of techniques to keep women out where they can, and to make them feel bad and out of place where they can't. First come the 'decent', legal, bureaucratic anti-woman tricks and manoeuvres. One of the most common and extensively practised *is widely known, and was criticised in an EEC report as long ago as 1974:*

> *In most industries at present, rates of pay are classified according to various categories, such as young persons; unskilled; semi-skilled and skilled male or female; male clerical; female clerical, etc. This often corresponds to segregated areas of work, at least in the manual trades. The Equal Pay Act may not make much difference therefore if there are no women doing 'the same or roughly equivalent' work to a man:* the name of the women's pay grade will be changed, *perhaps to Grade I . . . but job segregation will remain. Some firms are attempting to avoid increases to the lowest male rate [to avoid having to pay women more].* Others are fixing the lowest rate at a level below

which a man would be willing to work, or are moving men out of the lowest grades.

Evidence to Parliamentary Select Committees also shows that firms which are using job evaluation, and implementing Equal Pay for jobs 'rated of equal value', are doing it in such a way as to ensure that women's jobs are not rated equally with men's. *This can be done by giving lower points or 'weighting' to 'female' skills, such as dexterity, and more to physical strength job requirements. Alternatively,* men's jobs are re-named *even if involving the same work – eg. women remain 'shop assistants', men become 'warehousemen'.*

To get women's jobs classified as being of a high grade . . . is where the problem begins –

Women and Employment in the UK, Denmark and Ireland, Commission of the European Community, (1974).

And all these male-protecting, women-degrading tricks are perfectly *legal*, permitted by 'the system' – the masculine system, that is!

How the system does the dirty on women . . .

in thousands of ways that we've never even thought of. Pringle Smith has 'spent much time prodding and poking' at the bureaucratic bastions of male supremacy in the course of her work as a member of the University of Michigan's Commission for Women, and editor of the University Graduate School of Business Administration Magazine. She has identified some of the ways in which 'the system' and those who run it resist change:

*THEY REFUSE US THE FACTS
Smith herself was repeatedly blocked in simple attempts

to find out employment totals and dispersion by sex. Women in banking have complained through the Banking, Insurance and Finance Union that while males are encouraged to take all the promotion chances available, information about the courses and training opportunities that make promotion possible are *withheld from women*.

*THEY DISGUISE REAL REASONS WITH PHONEY ONES

Male managers will *never* say, 'We haven't promoted you because you're a woman.' They'll say it's because you're not old enough/too old, not experienced enough/too experienced, or even, in the last resort, your face wouldn't fit. One female reporter, with a good track record in British journalism and fluent in French and German, applied for a job with Reuters in Europe. She was told it was not that *this* head of department would not employ a woman, but that the agency's foreign contacts would not work with one. 'European men are very funny about these things', he said condescendingly. Not him, of course.

*THEY DISTRACT AND DIVERT US

Whenever you try to get a male to focus on discrimination against women, the standard evasion is, 'Ah, but what about blacks/homosexuals/ethnic minorities?' Does *he* care about these other disadvantaged groups? *Does he hell!* He's just trying to duck out of the argument by broadening the question to an impossibly wide and vague level – and also to score off you by implying that in selfishly pushing for *your* advantage, you don't care about the others. And faced with the inescapable facts about women's glaring pay inequality, they say, 'Ah, but there's a recession on!', piously pointing out how much it would cost to raise women's pay to the level of men's. This ploy is designed to make you feel

209

(a) *that there's nothing to be done about your pay disadvantage*

(b) *you are a grasping enemy of the hope of national economic recovery if you persist in trying to get equal with men*

*THEY GIVE US WORDS NOT DEEDS

All male leaders now are versed in the affirmative pronouncements and encouraging platitudes of getting women out of the closet and into

higher education	*science*	*technology*
industry	*commerce*	*banking*
the law	*parliament*	*public bodies*
etc.	*etc.*	*etc.*

Companies, too, play this game – they issue 'Equal Employment Opportunity Statements' as enthusiastically as confetti at a wedding, the more so as the mere *issuing* of these bromides gives them in the US a substantial measure of protection from legal action against them. Governments appoint commissions and committees to sit on/chew over/regurgitate the hardly unfamiliar facts of women's oppression, but deny them any legal sanctions, even the power to compel witnesses. Result? *Another* report. *It's all hot air*. It may make them feel better, but where does it leave women? Still running behind, with another faceful of masculine gas!

And then if all else fails . . .

*THEY RETALIATE

Women from all over the world are reporting the punches, kicks, gougings and woundings they've received in attempting to scrum down with the men:

A German librarian was assigned to the Children's Section despite her declared lack of interest in the

little readers, and her degree in Political Science. She repeatedly requested a transfer, and was put down as 'unco-operative', and 'disruptive'. When the Children's Section closed down in a rationalization, other colleagues were transferred to adult departments, but she was made redundant.

An American woman Director of Public Relations for her company enquired of the President how many women in the past had made it to Vice-President. He told her that none had, but then, none had 'presented themselves'. She decided to present herself, and did so in the form of a carefully-prepared document setting out her qualifications and achievements. This was received with everything from incomprehension to derision among the male VPs, and drew a total blank. But some time later she was told that the management felt that she had 'outgrown' her place in the organization, and that she should look for another job. This message was increasingly reinforced until she left.

A British woman was appointed to a London publishing house with special editorial responsibility for developing a 'women's list'. Interpreting this to mean Virago rather than Mills and Boone, she picked up on some projects which the largely male editorial board found 'political' and 'contentious'. When three of her suggested commissions had been stopped in a row by her immediate male boss, she challenged the rationale of his decision and tried to establish the basis on which she was working. She was told that her decisions were wrong – she didn't have an editorial 'nose' – and that her appointment had been made on a misunderstanding of the market – 'there's no mileage in women any more'. Her special responsibility was removed, and her work became so trivial, routine and disjointed that as she says, 'I didn't want to leave, but the job had left me'.

ALL THESE TECHNIQUES, TACTICS AND TRICKS
HOWEVER DIRTY AND DAMAGING
ARE LEGAL!

These men are professionals . . .

in every sense of the word. Lower down the power/
education scale, the men play even dirtier. Vebeka is a
Danish woman who worked as a crane driver for seven
months in Norway. Her foreman originally came on all
supportive – 'Why shouldn't women do the same work
as men?' But he resented Vebeka's criticizing the standard of safety procedures at the plant, where the men
ignored basic precautions not only with the huge
machines, but with cancer-inducing chemicals. He
obstructed and humiliated her in every way that he
could, and even though she was proved right when one
of the men died in an accident, did not change his
behaviour but only intensified it. Illogically, he was
even nasty to her when she said that she was leaving, as
he felt that it reflected badly on him!

Other women in non-traditional roles encounter their
own trials at the hands of male colleagues. Women in
engineering and industry have to suffer the dis-
appearance of their tools and implements, often expensive items and always essential to the work in hand – in
these areas, too, it is quite common for a female to be
sent to Coventry or otherwise ostracized if she commits
the unpardonable, unmentionable sin of passing out
higher than the males in any exams they all take. These
low-down tricks are threatening, disheartening, and
exhausting, as Sylvia, a London gardener, reports of her
workmates:

> Sometimes I want to strangle them. They wear me
> out with their teasing, their racist and sexist com-
> ments (this mostly from the three older blokes).
> I get physically very tired, but when they are on
> form I come home at night near to tears. At present

212

I am having a particularly difficult time with a
young bloke I work with . . .
I'm very tired of being so tired –

Women and Manual trades October 1981.

Yet Sylvia, in comparison with some, gets off lightly. An American woman on trial as a fork-lift operator had to move and stack 400 heavy lorry tyres by hand, while 'all the supervisors stood around and looked at me and laughed' – and a woman welder training in the US *had a hole drilled in her arm!*

Why do they do it?

Apart from the obvious reasons, you mean? US psychologists have tried to answer this question by researching the type of man most likely to obstruct women and oppose women's rights. He is:

concerned with his status
needing to look proper and respectable
rigid and inflexible
authoritarian and overcontrolling
deferential to male authority higher than his own
weak in ego-strength
illogical
fearful of and resistant to change

Does this sound like anyone you know? Or just all of them? Evelyn works as a receptionist in the car hire department of a large Oxford motor company. She devised a simple system whereby the girls who did this work could stagger their lunch-hours and thus avoid leaving the phone untended as happened at the time. Her manager refused point-blank even to consider it – 'You girls are only trying to wangle more time for yourselves . . . for shopping, getting your hair done . . . and going to the lavatory!' he accused.

Manners maketh man

In another research project, psychologist Philip Goldberg of Connecticut college isolated a group of misogynists who had high scores in tests of antipathy to women. Further experiments, including the aptly-named Rotter test, revealed that these men also scored highly in

> *hypochondria
> *hysteria
> *lying

Not surprisingly, they all romped home with high grades in tests designed to reveal 'general neuroticism'. Finally Goldberg demonstrated that *'misogyny is directly related to the need for power in men'*.

Tell them again, doctor.

Louder!

Numerous research studies have in fact confirmed that a man's level of self-esteem correlates directly to his attitude to the emancipation of women. The more logical, intelligent and secure in himself he is, the less he fears the forward movement of the other sex in terms of social and educational gains. But most men aren't any of these. As Benjamin Wolman, New York psychologist, puts it:

> *There are some people who for psychological reasons need to discriminate against others. They seem to feel that they have added some value or importance to themselves by assuming their superiority in regard to others, and displaying their hostile superiority feelings in apparent pursuit of easy self-aggrandisement . . .*
>
> *In my clinical practice I noticed that insecure men, under-achievers, men who are pushed around in their jobs, men who felt that they were not respected by their colleagues and associates, have been prone to discriminate against women. It*

seems that this was the only area where they could show their non-existent power . . .

Wolman concludes with a rallying cry that could be emblazoned in every woman's workplace in the world:

> *Defenceless people invite persecution. Weakness invites discrimination. The more women become aware of the fact that no one has the right to abuse his physical power against them, or to exploit them economically or sexually,* the more women will stand up to those who try to put them down, *the better will be the chance that discrimination against the largest human group will become extinct and fossilised.*

Got that, you women? Good!

Fight it – you're going to have to

When the natives are hostile, they do not content themselves with lurking and muttering in the undergrowth. *They attack.* And as they only attack you on the basis of sex difference, what better weapon against you than your sex? The savages of the work jungle aren't so ignorant but that they've perfected a variety of sexual strategies for use against women. They spring from a deep and unacknowledged well of anti-woman fear, hatred and hostility, latent in all men because endemic in our culture. These strategies are as old as the hills and as new-minted as today's transactions in thousands of shops, offices and factories all over the globe.

> *The men I work with sometimes get real mad and start calling me the worst thing they can imagine, and that is a cunt. That is very much like the way the men my father worked with responded to each*

215

*other – always competing and grading themselves
and using women to grade each other.* The lowest
grade is to be like a woman –

Andy Weissman, car mechanic, *The Women
Say The Men Say*, Evelyn Shapiro and Barry
M. Shapiro, 1979.

Sexual harassment . . .

is the name of the game. It has only recently come by its
distinctive brand name, and its identity is a shame
against working women and an indictment against the
men who practise it. From its emergence in America
around 1975, it has rapidly advanced in public awareness as a number of different studies have indicated the
scope and seriousness of the problem. Yet because of the
silly, smutty, page-three mentality of much of the
national press coverage (cartoons of women workers
complaining 'Sex harassment? *I* never get any!') the
result is that the newspapers have just continued
to reproduce the original offence – which is, in brief,
the offensive and degrading treatment of women's
sexuality.

You know what it is . . .

because according to survey statements of the spread of
sex harassment, you will have either experienced it, or
witnessed it, or both – unless you work in a nunnery. A
US Federal Survey of March 1981 offered the following
criteria of sexually harassing behaviour of one employee
to another:

Severe sexual harassment
1. *Letters, phone calls or materials of a sexual
   nature*
2. *Pressure for sexual favours*
3. *Touching, leaning over, cornering or pinching*

216

Less severe
4. *Pressure for dates*
5. *Sexually suggestive looks or gestures*
6. *Sexual teasing, jokes, remarks or questions*

This seems fairly comprehensive, but the investigators found that *it did not go far enough* – of the women surveyed, nearly 700,000 in all, a small but significant percentage reported harassment of a very severe nature, up to and including gross sexual assaults and even rape. *Nine thousand* American women in the survey had suffered in this way. The final results of this investigation were as follows:

Percentage of US Working Women Who Experienced Sexual Harassment between May 1978 and May 1980

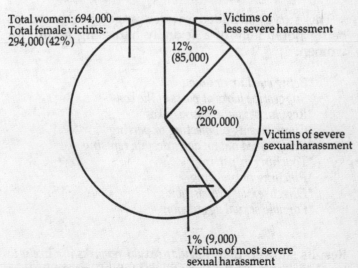

Total women: 694,000
Total female victims: 294,000 (42%)

Victims of less severe harassment

12% (85,000)

29% (200,000)

Victims of severe sexual harassment

1% (9,000)
Victims of most severe sexual harassment

SOURCE: *Sexual Harassment In The Federal Workplace:
Is It A Problem?*
A Report of the US Merit Systems Protection Board, March 1981.

Sex in the office

In England, the Alfred Marks Bureau has performed an inestimable service for its girls by helping to put the topic firmly on the map. As Bernard Marks ruefully confessed:

> *Nobody had more egg on their face than I had. I've been running this company for 36 years telling everyone that it doesn't happen, and clearly this survey shows that it does, in a big way.*
>
> Sexual harassment is a major problem. *It can cause people to leave their jobs, but they will not talk about it because they don't want to be thought of as someone without a sense of humour, a troublemaker, someone who in fact is the guilty party. Which is sad, because they are victims of something that can be extremely distressing.*

This survey included a wider range of behaviour as being potentially of a sexually harassing nature for women:

> **Being eyed up or down*
> **Suggestive looks at parts of the body*
> **Regular sexual remarks/jokes*
> **Cheek kissing on meeting or parting*
> **Being asked out on dates despite refusing*
> **Touching or patting*
> **Pinching or grabbing*
> **Direct sexual proposition*
> **Forcible sexual aggression*

Results showed that '*Regular sexual remarks are likely to upset 48% of employees* and will definitely upset a further 17% . . . *Female employees definitely do not like to be touched or patted* by their colleagues as 42% felt this was definitely sexual harassment . . . When it comes to pinching or grabbing it was universally accepted that *this behaviour is not acceptable . . .'*

*

Bassetlaw MP Joe Ashton's way for men to control a bossy woman is as follows: 'They've never been fancied . . . All you have to do is smile and blow her a kiss and then one day, preferably in front of a crowd of other women, just get behind her, put both hands on her bum, and say in a deep guttural voice, "Ooooooo, you're an exciting woman, Bertha"' –

Doncaster Evening Post

*

This is the message that needs to be got through to men loud and clear – women do not like or welcome this behaviour, they consider it to be harassment, and totally unacceptable. In other words, 'Ooooooo, you're an 'orrible man, Joe!'

You tell Cosmo, it's *not* a joke

The more information comes to light, the more epidemic the spread of sexual harassment appears. In the spring of 1982, *Cosmopolitan* magazine conducted a survey of what was described as 'a massive problem, but still not accepted as such'. It may be argued that Cosmo readers are more up-to-the-minute and aware than the majority of women, and more likely to be in touch with the American experience of the problem. Nevertheless, their results were still staggering – of 428 women, *only 16 had NOT been harassed at work.*

The size of the problem

Results from the different surveys at different times and in different countries show a varying percentage of women experiencing sexual harassment:

US Federal Survey: 42%
Alfred Marks Bureau: 51%
Cosmopolitan: 96%

Other results are similarly varied – a 1975 US survey found that 70% had had this experience, while a 1977 investigation from the University of Texas *failed to find one woman who had not!* Even when the question is heavily loaded, women will report their adverse experiences – a 1980 survey for the EEC among 3000 women asked them to state if they had been *'victims of sexual blackmail'*. Even with this melodramatic and lurid phraseology, 8% of French women and 7% of British women declared that they *had*. One thing is clear – this is a real, sizeable and sickening problem for a lot of working women, and constitutes literally *thousands* of the dirtiest of dirty tricks that men are capable of.

Sex harassment and you

So it's everywhere – but where do you stand? Many working girls are confused by the whole thing. They react strongly against the sordid press angle ('Slap and Tickle in the Work Place'; 'Office Romeos strike') yet want some sensible comment on what is a real problem wherever men and women work together. First, accept from the outset that sex will rear its head, ugly or otherwise, in your working life. 'You can't get away from sex at work', says Avis Lingard, a Midlands businesswoman, 'It's a fact of life.' Indeed, according to one authority, it's a fact *before* you enter your work life:

Male hiring authorities find it difficult to separate their aesthetic feelings about what a woman should

*look like from the technical aspects of the job. Men
have great difficulty with that. They often feel they
are judged by the women with whom they
surround themselves.*
*This kind of discrimination exists in all levels of
employment, regardless of whether it is an assistant in a chemistry lab or an executive in a corporate
office –*

Harvey Rubenstein, Chief Operating Officer
and Senior Partner, VIP Employment
Agency, Los Angeles, USA.

Consciously or unconsciously, men feel that they are the
overlords in the world of work. In their minds this gives
them something like the old-fashioned *droit de seigneur*,
the overlord's sexual perks, with every female they encounter. *They* are going to try it on. It's up to *you* to work
out what you are going to stand, and how much.

Sort out your standpoint

Different things are distressing to different people, and
sexual harassment goes in an ascending order of severity anyway. Let's start with the *verbal*. Many men enjoy
creating/obtain relief from tension by maintaining a
steady flow of sexual talk, innuendoes and jokes. These
can range from the apparently complimentary ('What a
figure! You wouldn't get two of those in a pound!') to the
frankly insulting ('Your nipple's sticking out' – which,
by the way, landed one Richard Smith in court and
among other things eventually cost him £954).

More problematical are the dirty jokes which are
usually both gross and unfunny – especially at 9.30 on a
Monday morning – but which are always carried on in
such a way as to make it very awkward, if not impossible, for a female victim to object or escape. But all too
often mucky-mouthed men don't even bother to
pretend that they are being friendly or fun. One woman

221

executive took a rare day off with a cold, and was greeted by a male chorus on her return of 'We missed you yesterday, *how was the abortion*?' Blue-collar or manual women workers entering 'male' territories routinely run the gauntlet of verbal assault to punish them for their intrusion and to ensure that they get out again as quickly as possible, so a male car worker at the Fisher Body Plant in Ohio reports:

> *Like every other man there I discuss and evaluate the physical appearance of every woman around me . . . Many men are completely unabashed about letting women know that they are being watched and discussed, and some men are quite open about the results of their analysis. Really attractive women have to put up with incredible harassment, from constant propositions to mindless and obscene grunts as they walk by. Men who call out these obscenities can't actually be trying to sleep with the women they are yelling at – they are simply making the women suffer for their beauty –*

John Lippert, *The Women Say The Men Say*, (1979).

As this shows, men do this lousy stuff not only to make themselves feel better, but to make the women feel *worse*. It is amazing that only *half* of Alfred Marks' survey sample objected!

One step up . . .

from verbal harassment is physical. As all the surveys show, women do not appreciate being grabbed, poked, felt, fingered, pinched or prodded. Yet few of the women who work with men get away without some at least of the manifestations of male 'interest':

222

* *Rosalie worked as a receptionist for a married couple, a doctor and an optician, both in their sixties. One morning as she was taking her coat off the husband suddenly squeezed her breast and said that she should keep her chest warm, as the weather was getting cold (she was wearing a thick polo-neck sweater). She shrugged this off, but he continued 'accidentally' to touch her body whenever he could, until she had to leave.*

* *Christine had only been a barmaid at the pub for a month when one day she was left alone with the landlord at closing time as his wife had gone out. 'He suddenly grabbed me, pulled me to him and was rubbing himself against my body', she said. 'I tried to pull away and reason with him, to no avail. He pulled his penis out of his trousers and asked me what I thought of it (I felt sick). I said he should be ashamed of himself—that he had a daughter the same age as me and how would he like some dirty old man doing this to her.' This made him release Christine immediately. He apologized and asked her to tell no one. But she could never work there again.*

Men don't have to touch women to make them feel physically degraded. Flashing is a fun kick for some of the brutes, especially if the recipient of the pretty sight is young and inexperienced. And one US woman executive reports a boss whose daily delight was to get one of the office girls in, talk to her and masturbate at the same time: 'He could do all these things and get away with them because he was a man, and I had to take it because I was a woman . . . I was intruding in the men's club' (*Male Chauvinism: How It Works*, Michael Korda 1972).

More problematic . . .

and more confusing are the occasions when the harasser

is too subtle for a crude physical assault, but tries for the same result by masquerading as your friend/counsellor/long-lost brother. Wanda had underestimated the sexual threat posed by her boss in local government, as he was so deeply unattractive ('short, fat, fifties, decaying – *ghastly*!) that it never occurred to her that he could think of *himself* as a possible sex object, even if he took her for one. His move, when it came, was both violent and unexpected. He cornered her in the office one lunch hour and threw her across the desk, ludicrously attempting to have sex with her there and then. She fought him off and ran weeping to another male superior who gently encouraged her to tell him the whole tale. When she had finished, he too got in on the act, trying to feel her up and propositioning her in no uncertain manner. When she protested, feeling doubly betrayed, he asked her what she had expected, turning a man on like that!

What do you expect?

You have the right to expect that your work environment will be free of this and other kinds of physical abuse, and that male colleagues or bosses will display the characteristics of a professional instead of the instincts of a predator. And whatever happens to you, do not make the mistake of thinking that this is just an individual problem – yours. First, the facts and figures show that it happens to vast numbers of women, no matter where or who. As the *Cosmopolitan* survey discovered: 'Sexual harrassment does not affect just young, attractive women bothered by young, over-sexed men. *Women of all ages, shapes and sizes reported being harassed by all kinds of men* – including the over-sixties.'

This also demonstrates that physical harassment has nothing to do with overwhelming physical attraction. 'I am forty-six', 'not well preserved', 'tall and ungainly', 'rather plain' run some of the touching self-put-downs of women subjected to these unwanted and unwelcome assaults. But what is the really clinching piece of evidence is that the US Federal survey of 1981 *exposed the harassers as 'repeat offenders'*. In other words, so far from having been swept off their feet by a sudden over-whelming passion for *you*, they have *bothered other women on a regular basis*. So much for:

* *'I just can't resist you in that red dress.'*
* *'What's that scent you're wearing, it's driving me wild?'*
* *'Do you know you have the sexiest dimple in your cheek/chin/lip?'*

and all the rest of what Lady Bracknell called 'meretricious persiflage'. Tell them to put *that* in their pipe and smoke it!

This thing is bigger than both of you . . .

in another way, too. Both you and your harasser are working within some kind of organization or in-stitution, and from the beginning to the end of the day it will be *on his side, rather than yours*. As one Federally-employed woman reported to a government subcom-mittee, 'I said no, I simply was not going out with him after work, and no, I was not going to have an affair with him because I thought I could rely on my job skills. I was fired with 25 minutes' notice on a Friday.' In Britain, the jealous wife of a senior barrister with an international steel company lodged accusations that her husband was having an affair with his secretary. Although the top brass accepted that this was not so, the secretary was 'asked to resign' anyway, 'to avoid any future un-pleasantness'.

The institution will close ranks against you to protect even its most crudely offending members. Boys will be boys, and no one understands this better than the boys who run the club. Its members derive their tactics, techniques, and even their ammunition from the or-ganization, because it gives them the power of hiring, firing, promoting or punishing. Not unusually, it puts the weapon they need right into their hands. One British actress had had steady employment as one of the regular characters in a famous long-running radio serial. She was distressed to be told by a senior BBC man that her character was likely to be written out, as the job had given her some much-needed security in an insecure profession. Her informant indicated that if she would 'pop into bed with him', he would use his influence to avert her departure. She did so, but was written out anyway. To make things even worse, she now thinks that the decision had already been taken when her blackmailer heard of it, and that he had no intention of trying to help her, but was simply capitalizing on a piece of advance information he had picked up by virtue of his position. 'I was shafted', she says with great bitterness, 'royally shafted. What do you do?' Her shafter is still a key man in the corporation.

What you don't do . . .

is keep it all to yourself. A July 1981 report of NALGO's Equal Opportunities Committee revealed that women conceal sex harassment at work because

> *they do not think that they will be believed*

> *they shrink from the embarrassment of publicity*

> *they fear that they will be punished by being*
>> *(1) down-graded*
>> *(2) given rotten jobs*
>> *(3) harassed more*
>> *(4) forced to leave*

Humiliated, isolated and undermined, you are far more likely to lose faith in your ability to cope, and simply leave. The Alfred Marks survey reveals that a staggering 53% *of victims changed jobs* as a result of male persecution, commenting 'in almost all cases, employees find it easier to leave harassment behind than to stay and fight it'. In the current shortage of jobs, however, this is to be viewed as very much a last resort – to leave your work miseries might be to run into the different miseries of unemployment – the devil and the deep blue sea.

What you do do . . .

is *something!* The great problem for most girls in this position is the victim mentality. It makes you feel so bad, so guilty, so complicit in the whole business that you lose your power to defend yourself and strike back. You are left in a state of what psychologists call 'negative panic', like a rabbit before a snake – frozen, cowering, and helplessly waiting for the blow to fall. *Shake it off.* Get the adrenalin going – anyhow, as long as you start to make yourself feel angry and strong rather than helpless and humiliated. Charlotte drew a cartoon caricature of her harasser in her desk drawer, and used to stick drawing pins in it whenever she felt like bursting into tears – 'especially the painful parts', she said with a grin. 'Worked wonders for my morale.' Brenda adopted a verbal approach: 'I used to stand in front of a mirror at night and just repeat to myself, "You don't have to take this. He has no right to do it to you. Are you going to spend the rest of your life putting up with it?" Even stupid things, like "Are you a man or a mouse? EEEEEK!" After a bit I managed to do it as if I was talking to *him*. I tried saying, "Look here, I mean, d'you know", and finally worked through all the ers and ums until I could tell him.'

Tell him

This has to be the first step, before you even consider any other sanctions. It's also the one that women find the most difficult, of course – looking a man in the eye and giving him either a direct order or an unpleasant piece of information is not something that most women have much practice in. But *it is absolutely vital*, and has to be got out of the way at once, or as soon as you can manage it. This is because in the first place, and being as charitable as possible, he may not know how you feel. In the *Cosmo* survey

> *Half the men who replied admitted they made sexual advances to colleagues.* Very few thought women disliked sexual advances at work.

As one American woman wrote to *MS* magazine (July 1978), 'My greatest sorrow in the aftermath of my own sexual harassment experience was that my boss had no idea how degrading his sexual advance was. He thought he was flattering me, but he was handing me the greatest insult a professional woman can receive'. Of *Cosmopolitan*'s women respondents

> *70% felt angry
> *59% felt embarrassed

Yet two-thirds of the men said the women they harassed became flirtatious in response to them! Their sexual confidence is truly impressive. They think we like it! They think we like *them*:

'The worst aspect is often the fact that harassers quite genuinely believe that they are offering you a compliment. Who do they think they are – Errol Flynn?' –

Cosmo woman.

The communication gap

Speak, that I may know thee – Ben Jonson

Bridge it. Communicate. Don't allow any room for them to interpret your behaviour as 'flirtatious' or flattered. It is *possible* (just) that some of these oiks are so thick-skinned, so sexually skill-less, that they can't tell a green light from a red. What is more likely is that in the absence of a firm refusal on your part, they'll do themselves the convenience of assuming your compliance – 'Silence gives *consent*' in the maxim of the law. For both these reasons, speak out – and the earlier the better, before it develops into a thing. What you say depends on the degree of the insult, how well you know your harasser, what power he has over you, and who else is likely to be there when you say it. Possible gambits are:

* *'I don't know what this is doing for you, but it isn't doing* anything *for me'*

* *'Have you thought of seeing a doctor about your condition?'*

* *'Didn't they tell you that cavemen are* out *this year?'*

* *'You know that big car-wash in town? You should put your mind/mouth through it'*

This is only if you feel like trying to keep the put-down light and jokey. If you use this approach, make sure you don't leave them with the impression that you think sex harassment itself is funny – just that *they* are. Other women favour a sincere attempt to state how they feel – an appeal to the male's sympathy. If you try this, work out in advance what you are going to say – and be prepared for *anything* he might throw back at you. One girl who tried this was dumbfounded when her harasser of nearly a year's standing turned on her indignantly with the line, 'I don't know what you're talking about! I'm a very happily married man!' Sure, John. On the other hand, an attractive Scotswoman who has been got at both North and South of the blood-soaked Borders, sees no point in beating about the short and curlies. 'Lean forward as if you're going to *thrapple* them', she advises, 'and then say slowly and menacingly "Will ye git yersel' and your donnie maulers *aff of me!*".'

Remember:

It's a woman's privilege to change his mind.

Telling him . . .

often does the trick – but be prepared to have to do it more than once. Just keep on kicking against the pricks, and you'll usually larn 'em in the end. If this doesn't work, you have to go further. There are a variety of options open to you, and you have to judge the right one for you – this often boils down to the requisite degree of force that needs to be applied. The possibilities can be divided into two sets of procedures, formal and informal.

Formal

(1) Write a letter to your harasser, spelling out what you object to (this advice comes from the US). Show it to a friend before sending it, to protect yourself from any mistakes or misunderstandings and keep a copy.

(2) Keep a diary of distressing incidents to show the grounds for your complaint. Accuracy and detail are essential. For instance, it may not look like harassment if a colleague casually offers you a lift home. But if he appears sniffing round your desk with a offer of his lift *five nights in a row*, then it's harassment. Get it all down, and get witnesses wherever possible.

(3) *Make it public* by talking to other women in the workplace. Tell your harasser's colleagues and boss – tell your boss. Brace yourself for oikish, embarrassed or inept responses, and the misplaced humour, either in the form of laughter and silly jokes, or appeals to you to 'see the funny side of things'. Stick to your story. Tell them it's not funny when the laugh is on/ all over *you*.

(4) *See a lawyer*. Under the so-called 'Green Form' in

Britain you are entitled to an initial consultation free, if your income is below a certain level, as it's likely to be. It is doubtful if the law in its present state of inadequacy can do much for you, but you still have the great common law of England on your side with things like assault, for instance. And even though you are unlikely to want to press charges, except in serious cases, a lawyer could do two things for you:

* *Help you to get things into perspective by giving you a completely objective, all-round detached view of events.*

* *Write a letter on your behalf to your harasser – it's amazing what a powerful effect even a non-committal legal communication has. Lawyers are good at writing the sort of 'My client has consulted me in regard to certain incidents' huff and puff, which several women report have blown the house down.*

But choose your lawyer with care! Don't go for the average conveyancer. It has to be someone versed in the newer regions of the law and of modern society, and someone who will be on your side, not the other. Just having a law degree does not prevent a man from being a prize nerd – in fact, some women have argued that it's a *training* in MC-piggery!

(5) *File a complaint.* Some women recommend an informal approach to management as a first step – put it either to or through the personnel department, with or without the help of your union rep. 'I told my union committeeman what was happening', said one American woman who worked on a construction site. 'And I told him if he didn't do

anything I would kick the SOB in the balls. He spoke to him fast, and that was it'. The 'having a quiet word' technique – one male policing another and feeling his collar – is surprisingly effective – provided that you have convinced him that you are really serious about your complaint.

If you fail to get any action unofficially, you may have no recourse but to lodge an official grievance procedure. This is tricky because so few British companies have as yet set up any machinery for handling sex harassment complaints – and in the Alfred Marks survey, in *one third* of cases where this behaviour was officially reported, the company took no action. Yet *three-quarters* of the women in this survey felt the need for proper channels through which women could proceed with these complaints:

* *49% called for any complaint to the personnel officer of sex harassment to be dealt with seriously and in strict confidence*

* *25% wanted the company to provide an independent counselling service to employees who felt victimized by sexual harassment*

As the US has led the way in raising awareness of this issue, so American women have struck out and achieved for themselves a far more substantial and varied measure of protection than is available here. But conversely, British women are years ahead of their counterparts in the rest of Europe, where the conservative, catholic, old-world oppressions still keep millions of women from full consciousness of their inferior and exploited position. So a complaint in Britain would be a pioneering attempt, but *not* a voyage into the unknown in the teeth of ignorance and reaction. And we do have the inestimable benefit of strong favourable winds blowing hard and often from the other side of the Atlantic!

That's one route . . .

you can take, the formal, official path. Difficulties arise when women either feel that they cannot pursue this course, through shortage of hard evidence, embarrassment or lack of advice *or* they try it, and it fails. Consider too the position of a woman working, as many are, in smaller and un-unionized outfits, or a man-and-a-lad joint where the man is the harasser, and the lad the keen observer. 'James always boasted that he had built his own business up "by hand"', said Mel, who works as his 'Girl Friday' in the electrical components trade. 'Trouble is, all the girls in the factory and the office are likely to get the "by hand" routine as well. We've no union, not even any management structure. We're all just praying he'll have a coronary before it gets too much to cope with!'

> *Sexual harassment has made the lives of many working women a sheer, bloody misery –*
>
> Anne Maclean, Society of Civil and Public Servants.

If for any of these reasons you can't take this route, you might like to know of some of the alternative put-downs, throw offs and joint-breakers developed by girls who have found themselves in an unwelcome half-nelson with an undesired member of the opposite gender (if you'll pardon the phrase) – you'll like them:

Informal

These are all tactics of anti-sex warfare which have been proved on the battlefield. Whether or not they are for you depends on what kind of a fighter you are (now go on, you've decided you'd rather be a combatant than a casualty, haven't you?). You don't have to be glorious Glenda Jackson to pull these off – just remember that with most men you are dealing with Bears of Very Little

Brain as Winnie the Pooh puts it. *Practise in advance*, and have a go!

> *To those who think I am suggesting that we have a*
> *war between the sexes, I say: 'But we've always had*
> *one – and women have always lost it'* –
> Phyllis Chesler, *Women and Madness*

(1) *Invent a lover* This is convenient as it is the ultimate excuse for not finding your harasser desirable, salvaging his eggshell male ego and exculpating you from any malicious charge of being a ball-breaker: 'I conveniently fall madly in love', as one *Cosmo* girl wrote, 'And acquire a live-in-lover and, because of our friendship, confide in the harasser my marvellous new-found happiness. It has worked every time. He sees himself as a valued friend and confidante, which takes the sting out of being rejected.'

(2) *Invent an ailment* This is for the more medically-minded (i.e. gruesome) among you. It can be either an interesting and permanent condition ('I have this er – well, my uterus/cervix/bladder', depending on how far you're prepared to go, 'means that I just . . .) or a nasty infectious disease ('It's been horrible, I don't know *where* I picked it up, but if you are prepared to risk it . . . Have you read all the stuff from America about genital herpes . . . ?') Dana, an American life guard, feels strongly that women shouldn't have to load themselves with imaginary illnesses to wriggle out of men's clutches. Her remedy is the Best Friend (don't say you've never suffered one) who undergoes gynaecological torments of the sort normally unmentionable – except she *mentions* them. In glorious technicolour, vista-vision and 3-D. 'When I get to the bit, ". . . and then she finally succeeded in *passing* this lump from her vagina, and I can tell you . . ." you should see them go green', she chortles.

(3) *Get tabs on him* There are various ways of doing this. If you work with at least one other woman, and know when at least some of your harassment is coming, get the sisters on your side. One girl working in a large grocery store where the manager regularly made a nuisance of himself to her, by dint of alerting some of her special friends in the shop, finally succeeded in getting him to compromise himself in front of witnesses. She had no intention of proceeding against him, but simply felt that if he had made a fool of himself in front of *other* girls, she could turn the tables. As it happened, the other girls' giggling gave them away. But the manager was so embarrassed and lost so much face in front of the female workforce, that *he* had to leave. Good, huh? I told you you'd like it!

Another more technical idea is to get your harasser to immortalize himself on tape. In a rare case from the EEC, a German girl working in the hotel industry had herself wired for sound in order to get a fix on a boss who was systematically propositioning her and undermining her working life. She had a brother in electronics, which helped. But you can do it. It is neither difficult, nor expensive. It is routinely used and recommended in the US:

> I would like to suggest a method [of countering sex harassment] that is perfectly legal – that is, unobtrusively to wire oneself for sound carrying a hidden tape recorder. Just think of all the possible ways to use the material. One could play back the tapes for the boss himself, or his wife, or the rest of the office staff, the human rights commission, or one's own union. This would not only ensure the boss's corrected conduct, but would change the conduct of other men in the office who might be similarly inclined –

Faith A. Seidenberg, Counselor at Law, Syracuse, New York.

235

In one case recorded by Lin Farley (*Sexual Shakedown*, 1980) a sheriff deputized a young girl, wired her for sound and obtained evidence to prosecute a manager of a fast-food restaurant. This technique has not so far been employed in Britain in a straight sex harassment case. You could make legal history!

(4) *Call his bluff* This one takes careful thought and a strong nerve – you don't want to bring on the very thing you're trying to avoid. Success depends on your accurate evaluation of the nature of your harasser – does he really mean business, or is he all p. and w.? 'You're not dealing with finalists in the International Sex Olympics', advises a London woman executive in the film business. 'Chance your arm – go for broke – and watch them scuttle squealing to *their* holes!' One American office worker told Michael Korda what she did: 'I just say "OK, let's stop talking" and it works like a charm. Sometimes I just walk over and lock the door, then sit down on the guy's sofa and ask him what he's waiting for. So far I've had no takers, and now they've stopped hassling me, and they even respect me. They think I'm a very tough chick indeed!' – (*Male Chauvinism: How It Works*).
Think carefully on this one. There might be a Gold Medallist lurking away in there – so don't try it unless you've worked out how you could handle any follow-through. But *think* about it!

(5) *Call his wife* Not recommended by some women on the grounds that it is a lowdown dirty trick. Warmly recommended by others on exactly the same grounds – he's doing the dirty on you, so why should you fight fair? This one depends on how much you feel that your back is to the wall, with no help in sight. But it's not as if she's enjoying an idyllically blissful marriage if her 'better half' is busy dogging other women – and Joanna, who did this, argued that she was doing the wife a favour by

236

letting her in on what was really going on while her busy husband 'worked late nights'. Weigh it up and see if the pay-off for you outweighs the dirt you'll have to dig if you do it.

Do something

Of all these options, there is some possible action that you can take. *If you don't, it won't go away.* When did the snake ever spare the rabbit, or the fox turn its back on the lamb? The sex harasser is not satisfied with one bite at you – the US Federal survey showed that the harassment continued from anything between one and six *months*, and even longer. Nor will it go away when you do. Two US music students trying to bring an action against their professor, who demanded intercourse as the price for being included in one of the department's performing groups (performing to perform), discovered that the same thing had happened to their predecessors. 'I have heard from friends still at the university that the same sequence of events occurred again last year', one of them wrote. And the next year. And the next.

Yet publicity and action *can* drive the wolves back to their lairs. Dr Joan Martin, Associate Dean of the University of Washington Graduate School and 'Adjustment Ombudsman' for sex harassment cases used to deal with at least one case a week. In 1980, the University's President John Hagness inserted an order into the University code stating that sexual harassment would be treated as an illegal coercion that would be punished with all the sanctions available, including firing. This together with some well-publicized campus scandals, has resulted in a dramatic drop in this behaviour – Martin now handles less than one case a month. If a get-tough policy can make the US professors pull their heads in, remember the old Russian remedy against wolves:

LIGHT A FEW FIRES!

Victoria Stevens, an 18-year-old Staffordshire telephonist, was dismissed when she reported that her boss had touched her breasts, unzipped her skirt, pulled her onto his knee and handed out advice about her sex life.

A Birmingham Industrial Tribunal ruled that she had been unfairly sacked, and ordered her boss to pay her compensation for unfair dismissal. Boss John Game (33) of Powerflame Combustion Services said 'I never fancied her in any shape or form' [Tut tut, Mr Game – isn't that even more un-Game to try it on with a woman you don't fancy?]

Ms Stevens was remarkable throughout for her calm, poise and dignity. 'I am not concerned with any award I may get', she said. 'I brought the case to clear my name, and for the sake of office girls everywhere' –

Morning Star, 19 April, 1980.

Women fight back . . .

in each and every way. Barmaids are particularly vulnerable to the crudest of sexual advances – especially in a conference hotel, according to Julie who works in a large hotel centre in Birmingham. 'They're all off the leash and trying to be top dog', she says. 'They still try the corny old "My wife doesn't understand me" line. Or they come up and put their room keys down in front of you, right there on the bar. They say things like, "I'm a busy man, I don't have a lot of time to waste, *do you screw?*" '

Julie and her friend Nicky on the bar had an arrangement to take these keys with a knowing wink as if accepting the assignation. Sometimes the keys were deposited in the jar of pickled eggs on the bar, or 'lost' inside the fridge or the glass-washing machine. 'Our best,' Julie stated, 'was when we had so many, we got them all muddled up, changed round, and locked in together. Then at the end of the night, we threw them all in a heap on the floor, shouted, "Sort 'em all out yourselves, boys, we're going, home'', and legged it for dear life. We thought they'd all complain. But they didn't.'

Fighting on all fronts

Liz is a sales representative travelling up to 60,000 miles a year selling computer software. 'It's murder for a woman on the road,' she said frankly. 'Women are meat. One man on his own can give you a hard time. It's a sort of test they think is funny – "OK, you're a saleswoman. Now sell me out of the fact that I'm going to make you before the night is out." That you can just walk away from. But more than two men together, they're dangerous. There's no limit to where they'll egg each other on. 'Liz's survival strategies contain the following hints:

> * *Don't have a drink before or after a meal on your own in the bar – that's construed as an open invitation.*
>
> * *Ask for a small table when you eat, and fill the rest of it with paperwork. This gives you something to look at other than the guy who keeps ogling at you, and it deters passing trade from just plonking down at your table with the pretence that you look lonely.*
>
> * *Stick to Post-House type places for your own peace of mind – it's worth it to spend two nights' expenses on one night, then drive through the night to get home, to be sure of safe, decent accommodation.*
>
> * *Don't smile, don't look round, don't be tempted to have 'just one drink'. You can't get away from their belief that a woman on her own just wants to be picked up. Better not to get stuck in than to have to shake them off at the end.*

Some women would argue that Liz's strategies are too defensive – why shouldn't you be able to buy a drink in a bar? But each woman learns how to handle the Dirty Tricks Brigade in her own way, to protect herself, and to be able to carry on doing her job of work. And make no mistake. It's a constant, on-going struggle which will not necessarily pass you by if you try however conscientiously to 'dress down', or as you get older. You need to put the whole issue of sexual harassment into the wider context of masculine behaviour, and behaviour at work.

*

> *Some thirty inches from my nose,*
> *The frontier of my person goes.*
> *Stranger, unless with bedroom eyes*
> *I beckon you to fraternise –*
> *Beware of rudely crossing it:*
> *I have no gun, but I can spit –*
> W. H. Auden

*

Contextualize sex at work

If, as the surveys all show, sex harassment has very little to do with sexual attraction between individuals, *what is it all about*? Power, is the short answer, rendered not only by the experts, but by the harassers and their victims too. As one US woman psychologist expressed it: 'Sexual attraction cannot explain the fact that men touch women so much more than women touch men, since women have to be considered to have as strong a sexual drive as men. Contrary to widespread propaganda, *men are not over-sexed, they are over-privileged'* – Nancy Henley, 'Touch and Space as Dominance,' *Body Politics*, 1980.

Henley has drawn up a checklist of the complementary gestures of dominance and submission which totally sums up men's behaviour to women in the work place, and women's reaction to them:

Dominance	Submission
Stare	Lower eyes, avert gaze, blink
Touch	'Cuddle to' or shrink from touch
Interrupt	Stop talking, fall silent
Crowd another's space	Yield, move away, back off
Frown, look stern	Smile
Point	Respond to gesture
Command	Obey
Use familiar speech	Use respectful address

Males have, too, a variety of sanctions for use against women who resist their touch:

* *'I was only being friendly – you are:*
    (a) too sensitive
    (b) over-sexed
    (c) dirty-minded'

* *'You've hurt my feelings'*

* *'What's the matter with you? You are*
    (a) a humourless bitch
    (b) a frigid bitch
    (c) a lesbian bitch'

Charming, isn't it? But touch is only one of the ways in which males will continue to assert their dominance in the world of work. Consider these two pieces of information in connection with one another:

In the barnyard the top chickens have the greatest freedom of space and can walk anywhere, whereas the lower birds are restricted to small areas *and can be pecked by the other birds wherever they go –*
Dr Robert Sommer, US behavioural
psychological.

The NBC spot sales department has 16 male sales-men and 16 female sales assistants. The salesmen hustle TV spots to advertisers. They sit in in-dividual windowed offices. The women are crowded (all 16 of them) on to the outer office floor. *The noise of the typewriters, telephones and voices on that outer floor is deafening –*
Ethel Strainchamps, *Rooms With A View, A Woman's Guide To The Media.*

Top chickens, huh? And how do you get to be a top chicken, able to coop the others up and peck them when you feel like it? *You get born with that extra, special 25%, that's how!*

If only this were all

But it's not. As Michael Korda stresses in his analysis of the nastier corners of the male psyche, 'to the person for whom work is the exercise of power, the place where it is done becomes the board on which power games are played, the central source from which power is derived' ('Office Power,' *New Yorker*, 13 January, 1975). Power predominates over sexual activity, in that sexual activity is brought into play to serve the power need. And guess who has the power need? Right! And guess who they use it against? Right again. The underlying drive has been identified by US researchers as follows:

242

> *For many [men in power] direct physical gratifica-*
> *tion is not enough. Some of them extend their*
> *dominion over the woman beyond the bedroom,*
> *controlling every aspect of her life . . . Indeed* the
> actual penetration of the woman sometimes
> becomes of secondary importance compared
> with the pleasure of invading her daily exist-
> ence. *The need to take possession of another's*
> *consciousness is called 'mind-fucking', and is a*
> *way of compensating for a devasating inner sense*
> *of impotence –*
> *A Sexual Profile of Men In Power*, Sam Janus,
> Ph.D, Barbara Bess, M.D., and Carol Saltus.

Men In Power

This doesn't only mean mighty males like Nelson
Rockefeller, whose New York desk had a large pull-out
drawer with steps in, so that he could ascend to the top
to harangue his female subordinates. There are few men
so lowly in the world of work that they don't have power
over some female. The ways in which they use it reveal
the *nexus* of sexual, psychological and economic
domination, which fosters women's inadequacy and
dependency, disabling, exploiting, and depriving them
of their personal and legal rights. An in-depth study of
one woman's all too typical experience illustrates clearly
the way that these strands are twisted together and
played out in the male boss's mind and behaviour.

Paula thought she was lucky to be offered a job in a
London advertising agency when her first job had
proved to be a dead-end. The firm was a small but thriv-
ing private business, and Paula's post was to be trainee
executive. As a Cambridge graduate, she had high
hopes and ambitions, and finding the salary good and
the work interesting she thought that she had embarked
on the career she had always planned for herself.

At this stage, her employer's behaviour was impeccable. Paula was impressed by his Old-School charm
and did not resent his paternalistic maner – 'And how's

my little Paula?' was his daily greeting. At 21, with plenty of boyfriends of her own age, she never considered him a romantic or sexual proposition at all, but looked on him as a kindly member of the older generation – 'avuncular' was the word she most often used of him in interview.

Wicked uncle

As the only trainee, and with her inexperience of business life, Paula did not find it odd that her desk was placed in the boss's office and close to his. Nor did she question the office custom whereby all the girls were required to kiss the boss on arrival at or departure from work. But her personal situation soon deteriorated from these 'norms'. The boss took to drawing his chair close to hers when they were working together. He would put his arm around her, or try to take her hand, usually with some line like 'It's cold in here – are you cold? Let's see/feel.' Passing in or out of the office he would take the opportunity to squeeze her from behind, or tickle the back of her neck. He began to make sure of kissing her full on the mouth, not just brushing her cheek. He proposed that on his next visit to America she should accompany him as part of her 'training' – 'purely on a work basis, of course.'

By this time Paula, taking the job as a long-term prospect, had committed herself to buying a house, and had taken on a hefty mortgage. But the dark side of the boss's playfulness meant that her career was not being taken seriously. Her 'executive post' was 'nothing more than a glorified p.a.'. Over a long period, Paula's requests for more specific responsibility, the promised training, or management experience, were either evaded, fobbed off, or satisfied by the granting of some advance which was later withdrawn.

Let's talk this over

Paula eventually demanded a show-down on her career

prospects. Decreeing that they needed somewhere quiet and private for this important talk, he took her to a noisy, busy wine bar. There, over several drinks, the boss sketched in a brilliant future for her with the company - directorship, own car, travel – if she played her cards right. He dwelt on his regard for her intellect, her ability, her personality. He then leaned across, grabbed her firmly and tried to put his hand up her skirt.

Paula's shock and resistance took him entirely by surprise – she left him muttering angrily, 'No but look here, you've got to play the game!' Thereafter at work the atmosphere was poisonous. He made every opportunity to pick on her, shout at her, force her to repeat trivial routine tasks, and humiliate her in front of clients. At her fall from grace she learned for the first time that all the other girls had believed that she was the boss's 'office wife' in the fullest sense, and that he had fostered this belief among employees and clients. Going to work became more and more of an ordeal, and as tension built up, she began to sleep badly, and had a road accident, seriously damaging her car. She had to get out.

Where to go

Paula could not simply leave, as her mortgage made her salary a necessity. She dared not let anyone know she was thinking of leaving, in case this precipitated the sack. For this reason, too, she could not ask for a reference from her present employer. She was further handicapped by the fact that she had received no management training at all in this period, and so was behind other girls in the intense competition for jobs. It says much for her desperation that she eventually found another post.

But her escape had been purchased at a high price. She had to leave the advertising business, in which she had become keenly interested, to take a drop in salary and a reduction in the variety and range of her work. She had in fact to return to an unfulfilling secretarial/clerical post in a section with four other women. The boss's rage when she handed in her notice knew no bounds. In the course of what she described as 'a terrible row' he alternately abused her for 'betraying him', and offered her almost any inducement to stay. He promised to make her a director within two years – 'You could be running this company within the decade, I'm looking for an intelligent person to succeed me.' As a short-term sweetener, he offered her £1,000 cash down, to enable her to trade in her crashed car for a new one.

Poor but honest

Paula hung onto her principles, and left. She resents now not so much the sexual harassment, although she found that increasingly repulsive, but the general exploitation of her inexperience – the creation of a phoney job, the denial of training, the promises of job improvements that never came. She sees too, a deliberate maintenance of her dependent status, the requirement to feed his ego at the expense of hers, and a constant psychological intimidation. 'I did feel obliged to him. I did feel under him', she says unconsciously.

She has since learned, too, the other areas in which he was depriving and defrauding her – her contract of employment, for instance, simply bound *her* to work for *him*, but did not bind him to any of the normal obligations of an employer. Hence she would have received under this document:

* No sick pay if she was ill
* No maternity rights or benefits
* No pension rights or schemes

She never had a job description, or any agreement as to her prospects and promotion. She has invested four key years in a 'career' which not only denied her the training promised, but also the chance of training on a job elsewhere. Above all, her confidence has been badly undermined by the whole episode, and she feels that she has lost ground that she may never make up.

Watch your step

Paula's boss is just one of the many revolting natives with which the work jungle crawls. Tread carefully to avoid these and other woman-traps which they have ingeniously scattered in your path. Wise up to the whole repertoire of dirty tricks, and make it plain that you aren't going to stand for any of them. This is the message with which to massage any savage masculine egos around:

> The chickens are coming home to roost for many men right now. We've tied ourselves in knots trying to perform sexually, and sacrificed women on the altar of masculinity. Now we're paying the price. Things are now wreaking havoc up front with men's psyches and sexuality as we have done to women –

> Michael Novick, *Brother: A Forum Against Sexism*, (1978).

Right, all you girl chickens – no more chickening out to the top chickens, OK?

6

When Things Go Wrong

How wrong can they go?

Things can go wrong for you at work in any number of ways, ranging from the running trial of your friendly harasser, to the ultimate sanction – losing your job. Here again, you are disadvantaged by the simple fact of being a *female* chicken rather than one of the top honchos. The much-vaunted break-through of women into the labour force has been more than compensated for by an *increase in female unemployment*. In January 1976, women made up 22% of the registered unemployed – by January 1981, this figure had risen steeply to nearly 30%, while the rise in *male* unemployment was nothing like so rapid:

Unemployed people in Britain, 1976-1981

	Males	Females
1976	981,300	270,500
1977	1,034,000	356,200
1978	1,070,200	414,500
1979	989,900	401,300
1980	970,400	434,000
1981	1,647,100	673,400

SOURCE: *Department of Employment Gazette, February 1979 and 1981.*

These bad news figures for women are supported from other government sources. According to the 1980 statistics from the Department of Employment and Productivity, 6% of working women are now unemployed, as against 9% of working men. The soaring rate of

248

women's loss of work means that

> * *there were 6 women unemployed in 1980*
> *for every 2 women unemployed in 1975*

Conversely, there are only *3 men* unemployed today, against *every* 2 unemployed five years ago.

Around the world . . .

The same bleak picture holds true for working girls. In France, six out of ten unemployed workers are female, and in the European Community as a whole, women account for almost *half* of the registered unemployed – even though they represent little more than *a third* of the Community's working population. And even those women in work are hanging on by the skin of their teeth – EEC reports have stressed that the majority of European women are in what they call 'precarious' forms of employment, i.e., part-time, unskilled and temporary.

The disadvantage of women in Europe is paralleled by the situation of women in America. By a cruel irony the US, home and heartland of women's liberation, is experiencing rocketing female unemployment like nothing before in its crowded history. In 1947, according to the Women's Bureau *1975 Handbook on Women Workers*, women constituted 27% of the unemployed. *By 1973 this had risen to 48%*. Think of *that* next time some schmuck tells you that women have it all their own way in the Land of the Free! The fuller statistical picture bears this out (see overleaf).

Why are women hit so hard?

The short answer is, because they're women! The longer answer unravels the complex interlocking of factors that makes women far more vulnerable than men in the work force. From France, a 1980 survey argued that women had been knocked out of the labour market more easily than men for these reasons:

The number of unemployed women in America, as a percentage of all unemployed people, over the last 25 year period

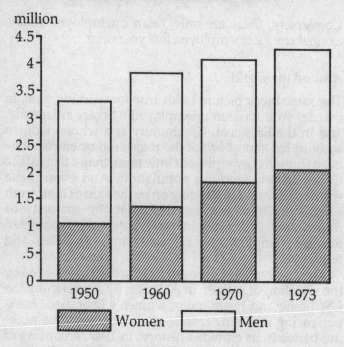

SOURCE: US Department of Labor, Bureau of Labor Statistics

* women have a lower skills level than men — because they are neither educated nor trained to anything like the standard the men achieve

* working women have less seniority at work than men — because they are held back from winning advancement in a thousand different ways

* women carrying the lion's share of the domestic burden in addition to their work load are more likely either to have to give up work to care for a family member or be tainted with the

> *discriminatory belief that women have families, which a) makes them inherently unreliable and b) gives them something to fall back on, so unemployment does not matter to them*

> * *a spasmodic, uncommitted, and generally poor Trades Unions defence of women's rights – when at best French women's wages are only two-thirds of their men's (compare British women's 75%)*

Unemployment is greatest in France among women under twenty-five, who can neither be sure of getting jobs, nor sail uncritically into the by-pass/cul de sac of early marriage, in the way that earlier generations did. 'My mother and my grandmother were both married at nineteen – a whole year before my age now,' says Francoise, a philosophy student from Bordeaux. 'I want my own life – but that calls for a job, a real job too, not one a young girl just plays at. *Que faire?*'

Sauce for the French women . . .

is sauce for the English too – you don't have to be Descartes to grasp the application of all this to your working life. The recession has combined with the onward march of the new technology to shrink the pool of what were traditionally women's jobs – clerical and service work are being phased out by machines; clothing footwear and textile industries are all cutting production and with it jobs; and even teachers are put on the scrap heap as education spending falls to yet another disastrous low.

Employers respond by attempting to reduce the work force according to certain recognized principles:

> * *voluntary redundancy*
> * *natural wastage*
> * *early retirement*

* *last in first out*
* *part-timers before full-timers*

With the possible exception of voluntary redundancy, all these operate *to work against women, and to the advantage of men at work.* They are not the objective criteria which they purport to be, when they are one-sidedly loaded against us, in these ways:

1) *Natural wastage* i.e. the normal turnover of jobs as people move around the labour market, means that more women lose their jobs than men, since women are more likely to have to give up a job in the first place. Leaving to follow a husband or lover/partner when he makes a career move; to have a baby or care for an elderly dependant; to take a further qualification to catch up with the men; to take a much-needed break from the multiple problems of carrying the woman's traditional double burden, at home and at work – all or any of these mean that you get 'wasted', while *none* of them would make a man have to give up on his job. 'I thought it was roses round the door when I packed in work to come with Steve to Durham,' said Josie, a primary school teacher. 'It never occurred to me I might not get another post. But I've tried everywhere round here, and there's nothing doing. What really riles me, though, is I read in one report about women teachers "deemed to have left the profession". I didn't leave the profession – I've been locked out!'

2) *Early retirement* Here again, as the 'weaker' sex, women go to the wall. The tender concern of the patriarchs who long ago decreed that women retire at 60, while men go on till 65 even though we live longer than they do, means that 'early retirement', if it comes, *comes earlier for women than it does for men.* Because women are made to give up five years earlier, they are always nearer to the end of their working life than men are. Being deprived of that final five years robs working women of the ultimate clout that they need to save their

jobs. 'I was exactly the same age as Peter', said Elsie, a department manager in a big Liverpool store, 'And we were both on the same grade. But at 53, I "only had another seven years in me", while he had almost twice as long to go. So *I* got the early retirement, would you believe.'

3) *Last in first out* quite brutally weeds out women in preference to men – women join the work force later, have more interrupted work lives, and as less skilled and less qualified workers move out of jobs and around the labour market more than men. For all these reasons, when an individual firm or company turns the spotlight on its workers in the search for disposables, women are the first to be picked up, as they will have joined there more recently than the men. 'How could I have been "first in"?' asks Rita, a 43-year-old worker in the car accessory trade. 'When *he* came in [pointing to a male colleague] I was working in a shop and trying to get my City and Guilds at night school. When *he* came in, I'd had to go with Trevor when he was transferred to Wolverhampton. When *he* came in, I was having kids. There isn't a woman here that isn't *ten to fifteen years* behind these blokes.'

4) *Part-timers before full-timers* is another euphemism for 'women out first'. Far more women than men work as part-timers – indeed, the vast majority of the part-time work force is female. This is not because women take their work any less seriously than men do, but because handicapped with the traditional double burden of work and family, and confined to the lower end of the labour market through shortage of marketable skills, part-time work is often all that women can get. And *as a part-timer, you lose out in another way, too* – you have to have worked for at least five years for your present employer before you are eligible for consideration for redundancy money, as against two years for a full-timer. 'We were just chopped', Maureen said when she lost her job as a data puncher on the 6-10 pm shift at a

Coventry car works. 'No consultation, no nothing. They just decided to close down the evening shift to save money, and we were out before you could say knife.'

'A slimmer and more efficient economy'

All these methods of thinning down the work force operate to cut off the female fat before the male, and are directly and inescapably discriminatory against women. Taken together, they form a battering ram which is ruthlessly driving women out into the cold, and *in far larger numbers than men*. Yet all this is taking place against a backdrop of complacent male attitudes which claim that

* *women are workers non-essential to the economy, and readily dispensable when things get tight*

* *women are better out of the work force in a recession, since they are only taking men's jobs*

Like those jobs that the Germans could not even get their *Gastarbeiter* to do, you mean? These anti-women attitudes further ensure that an unemployed woman has a harder time getting another job, if she can be seen as in any way competing with men, or threatening to 'take a man's job' – and at the end of the day they see to it that the only unemployment that the government, the media, and the powers-that-be ever take seriously is *men's*. Wouldn't you know it!

> *Whilst the official unemployment figures are given as* 2½ *million, the reality is considerably higher* . . . The hidden unemployment is in the main made up of women who, as part-time workers, are ineligible to register. *Little reference is also made to the fact that* unemploy-

ment among women is rising much faster than among men. *Since 1975, male unemployment has risen by 61%, but* female unemployment has risen by a staggering 207%. *Women are more vulnerable –*
Women's Rights, National Labour Women's Committee statement to the National Conference of Labour Women, June 1981.

Unemployment as a reality

Face the harsh fact that it *could* happen to you, and that it is *more likely* to happen to you, because you are female. Losing your job is a grave crisis in anybody's life, as these comments show:

* *It's a marvellous lesson in humility. You realize that you are just a cog in the wheel. Bosses complain about staff loyalty when workers go on strike, but generally speaking they've got even less loyalty. They're not interested in your pathetic little destiny –*

Nicola Tyrer, journalist

* *It's very difficult to disentangle your personal life from your job, which means losing your job is like a very complicated divorce case. For four to five months I was in total shock –*
Victor Lowndes, Head Playboy, UK, 'Lost Your Job?', *Cosmopolitan,* March 1982.

People who become unemployed normally go through a series of emotional stages – initial shock and panic release painful negative feelings, but usually give way in time to a determination to explore the situation in full and if possible to fight.

Where to turn for help

The classic resort for any member of the work force throughout the world in modern times has been the union. From the historic stand of the Tolpuddle Martyrs, the unions have uncompromisingly asserted the right to fight for the workers against the bosses, and have some signal victories to their credit. Women's growing participation in the work force has been matched by the rising female membership of the different unions – so much so that NALGO and APEX now have a 50/50 male/female membership, while 15 unions have *more females than males*, including some of the biggest, best known or most important professional associations:

Union	% Members Female
Union of Shop, Distributive and Allied Workers (USDAW)	63
National Union of Teachers (NUT)	66
National Union of Public Employees (NUPE)	67
National Union of Tailor and Garment Workers (NUTGW)	92

Women also predominate numerically in the Civil and Public Service Association, the Inland Revenue Staffs Federation, and the Professional, Executive, Clerical and Computer Staffs Association.

But only numerically

Once again, no matter how many female chickens there are in the pen, the top chickens *are all male*. Consider this pictorial representation of women's union *power*, in comparison with women's union *membership*:

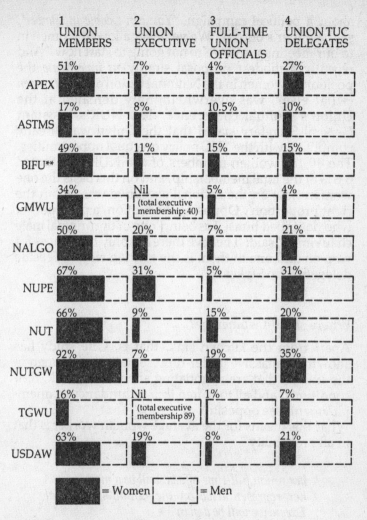

	1 UNION MEMBERS	2 UNION EXECUTIVE	3 FULL-TIME UNION OFFICIALS	4 UNION TUC DELEGATES
APEX	51%	7%	4%	27%
ASTMS	17%	8%	10.5%	10%
BIFU**	49%	11%	15%	15%
GMWU	34%	Nil (total executive membership: 40)	5%	4%
NALGO	50%	20%	7%	21%
NUPE	67%	31%	5%	31%
NUT	66%	9%	15%	20%
NUTGW	92%	7%	19%	35%
TGWU	16%	Nil (total executive membership 89)	1%	7%
USDAW	63%	19%	8%	21%

■ = Women   ⬚ = Men

SOURCE: *Women At Work, Chris Aldred,*
Pan Trade Union Studies, 1981

Many women workers and activists tell stories of the gross anti-feminism and discriminatory tactics of their 'brothers' in the Trades Union movement. Beatrix Campbell has written of one North Eastern woman who tried to visit a local miner's lodge with some documents

257

about a political campaign. *'You can't come in, flower'*, said a miner's official. 'We've never allowed women in to our meetings, and we're not going to start now.' And recently a modest proposal simply to *investigate* the position of women in the National Union of Railway*men* (what else?) was overwhelmingly defeated at the Union's Annual conference. The NUR's assistant General Secretary stated that the Union was already complying with the TUC policy on equal opportunities. The 10,186 women members of the NUR constituted 6·6% of the total membership, and on this basis the one woman now on the national executive was 'about the right proportion'. Opposing the motion, a prize porker who described himself as being 'one of the original male chauvinists' said: 'I believe there are only two places for women and one of them is the kitchen sink' – Teeside delegate John Stokes.

Where should women be?

Apart from the kitchen sink, that is. One study has shown the massive under-representation of women in the unions that are negotiating about *their* work, *their* conditions, and all too often *their* redundancy or unemployment (see opposite).
What this means for the average woman worker is that in all probability

* *her union full-time official will be a man*
* *her representative on the Union's National Executive will be a man*
* *the representative her union sends to the TUC will be a man*

Women's union mis-representation . . .

was highlighted by researcher Anna Pollert in her study of women workers in a Bristol tobacco factory:

258

'For the women there was the problem that they were
represented by men . . . there was a consensus among
the men in the factory – workers, stewards, foremen and
managers – that women were different from men. They
were not like other workers: they were primarily
housewives, their place in the home, their wages 'pin-
money'. The stewards frankly thought that women
were not too bothered about money. Mike: "You ask any
of the girls in here if they know anything about this pay
claim, and I'll lay a pound to a penny they don't know
what it's about. Mm? Do they?" '

'Some were actually antagonistic to the women:
others simply did not understand them. They did different jobs – not 'women's work' on the production line.
And they were not women . . . Mike, already over-
loaded with sixty-odd girls, now became *de facto* steward
for all the women in the factory. *Consequently the men
were reasonably represented and the women badly . . .*'

Women In The Unions

Figures in brackets show how many women there would be if they were represented according to their share of the membership.

Union	Membership		%F	Executive members		Full time officials		TUC delegates	
	Total	F		Total	F	Total	F	Total	F
APEX (Professional, Executive, Clerical, Computer)	150,000	77,000	51%	15	1(8)	55	2(28)	15	4(8)
ASTMS (Technical, Managerial)	472,000	82,000	17%	24	2(4)	63	6(11)	30	3(5)
BIFU (Banking, Insurance Finance)	132,000	64,000	49%	27	3(13)	41	6(20)	20	3(10)
GMWU (General & Municipal)	956,000	327,000	34%	40	0(14)	243	13(83)	73	3(25)
NALGO (Local Govt Officers)	705,000	356,000	50%	70	14(35)	165	11(83)	72	15(36)
NUPE (Public Employees)	700,000	470,000	67%	26	8(17)	150	7(101)	32	10(22)
NUT (Teachers)	258,000	170,000	66%	44	4(29)	110	17(73)	36	7(24)
NUTGW (Tailor & Garment)	117,000	108,000	92%	15	5(14)	47	9(43)	17	7(16)
TGWU (Transport & General)	2,070,000	330,000	16%	39	0(6)	600	6(96)	85	6(14)
USDAW (Shop, Distributive Allied)	462,000	281,000	63%	16	3(10)	162	13(102)	38	8(24)
Totals	6,022,000	2,265,000	38%	316	40(150)	1,636	90(640)	418	66(174)

All figures are approximate, and the most recent that were available in November 1980.
SOURCE *Hear this, brother, by Anna Coote and Peter Kellner, New Statesman Reports No 1, 1980.*

Just how badly . . .

became clear when Imperial Tobacco introduced its grandiosely-titled Proficiency Pay Scheme, a productivity and incentive scheme to 'rationalize' the work and step up the output. Pollert describes the job alterations as they affected two groups of the women workers both engaged in stripping the tobacco:

> The hand-strippers had been made to forfeit to the machine strippers a specially skilled type of stripping for which they had earned extra 'plusage'. Both lost out: the hand-strippers because they lost 'skill points' [for which they had received extra money] and the machine strippers who, although in a higher job group, got no extra money for the extra work. In this case, the women were ignored by their shop steward, and totally mystified by their union official, who supported the PPS scheme, and felt the women too ignorant to 'appreciate' that because the new points sytem simplified pay, it was 'better' for them – even if they earned less! –
>
> Girls, Wives, Factory Lives, (1981).

Brothers under the skin

Women everywhere recount examples of the failure of 'their' representatives to represent *their* interests. Maybelle, a Detroit car-trade worker, got so frustrated with the way that her union 'bozo' was 'boogying around' with a complaint of hers, that she 'bust him on the schnoz. And he never even filed suit against me!' she said. 'But I had to shake the fillings right out of his teeth to get any action – and when the SOB did get on the stick, what happens? Zero, zilch, *nothing!*'

In Europe, too, there is a general recognition that women are losing out in the only area where they could hope for some clout against the might of management and bosses. In France, at a congress of confederated unions held at Metz in the summer of 1982, the union CFDT voted to promote women's union interests via positive action. One out of every three CFDT members is a woman, but only around 10% of union jobs are held by women. The number of women's seats on the CFDT National Council is to be raised from 31 to 39.

> *It's all very well talking about how you're going to change things, but you've got to be in a position to make people listen –*
> Hazel Simmons, union activist and member
>   of TASS national women's sub-committee

All the union top brass are making the right noises – naturally. At the regular conference of the European Trades Union Confederation in the Hague in 1982, the situation of women in the labour force 'was mentioned at the meeting several times': 'Their job insecurity, the threats to existing jobs through the introduction of new technologies, and the way women were exploited by "temporary" employment agencies, were all deplored – *Women of Europe* 26, May–July 1982.

But the faith that the women of Europe have in these windy pieties is shown by the fact that the first ever Women's Trade Union Confederation (Confederation Syndicale des Femmes) has just been established in France. It has been launched by the official wing of the Women's Movement, the MLF, to provide the *specific, informed and caring representation* that women workers need. This women's union, the CSDF, is committed to attacking what it sees as women's triple and simultaneous exploitation:

* *as workers*
* *as houseworkers*
* *as producers of children*

262

Ironically, women's unions were orginally an important feature of the French Trades Union picture. But after the Liberation in 1945, women workers were given the choice of remaining in their own unions, or joining a mixed one. For the sake of solidarity they took the second option. But this *pis-aller* soon revealed itself as a *faux pas* when women were ousted from positions of power, and forced to hand over the reins of union politicians to men. Nearly forty years later, they are reclaiming the right to run their own union affairs. 'Allez-y, mesdames – la lutte continue!' [Go to it, girls – the fight goes on] was the comment of Jeanne, a veteran woman unionist of pre-WW2 days.

The brotherhood of man

The French solution could provide a useful model for British women seeking to gain their union rights. Unions have traditionally insisted that representatives should be workers well versed in the trade of their colleagues, with personal experience of the details and difficulties of their working lives. Full-time union officials are expected to fill in any gaps in their knowledge by learning about any aspects of the work that they are unfamiliar with. Great. Yet 3½ *million* British women workers are represented by men who are blithely unconcerned by their ignorance of women's work, and women's jobs – ignorant even of their own ignorance – and who under the comforting nit-brained notion of representing *all* workers, can sweep the women under the carpet.

All this takes place against a background of verbal placebos for women workers. As long ago as 1975 the TUC General Council published a Charter for Women, some of whose key demands were:

* *equality of job* opportunities *for women*

* *equal* promotion *opportunities for women*

263

* *an end to* pay differentials *between women and men*

* *women to be* full and equal members of the work community *and all discrimination against them to be abolished*

Right on, brothers!

More recently the TUC has promulgated a special charter of its own to cover the points raised in criticism of the TUC's record:

'Equality for women within Trade Unions'

1 The National Executive Committee of the union should publicly declare to all its members the commitment of the union to involving women members in the activities of the union at all levels.

2 The structure of the union should be examined to see whether it prevents women from reaching the decision-making bodies.

3 Where there are large women's memberships but no women on the decision-making bodies special provision should be made to ensure that women's views are represented, either through the creation of additional seats or by co-option.

4 The National Executive Committee of each union should consider the desirability of setting up advisory committees within its constitutional machinery to ensure that the special interests of its women members are protected.

5 Similar committees at regional, divisional, and district level could also assist by encouraging the active involvement of women in the general activities of the union.

6 Efforts should be made to include in collective agreements provision for time off without loss of pay to attend branch meetings during working hours where that is practicable.

7 Where it is not practicable to hold meetings during working hours every effort should be made to provide child-care facilities for use by either parent.

8 Child-care facilities, for use by either parent, should be provided at all district divisional and regional meetings and particularly at the union's annual conference, and for training courses organized by the union.

9 Although it may be open to any member of either sex to go to union training courses, special encouragement should be given to women to attend.

10 The contents of journals and other union publications should be presented in non-sexist terms.

But are they doing this for you? How effective is this charter lower down the union movement? How many male unionists are even passingly aware of it? And when did any union encourage its male officials to give some attention to, and learn something about, *women's work*, your work?

You're on your own, sister

You can't rely on, or even necessarily trust, your union 'brother'. In their survey of women in the unions, Anna Coote and Peter Kellner relate what happened when the National Women's Advisory Committee of ASTMS (Association of Scientific, Technical and Managerial Staff) sent out a letter to all members. Concerned at the lack of response, the committee investigated:

> *It was discovered that some secretaries* were not passing on the information at all, *and others, instead of reading from the letter (which was deliberately low key) were mentioning in passing that 'two women's libbers want to come and talk to you about women's lib', which got the reaction it was geared to receive* – rejection –
> *Hear this, brother!* 1980.

But there's worse than this. Male unionists' readiness to agree to management redundancy proposals on a 'part-timers before full-timers' basis was an act of naked self-interest which has left hundreds of thousands of women washed up. When the all-female 6-10 shift at the Talbot Whitley plant outside Coventry was dismantled, the girls turned immediately to their union reps. 'But they didn't want to know. They just didn't bloody want to know. After all, they'd all agreed it, *arranged* it,' said Gaynor in disgust. In another 1982 case, Brenda Clarke had worked a 25-30 hour week for 14 years at a Birmingham munitions factory when she was made redundant as a part-timer. She discovered that her union, the Transport and General Workers, had made an agreement that part-timers should go first, after a mass meeting at which the 400 full-time men easily out-voted the 70 part-time women workers. As she commented: *'We paid the T and G our full dues, for all those years, and they made an agreement to sack us first.'*

Well, *they would*, wouldn't they?

If you can't beat them . . .

What happens when you join them? An Equal Pay case which came before a Birmingham Industrial Tribunal threw into relief the difficulties of Mrs P. C. Price, described as 'the only lady union representative present at the [Equal Pay] negotiations.' As the judgement of the Industrial Tribunal tells it:

> *[Mrs Price] advocated equal pay and others [male] were not really interested as they wanted to keep out of it; there was little support from other shop stewards . . . The new scheme [which preserved women's rates at a lower level than men's] was implemented from January 1976; she was against it and always had been. When she told her colleagues on the day shift, they were furious. The attitude of Mr Lashwood [union branch secretary] and the chairman of the union branch was that they thought that the equal pay proposal satisfied the* majority of the workforce, *therefore the proposal should be adopted.*
>
> *For several months she did not know what to do. She had tried to get a discussion with management for negotiations, but Mr Lashwood was not interested. They went to negotiate as a team and she had to accept the majority decision of the [male] shop stewards before they attended the meeting, and could do nothing to 'rock the boat'. The decision of the shop stewards to accept the schedule*

was not referred back to the lodge and no type of branch meeting took place . . . She had said that the girls in the grinding room totally disagreed with the proposal. *She was 'shot down' because the others said that it was a majority decision . . .*

We accept that she did protest to her fellow negotiators and did vote against the proposals but was outvoted by them and that when negotiations with management took place, she had to act as a member of a 'team', abide by the majority decision, and vote with the fellow negotiators.

The male majority

Masculine short-sightedness here landed them all in court, where Mrs Price and others pursued a successful claim for this *un*-equal pay scheme to be reversed. But it clearly shows how the simple, everyday process of union politics actively discriminates against women and women's interests. This pattern is so deeply entrenched that males in trades unions can't even see when selling the women down the river means selling *themselves* as well. Union workers at a carpet plant in Ontario, negotiating a new contract, decided that their own wage demand would be jeopardized if they supported the lower-graded women workers in their demand for a six-cents-an-hour rise. A female union official tried to insist that if the women's right to a proper wage were not recognized, the men's wages would be adversely affected at some point. She was ignored. Shortly afterwards *the men's jobs were reclassified downwards and their wages decreased.*

Moral: *the fight* for *women's pay is a fight* against *low pay in general. It is not in men's interests to preserve the lower wage status of women, since they can and will be undercut.*

Then hear this

Women trades union activists speak:

> * *I always thought that Equal Pay was a safeguard for the men – instead of women being used as cheap labour, we were going to be used on a basis of equality –*
> Kath Smith, TGWU branch chairman and TUC gold medallist for outstanding service to the Trades Union Movement.

> * *Many women have come to me and said they are very pleased to have a woman convenor. I regard myself as equal to any man –*
> Colleen Mansfield, convenor and president of Enfield Trades Council.

> * *It's good for members to be able to go to a woman steward and discuss their problems. Men are not always as tolerant. I'm against saying that there should be special rights for women, but when you're fighting a losing battle to give women experience in the union, perhaps there should be –*
> Sylvia Greenwood, Sheffield convenor and Industrial Tribunal member.

Perhaps there should

What can you do about it all? First, be sure to check out any and every agreement that your union has made with the employer which affects your rights, or your chances of being fingered for redundancy or dismissal. If this happens, go to your union and *keep on going* – enough women enforcing their justifiable grievance will demonstrate to the union that they were on the wrong track in making the original agreement. Don't let the patchy and unimpressive record of the unions on women's rights deter you – they have all acknowledged the issues, and formulated reasonable anti-discrimination policies that could be a real source of strength when made to work.

Anne Sedley, Women's Rights Officer at the National Council for Civil Liberties, says: 'The Trades Unions have the policies – the only problem is getting it down to grass roots level. *It is absolutely essential that young women join their union*, find out the policy and get it implemented, and be as active as possible.'

What about it? Why not seriously consider joining actively in union politics yourself, possibly with a female workmate for that solidarity that the brothers seem to think is a masculine prerogative. After all, you can't safely leave it to the men, can you? – look what a mess they've made of it!

If union power fails

or if it fails you, what then? There are two national organizations that can help (for addresses, see back of book):

* *The Equal Opportunities Commission (EOC)*
* *The National Council for Civil Liberties (NCCL)*

As their names imply, these are two very different outfits. The first is a regular Civil Service organization plushly housed in downtown Manchester, a stone's throw from Granada TV, and just up the street from the private speakeasy where Granada personnel can get luxuriously boiled of a lunchtime. The NCCL by contrast is a shoestring operation in darkest Southwark, which may have been the 'in' place when Chaucer lay at the Tabard on his way to Canterbury, but certainly isn't now.

These two bodies work to advance the cause of women in rather different ways. The NCCL has a tradition of radical questioning and opposition that reaches back to 1934, and its Women's Rights Unit has been active as a separate section since 1973. It has led a number of key campaigns not only to defend, but to *extend* women's rights, taking up the case of Mrs Brenda Clarke when the TGWU would not, and winning a famous victory for her and all part-timers. As it pursues a test case strategy (i.e. a policy of fighting those cases which break new ground, or turn on a point of law) the NCCL would not normally take up the cudgels on your behalf. *But advice and assistance are freely given to hundreds of women who contact them every year*. On the basis of what emerges about your situation, the NCCL can give you direction, or refer you elsewhere for the next stage.

They also have available a number of books and pamphlets on particular aspects of women's work lives, rights and benefits (see booklist at back of book). These are not only very reasonably priced – they are exceptionally well-written, clear and helpful. If you are in a specific difficulty at work, it's a good idea to send for the relevant booklet as a first step. It may answer your questions by itself – or if not, you'll find it helpful to have covered some of the groundwork before you seek further help.

Rights for women . . .

are not the sole concern of the EOC, which since its inception in 1975 has had within its purview discriminations against men, and ethnic groups. Critics have considered that these other preoccupations distort and diminish its concern with the only continuously oppressed *majority* in the history of the humam race, i.e. women. The EOC has been attacked for its dedication to equal opportunities for men and for women when

> a) *women are so severely disadvantaged in comparison with men*
> b) *any given reform will have a totally different* impact *on women and on men*

A recent issue has been the question of the protective legislation which restricts the hours that women may work in industry (see previous discussion of this in Chapter 3). The EOC has concluded that: 'there is no longer justification for maintaining legal provision on hours of work which require men and women to be treated differently . . . the legislation should be removed, or, where health, safety and welfare demand it, replaced so that it applies equally to men and women.'

Equalizing down

How equal can you get at the bottom of the heap? The NCCL was quick to grasp that the 'equal opportunity' to do dirty, heavy, dangerous industrial work, in shifts or antisocial hours, is one that working women can do without, thank you. Its response is more in line with European thinking on the subject; *Equality is blindly pursued by the EOC for its own sake*, without regard to the relative impact on men and women of equal provisions under the law. It should be the EOC's aim to achieve equality for women without deterioration of their working conditions, instead of equalising "down".

'The EOC has long tried to excuse its reluctance to use its enforcement powers by pointing to the greater importance of its longer-term strategic role: yet its approach to the review of protective laws amounts to a completely wasted opportunity to make an important strategic contribution to both an analysis of and the improvement of working conditions for women.

'If the EOC's recommendations were implemented, women would simply be equally vulnerable with men to the pressures of working long and unsocial hours to gain a decent wage. It is an insult to women for the EOC to campaign on their behalf for this spurious kind of equality' – *The Shift Work Swindle*, Jean Coussins, NCCL (1979).

Mistaken, even harmful policies are not the only charges laid against the EOC. The Commission has also come in for a good deal of criticism for its cautious progress, and timorous refusal to use the considerable power of investigation and enforcement which it was given when the legislators rightly foresaw that you cannot right injustices by persuasion alone. A distinguished legal figure comments:

> *The Equal Opportunities lot have picked the wrong causes – they've gone for isolated incidents and put one woman up, when they should have gone for group cases as in the US. And they supported a case where women were allowed into a night club free, and men had to pay £1 to get in. They won the case, but were given 1p damages. That did them a lot of harm. Right-thinking people thought what a waste of time and money.*
>
> *The real trouble is that they are not prepared to campaign. They saw the dangers of being too political, and went the other way. But to change attitudes entrenched since the Industrial Revolution you've got to be political. You've got to try to change public opinion. It needs a lot of educating.*

Educating public opinion . . .

is a long, slow job, and the EOC has undoubtedly suffered from its policy of not doing PR work on its own behalf, not giving interviews or blowing its own trumpet. Much valuable education of individuals and companies has gone on behind the scenes, and there is no underestimating the magnitude of this task. There is a massive ignorance among employers and workers alike about the new legislation and how it works – so much so that on occasions the only action required is a letter pointing out the breach of the Equal Pay and Sex Discrimination Act of 1975. Cases are on record where the employer, informed that he has broken the law by rejecting a candidate for employment, has immediately offered them the job. That does not necessarily protect

272

the employer from legal proceedings – ignorance of the law is no defence – but it makes a considerable difference to the final allocation of compensation or whatever.

Going to law

If sabre-rattling fails, your last option is to go to law. Despite the often sharp differences between them, the EOC and the NCCL are not so far apart – the EOC is one of the bodies that actually funds the NCCL – and both exist to give women 'a helping hand', in the words of an EOC pamphlet. This asks, 'Are you thinking of making a complaint about sex discrimination or equal pay?' and answers encouragingly, 'If you are we can help. We can help you to use these two Acts of Parliament . . . Women and men too have the right to take their own complaints to an Industrial Tribunal or a court . . . Why not ask us?'

You can get help . . .

to take your case to law – and in this case you're going to need all the help you can get. For the law itself – strictly, the *Equal Pay Act* which, though entered on the Statute Book in 1970, did not become law until the end of 1975 along with the *Sex Discrimination Act* – as a new piece of legislation is full of pitfalls and woman-traps. David Pannick, barrister and Fellow of All Souls College, Oxford, has drawn attention to 'what is already obvious to all except the Government: that *the Equal Pay Act 1970 is grossly defective and that amending legislation is essential.*' He adds:

> The 1970 Act provides that a woman employed on like work with a man in the same establishment is entitled to equal pay (unless the employer can prove that any variation is due to a material difference other than sex). Unfortunately, 'like work' is narrowly defined to mean work that is 'of the same or a broadly similar nature'. It is not sufficient for a woman to prove that she is doing

273

work of equal value to that done by man in the same establishment who is paid more than her (*unless a job evaluation study has been carried out with the consent of the employer*).

Because *occupational segregation by sex remains endemic*, many women cannot bring equal pay claims: *there are no men doing 'like work'. Nor does the 1970 Act entitle a woman to more pay because she can prove that she would receive higher wages if she were a man.*

In other words, if you are getting penalized simply for being a woman, there's nothing you can do about it! This has produced some decisions of the highest absurdity, as in the cases of Reaney and Turley, where two women *failed* to prove that they had suffered sex discrimination when dismissed because they were pregnant – on the grounds that no man could ever be in comparable circumstances!

The law's an ass . . .

but it's a donkey with a man's head. The dice are loaded against woman who have to pursue a claim through the good offices of a profession in which women number only 8% of barristers, and 7% of solicitors, while female judges, recorders and registrars are counted in ones and twos. At Industrial Tribunal level, where your case would be heard, you'll be faced with an overwhelming preponderance of men. In Birmingham, for instance, there are 6 full-time IT chairmen and 7 part-time, all men, and the composition of the members looks like this:

Members	CBI	TUC	Total
Men	72	82	154
Women	20	18	38
% female	22%	18%	19%

Set this dismal female representation against the female

percentage of the workforce – over 40% and rising – or of the population as a whole, 51%, and you will see why individual women claimants feel hopelessly at a loss. One woman described the experience of going into an all-male court as 'like being arrested and taken to prison'. For another 'it was horrible, terrible. I just knew that I would not get them to understand'. Individual IT men may be wise, humane and disinterested. There is also no evidence that they will show undue sympathy to male claimants – one clerk remarked approvingly of his chairman's deft handling of an obviously fraudulent claimant, 'This is a clever one, but he's not going to wriggle past my old fox!' But until the women's membership and presence balances that of the men, ITs will inevitably appear to represent and reinforce the masculine domination of society which is what women are complaining about in the first place.

By men, for men

Not only are the ITs overwhelmingly manned by men, as chairs, clerks, legal representatives and even court officials – they are also primarily *used* by men to push their claims. Of one hundred cases on record in Birmingham between 1979 and 1982, 105 men had pursued claims as against only 40 women (this 40 including two class actions, one by eight and one by 14 women, while the men tended to act for themselves alone). Women's claims constituted only 27½% of the total. This means that *a piece of legislation designed to redress the injustices of women is being used for the benefit of men.* Meanwhile women remain as far behind in the work force as ever. Wonderful, isn't it?

The masculine bias of the ITs comes over in a number of ways. Consider the case that Miss S. King brought against Amey Roadstone Corporation in 1981, where the final judgment ran as follows:

> *There is no doubt that the applicant was working in what is still very much a man's world [materials*

275

*supplier to the contracting industry]. She often
went to large meetings involving not just the Western
Region where everyone else who attended was
a man.* None of the other marketing officers
(those employed in other regions – all men)
*has been dismissed. In these circumstances it is not
surprising that the applicant should genuinely
believe that she was chosen because she was a
woman, and that if she had happened to be a man
she would still be in the respondent's employment
It is right to say that the applicant created an
extremely favourable impression upon all of us.
She was in no way militant. On the contrary, she
was plainly extremely emotionally upset at what
happened.*

THIS CASE FAILED. 'We believe that if she had been a
man she would still have been the person chosen for
dismissal.' Oh, sure. This woman fell foul of the legal
requirement that the burden of proving sex discrimination falls upon the applicant. So even though she
received the patronizing pat on the head for not being
'militant' (would she have been penalized if she had
been? She obviously gets full marks for being 'extremely
emotionally upset'. Can you imagine these things being
said of a male applicant? A Trades Unionist?) she did not
convince the court.

But how do you convince them of something they don't recognise?

At a 1982 hearing in a London Industrial Tribunal Mrs
Langbant brought a case against her employer of sexual
discrimination and harassment under the 1975 Act.
Immediately before the hearing, the company withdrew
from the action – effectively a concession of the sub-
stance of Mrs Langbant's case – although the stated
reason was the desire to avoid the expense of bringing
their witnesses to the hearing.

It was agreed by both sides to issue a joint statement,

and the company met Mrs Langbant and the NCCL Women's Rights officer involved in the case to prepare this, at the Industrial Tribunal headquarters. At this stage the court called the parties in and asked to know what was going on. It appeared to be sympathetic to the employer in querying the meaning of sexual harassment under the Sex Discrimination Act 1975, and even doubting its existence at all – *'Isn't it just something that's been dreamed up by the newspapers?'* the Chairman asked.

After some discussion the court was persuaded that the case did fall within the provisions of the Sex Discrimination Act. But doubts about the reality of sex harassment clearly persisted. Although the two sides were allowed to go away to work on the agreement, they were subsequently called back to be told that it was the opinion of the Industrial Court that Mrs Langbant should withdraw her complaint. Yet the company had agreed to pay her £500 compensation, with the offer of an interview for another job, and were ready to sign to this.

The court then required Mrs Langbant to read the agreement out loud to them on oath, even though they had been supplied with written copies, and though this was not her work alone, but a joint negotiated agreement. After an adjournment of half an hour, the court returned to announce that the matter was not well founded, despite not having heard the case. The decision was that the court had only three options:

1) *to hear the whole case through*
2) *to require Mrs Langbant to withdraw and make a private argument*
3) *to find against her*

This action by the court succeeded in snatching defeat for Mrs Langbant from the jaws of victory. She could not take the first option, since her opponents had withdrawn – and she could hardly be expected to take the last one. She had no choice but to be forced into accepting a private agreement when the company had already demonstrated its willingness to make a public statement.

Mrs Langbant's complaints of sex discrimination and harassment involved the abuse of authority by a hostile male one step up from her on the management ladder, who had sought to prevent her from enjoying the privileges to which she was entitled on her grade. He had also subjected her to written comments of a gross personal and sexual nature. Following her complaints, she was moved from her post which she enjoyed, with good long-term prospects, to a dead-end job, while her harasser remained where he was. Had this case not been subjected to interference and succeeded, it would have been the first and only one to do so in the 7 years since the 1975 Act. Yet such cases are now commonplace in the US, where a body of relevant case law stretches back over the last *decade*. At the very least it is appalling that Industrial Tribunals, placed as they are on the frontiers of new legislative and social developments, are so ignorant of related matters elsewhere. As David Pannick states:

> Women at work are habitually subjected to unwelcome sexual advances, requests for sexual favours and other verbal and physical conduct of a sexual nature. In many cases submission to such conduct is expressly or impliedly made a term or condition of employment. Often the woman's response will determine whether she is taken on in the job, promoted or dismissed. Even more frequently, sexual harassment has the effect or purpose of unreasonable interfering with her work or creating an intimidating, hostile or offensive work environment. When sexual harassment takes one of these forms, it is, far from being being a joke, an important contributory factor to the stereotype of a woman's role at work and a violation of legal rights . . .
>
> There have, as yet, been no cases brought under the 1975 Act for sexual harassment at work. But

*there is every prospect that our courts and
tribunals will follow the approach of the US
Federal courts which have decided that* sexual
harassment in employment is sex discrimination contrary to Title VII of the Civil Rights
Act 1964. *After early cases which rejected
women's claims because of judicial fears that 'an
invitation to dinner could become an invitation to
a federal lawsuit', and that 'the only sure way an
employer could avoid such charges would be to
have employees who were asexual',* American
courts have moved on to an understanding of
the misery caused to women by persistent
and unwelcome sexual demands made of
them at work, and have recognised the un-
lawful nature of such conduct. *So far has the
American jurisprudence developed that, in a recent case, a US district court issued an injunction
to restrain male employees from making female
employees' working lives intolerable by continu-
ally harassing them with comments such as 'Did
you get any over the weekend?'*

Did you get any justice in an Industrial Tribunal?

Sarah Crompton, a journalist experienced in reporting
IT cases, says, 'Women can't win at the moment, the
way things stand.' From a survey of cases in a number of
IT courts, it is clear that woman will only win a case
where the discrimination against her is gross and palp-
able. Mrs Stubbs, a restaurant worker sacked by a
22-year old chef, only succeeded in proving sex
discrimination against him because the owner's wife
had told her that her sacking was inevitable because 'he
had got to have his own way, because he was the chef'.
The court found that 'he did not like working with
women in the kitchen'. So he sacked them! Just like that!
Other victims of vicious sexual prejudice were Trudy Pos-
nette and Joy Shingler. These women worked for Barratt
Developments Ltd as sales negotiators, selling new

houses to buyers with considerable success, until one Mr Symonds was appointed as sales manager. As the Chairman of the Industrial Tribunal takes up the story:

> *This job of sales negotiator had normally been done by women. It did so happen that when Mr Symonds was first employed he was a sales negotiator, and of course he was a man, and he was one of very few male persons to do this job. When he came to the respondents' company, he saw that most of the sales negotiators were female. Apparently he believed in aggression . . . women are not normally associated with that particular characteristic . . . he decided immediately that the two applicants, who are women, and whose record was satisfactory, and that is our finding of fact, should no longer remain in the respondents' employment.*

The aggressive Mr Symonds was, as the Tribunal found, 'moved quite irrationally by sex discrimination'. In the course of 'this miserable saga' he first revamped the sales force – where previous adverts for vacancies had stated that the job was 'an ideal opportunity for a man or woman', the new ads read that the company 'needed ambitious recruits'. This wording, together with an increase of £1,000 on the previous salary offered, had the desired effect of bringing male applicants flooding in and drowning the females. He then sacked the two women on the grounds that they were not 'aggressive' enough, even though one had just pulled off the difficult sale of some highly-priced houses. They were hustled off the premises immediately, and *on the very same day* two men started work in their jobs.

These women were lucky

They won their case. Even so, they were only awarded a paltry £600 compensation, when they had been put out of their jobs like this. But at least they won. *The majority of women lose*. Of fifty cases on record in Birmingham Industrial Tribunal between 1978 and 1982, only *five* succeeded. Nationwide, this depressing picture continues. The number of cases heard by Industrial Tribunals under the Equal Pay and Sex Discrimination Act were down to a record low of *119* in 1981. Equal Pay applications have crashed down every year from 1,742 in 1976, to only *54* last year, according to the Department of Employment Gazette – and of those, *only a quarter were successful*. In Sex Discriminations cases, *82% were dismissed*. What's going on? An Industrial Tribunal judge commented, 'We think that there aren't as many cases as there could have been.' His unease echoes the feelings of many, from the very highest level in the land. Lord Justice Scarman comments on this issue:

> With such a simple concept as equal opportunity and equal pay, it is discouraging that all that the Equal Opportunities Commission can report is 'some progress'. The Commission has had to invoke the jurisdiction of the European Court in order to get the equal rights of pensioners sorted out.
>
> When we come to the two Equal Opportunity statutes, the Commission has come to the not surprising conclusion that these statutes need amending – but when, how and by whom? We are discussing a fundamental human right.

It is not all well, with this obscurity and delay.

Not all well . . .

but it's the best we've got. There are difficulties, throughout the world, in enforcing the new legislation – in the first eight years of Equal Opportunities action in the US, the Department of Labor found *$47 million* to be owing in back pay to 113,000 women. By the end of 1972, only about a third of this had actually been paid, sometimes only after costly court action. 'Equality is

281

much more difficult than we thought,' says Birgitta Wistrand, president of Sweden's venerable and prestigious women's organization, the Frederika Bremer Association. But the law exists to help us bring it about – use it, and make it work for you. Once again the lead comes from the US, where a number of law cases have opened doors for women that were previously firmly closed.

* *A major sex discrimination suit was settled against the Chase Manhattan Bank, by which the Bank, although not admitting to any wrongdoing, agreed to adopt Positive Action Goals for women in future years. The money value of this settlement exceeded $2 million – to be used to enable women to enhance their business and professional skills.*

* *Jeanne King, an experienced waitress refused work at New York's haute cuisine restaurants, filed suit against them and against her local branch of the Hotel and Restaurant Employees Union for their pusillanimous acceptance of discriminatory practices against their members, the majority of whom are women. Despite well-funded resistance from what are among the priciest chop-houses in the world, King won hands down. As a further result of this case the US Department of Labor undertook a major investigation into the internal management of the union. Although deemed unable to lift a tray (one of the reasons given for not hiring her) King knocked down the first domino to produce a massive and far-reaching change.*

* *Tony Gilbertson filed charges of sex harassment after an interview at which she was asked by the male interviewer whether or not she wore a bra, what size it was, and told that her breasts were*

too large for the job [in the timber *trade? what job?]. When the judge found in her favour he noted that four other charges of sex discrimination had been brought against the company in the past. Gilbertson's victory also ended a sympathy strike by the local branch of the International Woodworkers' Union of America – the first time that this union had ever called a strike in support of a woman.*

Fall back on the law

With all its faults, the law has been framed to defend and to extend your rights as a woman and as a worker. Don't be afraid to fight for them. Get the EOC booklet on how to prepare your own case – remember that you don't need to be *legally* represented, but can be assisted by any one you nominate. At a recent Midlands tribunal, one girl was represented by her mother. 'A lioness fighting for her young', said the Chairman admiringly. She won the case. Or get a friend to assist you – Anne Sedley, Women's Rights Officer of the NCCL, advises always to have a woman friend with you when 'the man from ACAS' comes round as part of the preliminary process. 'Research has shown a biassed attitude on the part of the largely male officials', she says. Pressure is put on women claimants to withdraw their cases by the suggestion that theirs is a bad case, or they have no hope of succeeding. So when you hear that 50% of cases are settled before the hearing, by 'mediation' or 'conciliation', it can mean simply that women have been psyched out of it. Be prepared, and don't let this happen to you!

How to pay

You will need the help of your friend, sister, mother or union official at the Tribunal stage, as you are not entitled to legal aid actually to fight your case. Solicitors can and do give preliminary advice under the 'Green

Form' scheme – they can sort it out and put it together for you to take to the Tribunal. You can also be entitled to legal aid if your case goes from the IT and Employment Appeals Tribunal. But the idea of the Industrial Tribunals is that they are not bound by legalistic and formal requirements like criminal courts. They were originally designed to be 'people's courts', where justice could be dispensed with the minimum of pomp and ceremony.

Women are people too . . .

and must assume their rights in these courts, both as members and users of the process which at the moment is working against them. The effort must be made to reverse this process. This warning comes from Judge Constance Baker Motley: 'As women move up, the resistance is going to stiffen. *Court action will continue to be necessary*'.

The individual victories of brave and determined women, with the help of the EOC and NCCL, are inching open the closed doors that block our way. Get behind these pioneers, and take action too!

7

Think Positive

Positive Action – have *you* tried it yet?

is an EOC challenge in the form of a hand-out for
industry, management and individual workers. It's a
good question, and one which leads to the sunny side of
the work jungle, away from the thickets where am-
bushes and pitfalls lurk to snare the unwary. In Positive
Action a deliberate and sustained attempt is made to
advantage women – to provide new avenues, to make
straight the way, and to remove obstacles. Sounds like
discrimination all over again, only this time against men
instead of against women? Not quite. That is illegal.
Employers are not allowed to practise *reverse discrimination* – for example where a male and a female are both up
for the same job, and the employer decides to give it to
the girl, to make up for the fact that they've always
before had a man in that post. In this situation, the man
is deliberately rejected *solely on the grounds of his sex*, and
as such illegally discriminated against.

Women have been used to this . . .

but men can't stand it! Their active resentment, however, has a knock-on benefit for women in the jungle
war. US males recently used their country's legislation
to clip the wings of Southwest Airlines, whose female
employees had become the prisoners of a crudely sexist
and obscene advertising campaign. When Southwest, a
short-haul airline serving the southern states of America
began business in 1971, it adopted a 'love personality'
dreamed up by its agency – the campaign was designed
to win businessmen travellers by the *blatant exploitation*

of sex appeal. TV commercials for Southwest featured female attendants in tight dresses catering to male passengers, while an alluring female voice promised 'tender loving care'. On board, girls in hot pants served 'love bites' and 'love potions' (toasted almonds and cocktails to you and me). Even the airline's ticketing system was billed as a 'quickie machine' to provide 'instant gratification'!

Ladies only

To keep up this nudge-nudge image, Southwest hired only women for flight attendant and ticket agent positions. But more than 100 men challenged this hiring policy as a violation of the famous Title VII of the 1964 Civil Rights Act. In June 1981 the company defended their policy in court, claiming that it was crucial to their financial success. But a federal judge found against them, and concluded that being female was *not* a qualification required for the job: 'Southwest is not a business where vicarious sex entertainment is the primary service provided. Accordingly, the ability of the airline to perform its primary business function (the transportation of passengers) would not be jeopardised by hiring males. *To hold otherwise would open the door for other employers freely to discriminate by tacking on sex appeal as a qualification for any public contact position.*' – Judge J. D. Higginbotham.

So, fighting for themselves, the males won positive advances for the women. First, with male stewards aboard, the in-flight love-ins had to be abandoned, at the risk of turning the plane into Sodom and Gomorrah – and second, by establishing the principle that a public contact person does *not* have to be a woman whose sexuality is being peddled to get male customers to trade.

Positive women

In general, though, Positive Action *directly* benefits you

by enabling you to think of jobs or training schemes which women have always been excluded from before. The lifting of the 'Women Keep Out!' signs is proceeding steadily in a number of ways which *are lawful*. The Sex Discrimination Act 1975 rightly recognizes that it is necessary to *take action* to overcome the effects of past discrimination, and its legacy in the negative effect that education and society still have on girls' chances in life. So the law makes possible what the EOC actively recommends, a package of positive programmes on the part of those whose attitude determines failure or success for women:

* *Official bodies running training schemes: the Manpower Services Commission, the Training Services Agency, the Employment Service Agency, and industrial training boards.*

* *Employers, especially where their workforce is heavily biassed in favour of one sex.*

* *Trade unions and employers' organizations, again where a fairer balance of the sexes needs to be achieved.*

How this works

These provisions are wide enough to permit a variety of exciting new initiatives for women:

Education

A national body has been formed to promote maths for girls. The Girls and Mathematics Association (GAMMA) is the brainchild of Zelda Isaacson, Senior Lecturer in Maths Education at the Polytechnic of North London. *'We want to tell the world that girls have ability in maths – they can achieve with encouragement'*, she says. The

EOC thinks so too – the Commission has just been given £4,770 to further GAMMA's positive work.

The EOC is also taking steps of its own to get down to the bedrock of sex discrimination where it first affects girls, in the schools. From the volume of complaints received by the EOC, it emerges that *one third of the nation's Education Authorities have been breaking the law* by not giving girls the same opportunities as boys to study the subjects of their choice. The Commission has therefore embarked on a major advertising campaign to persuade parents, teachers and pupils that by giving up sciences, girls damage their job prospects.

Training

Government TOPS courses are opening their doors wider all the time to women who want to escape from the traditional female job ghettoes like office work. You can now train as a welder, brickie, bookbinder or what have you, where only men and lads went before – more than this, you have the right to demand entry on the Positive Action programme to any area of work which is substantially dominated by male workers at the moment.

Bristol Women's Workshop teaches woodwork and canework, and is beginning to give instruction in plumbing, electricity, and building. The Workshop's founder, Anne Harding, pointed to its tremendous success story: *'Three hundred women have come here to study carpentry in under two years* – extraordinary', she said.

Management

An exploding opportunities area for women, since even the most short-sighted scrutiny reveals women's gross disadvantages here in the past, where women hold fewer than 5% of middle or senior management jobs. Recent developments include:

The establishment of the National Organization

for Women's Management Education, to promote positive action and to forge links between women managers via conferences, news letters and a members' directory.

* *Management development courses for women are being run by the Manpower Services Commission as TOPS courses throughout the country. Special scholarships are being offered for women taking general management courses at Henley College, Henley-on-Thames. And many of these are taking advantage both of the Sex Discrimination Act and of recent research which shows that women do better on a 'Women Only' course* – male macho is much more fervently dramatized and acted out by numerically dominant males in the presence of a minority group of women. *Gill Howison, Head of the Department of Management Studies at the Gloucester college where one such course has run, comments, 'We've recognized that there is a great need for women's training in this area.'*

Professions

A world which like science and engineering cannot escape the 'very poor record: must try harder' verdict on its achievements to date. But things are beginning to stir in this primeval patriarchal ooze:

* *Women in Banking has come together to improve women's career prospects through a series of training sessions, workshops and lectures. And the NatWest Bank, recognizing that only 3% of top posts in banking are held by women, have started an experimental re-entry scheme for women leavers, permitting women with management potential to take up to five years off, then return to banking at the same grade. Jane Adams,*

289

NatWest's career planning adviser, says that 20
women have applied for this in only the first year
of the scheme.

* *The British Association of Women Executives,*
already linked to the 13-country strong Femmes
Chefs d'Enterprises Mondiales is expanding its
range of activities. A trust fund is being set up to
make an annual travel bursary award to an out-
standing woman entrepreneur.

And finally

there are new job opportunities for women in the
positive action field itself. Following the lead of the
GLC, where Judith Hunt recently took up her position
as the first Equal Opportunities Officer in the history of
the Council, Leeds City Council has established a post
whose responsibility is 'to assist in the development of
council policy on securing equal treatment for women in
employment, including recruitment, education, training and welfare'. Other women-based projects are
afoot, too – the NCCL reports an investigation going
forward into the career development of women, and an
agreement with the National Union of Journalists for a
project based in Manchester which will look at women's
opportunities in newspapers.

IT'S ALL STARTING TO HAPPEN!

It's happening now . . .

for women at Thames Television, after the company
boldly undertook its own Positive Action project. It's a
cherished part of media mythology that these industries
are wide open to any people with talent. In practice, this
means *male* people with talent, while *female* people,
however talented, fetch up in support roles as
secretaries, p.a.s, dogsbodies and gofers. Additionally,
poor scientific education combines with sex role stereo-

typing to decree that all the technical side of TV production is a male province too. And these glamorous and highly competitive industries can afford to 'waste' the frustrated or disillusioned employee, since there are always thousands of hopefuls queuing up to take her place.

*

> *Telly men go into telly because they fall madly in love with the medium. In TV there's an orgasmic interest in the product, and not so much in the human resources –*
>
> female television executive.

*

An Action Research report by Sadie Robarts on the structure of Thames Television demonstrated that the company's workforce was segregated by sex, that women were clustered in the lower-paid jobs, and that numbers of them wanted a chance to move up and out into the non-traditional job areas. But as the report states: '... Thames is not markedly better or worse than any other Television company. In the BBC in December 1979, 86% of the secretarial and clerical staff were female, while only 17% of the management/ professional grades were filled by women. Furthermore, in the very highest management grades of the BBC, women filled only two of 151 positions' – *Account of the Thames Positive Action Programme 1980-81.*

Where Thames scores . . .

is in its frank acceptance of Robart's discovery of these discriminatory patterns, and in its determination to do something about it. A Women's Employment Officer was appointed early in 1982, and a Positive Action Committee formed. Among the resulting changes, prominent are:

* *the introduction of training courses for all managers and personnel management on Equal Opportunities*

* *the monitoring of all job applications, internal and external*

* *the establishing of Television Training Courses open to any staff to learn the basics of television programme making*

* *the creation of a Code of Practice for non-sexist interviewing, and an Equal Opportunities booklet for distribution to all staff*

* *the drawing up of a company profile, and the continuation of research and discovery*

Inevitably, there has been some resistance and opposition to these changes. But Sue Hackett, Women's Employment Officer and in charge of the programme finds this a healthy sign. 'Apathy is the worst enemy', she says. 'Hostility keeps it alive. The men talk about it in the bar.' The success of the scheme overall is shown in a number of different ways. The Television Training Course answered a very deeply-felt need among the women – 'it was like taking the lid off a cauldron' as Sue recalled. It worked so well that the original group went on to a second stage, and then to a third-level course. *Thames women as a result are winning their spurs* not only in terms of promotion to management, but as electricians, camera operators and researchers, while all those who attend the training courses receive follow-up career counselling.

Thames's swift and successful response to the

Positive Action Report has also put the company on the map as a pioneer in this crucial area of industrial relations. Enquiries are now coming in from training bodies in industry, commerce and business, and from individual companies throughout Great Britain and the EEC. Is the Thames programme unique in Britain? 'We have gone the farthest', observed Sue. 'Local Authorities have gone quite far, but in the private sector, no, there is no *total* company programme.' But perhaps the greatest achievement lies in the winning of hearts and minds within Thames itself. *'The men are coming round,'* Sue states. 'It all takes time, and you'll always get the person who can't take the change. But lots are coming round.' Sue also points to the tremendous potential for change in a Positive Action project within a TV company. 'If you were to *revolutionize* Shell Oil, it won't have the same knock-on effect as in a communications industry. Here you can potentially affect programming and the product – eventually even advertising, the worst of the prime sites of women's stereotyping!' Right on, Thames – keep up the good work!

Positive Action for you

The vast majority of companies and organizations have yet to follow Thames's bold and imaginative lead. If, as is likely, you work in one of the others, how do you set about taking them and yourself down this road? The first task is to *identify any areas in which women are under-represented*. Use existing personnel records to find out where the women are located – they will almost certainly show that

* *women are confined to a restricted number of occupations*
* *the proportion of women declines in relation to the seniority of the grade.*

Enlisting the help of other interested women, either informally or as a regular working party, you then go on

293

to *investigate the causes of this segregated structure* of your outfit, and the discriminatory effect against women. They are probably any or all of the following:

* *discriminatory recruitment procedures*
* *unfair wage and salary structures*
* *male-biased criteria for promotion*
* *insensitive appraisal systems*
* *inflexible job segregation*
* *inadequate training facilities*
* *persistence of sex-stereotyped thinking in male management*

Research all this thoroughly, collect as much material evidence as you can, and get together a portfolio establishing the case. Then:

Design your own Positive Action programme

How much work you are able to put into this depends on how much time and energy you have to spare – Sue Hackett's job at Thames is a full-time one, and the rest, as its demands spill over into her evenings and weekends. Don't try to take on the whole of your company's procedures single-handed – you'll only finish up with what Americans have called 'feminist burnout'. On the public level, you may have done enough by raising awareness of these issues (often carried on quite unconsciously because unquestioned) and by fingering the particular black spots in your outfit. Once you've stigmatized recruitment or selection procedures, age bars or restrictions on training opportunities, you should be able to leave it to someone else (eg. your union) to follow it through.

With a little help from female friends . . .

you may find that it just disappears by itself. 'My firm had this awful section on the application form', said Molly, who works in personnel in a large industrial bakers, ' "For Females Only". You had to put down your marital status, maiden name, how many children, all your past history. When we complained, they agreed to phase it out. Then one girl applied, she was a student or something, anyway she didn't really want the job. She not only made up a lot of marriages, divorces and children – she filled it with revolting stuff about all her miscarriages, caesarians, oh, gruesome! Well, the forms went out pretty quickly after that!'

On the private level

work out your own tailor-made Positive Action programme to counteract the disadvantages of your sex, and to take the chance offered by the current impetus to advance yourself and your career, as follows:

* *ask about your employer's policy on Positive Action for women – especially on staff development and training. If you draw a blank –* a staggering 37% of employers have no training policies *– ask for one to be developed, pointing out that both legal and financial backing now exist for this.*

* *speak to your immediate boss about your career development and training needs. Enquire in depth as to what is available, and make sure that s/he knows that you want to know* whatever is going *(even if it's something that they may not have thought of for you) and that you are willing to travel/move around/stay away evenings or weekends to do it.*

* *find out where and how other opportunities are open to you, whoever may have an Action Programme that you could benefit from – check professional bodies, trade associations, government schemes.*

* establish who else in your department or company is interested in the same thing as you are – take joint action to get your employer moving by demonstrating the demand.

* check out funding from other sources if your employer won't pay – the European Social Fund, for instance, opened a special section 'to finance specific action for the training of women in response to the deteriorating position of women in the labour market', which in 1980 benefitted 10,500 women.

* don't be fobbed off with 'policy outlines', 'statements of support', 'Equal Opportunity/Positive Action declarations' and the like. These simply substitute the will for the deed. Press for implementation of suggestions, fulfilment of promises – in a word, action!

The lights are going on all over Europe . . .

as different countries realize and attempt to fulfil their obligations to women. On 1 May 1981 (the first time in history that Labour Day has packed a punch for women workers!) 14 special advisers on Equal Rights started work in employment bureaux in different regions of *Denmark*. Their main tasks are to promote equality between men and women in the labour market, by finding jobs and initiating schemes for unemployed women.

In *France* the first ever Minister of Women's Rights was appointed in 1981, 'to eliminate any form of discrimination against women, and to increase their guarantees of equality in the political, economic, social and cultural domains'. The Minister, Yvette Roudy, is especially to 'guide and co-ordinate' work done in employment, and to undertake to enact the decision of the Council of Ministers to 'abolish sexist discrimination' in the labour market. One immediate step will be the reservation of *at least 60%* of places on training courses for young women, unemployment among French women under 25 being so severe as to demand positive remedial action without delay.

*

> *It is coming at last, for women. Only the most stupid men would now doubt this, or dare to oppose it – dodos, dinosaurs, you would call them. They are still powerful, but their days are numbered. And then,* kaputt! –
> German Professor of International Law

*

The EEC launched a new Action Programme on 9 December 1981 to strengthen women's rights and promote Equal Opportunities throughout the member states. A 16-point programme is to be implemented in stages over the next three years. A highly significant feature of the programme includes specific steps to desegregate women's employment, to analyse its trends and *protect women from it!*

Under the European Social Fund, France, Germany and Italy have received grants for training women in 'men's' skills, and for re-training those scrapped in reorganisation or redundancy schemes. Courses that have proved both popular and successful with women include:

* *maintenance engineering*
* *toolmaking*
* *car maintenance*
* *computer programming*
* *micro-processing*

But when the Dunkirk Chamber of Commerce ran a number of training programmes for unemployed women in 1981, offering a wide range of skills, the

297

women showed a marked preference for the jobs of light and heavy vehicle drivers, and fork-lift truck operators. Truck on, mesdames! *Bonne route!*

To the barricades!

Today's women are not just sitting back and waiting for the legal and social machinery to grind their male opponents down in the course of time. They are fighting back in their own right, with guts, with strength, with humour. Mrs Kathleen Martin was stocking shelves in a small Nottinghamshire Post Office when a man rushed in and fired a pistol over her head. He shouted to her colleague, Mrs Jean Hawker, 'If you don't want me to kill her, give me the money.' The Postmaster was out at the time, taking the three guard dogs for a walk. But Mrs Hawker shouted, 'Katy, let the dogs out!' and in her own words: 'The man panicked. I pushed him out from behind the counter, and we pushed him out of the shop, Katy slung the bread tray at him.'

A man with a gun! For this coolness and bravery, these two examples of 'the weaker sex' were awarded £250 each in August of 1982. Bang on!

Women fight back . . .

in the toughest of all cities, New York. In September 1982, 70 female candidates passed a physical endurance test for the City Fire Department which required them to:

* drag a dummy weighing 120 lbs
* scale a 5 ft wall
* drag an 80 lb fire hose for 145 ft
* lift a 20 ft ladder
* climb to the fourth floor of a building
* break into a building with a sledge hammer

'It took five months of daily jogging, sit-ups and knee bends, to pull me through this', said Ms Katrina Cannon, a 25-year-old accountant. 'All I want to do now is to raise my right hand, and take that oath to be a New York City fire-fighter.' She and the other successful women only won the right to *take* the test after a Federal Judge had thrown out a previous physical test on the grounds that it was discriminatory. This test, vigorously defended by the firemen's union as a way of keeping women out, did not only discriminate against women. It emerged during the hearing that half the *men* who took it failed! What's that again about the weaker sex . . . ?

Fighting male machismo

Some women find themselves right in the firing-line because of their jobs, and taken to be an easy target by every dead-eye Dick, the local scorer. 'Part of the life of a barmaid is coping with the dreadful stigma of being a pushover', says Lallie, who works evenings in the bar of a super-de-luxe country hotel in Warwickshire. Hardly a night passed without some drunken buffoon making an inept pass at her: 'Honestly, you'd think he'd only just discovered sex, made it all up by himself', she grinned. 'But the stupid thing is, there's nothing harder than a barmaid to pull, because she's heard it *all* before!'

The Barmaid's Revenge

Lallie took most of this in her stride, even enjoying the spectacle of the master race making fools of themselves. 'You wouldn't believe what they do when they're boozed up,' she chuckled. 'I mean, trouser-taking-off competitions – and worse – the lot. It's pathetic. Truly pathetic. It's like aversion therapy really – it'd put you off sex for life if you let it.'

Sometimes, though, a customer overstepped the mark by a mile, and the barmaids were put in the impossible position of having to continue to be 'nice' to a man whom they could only discourage by being nasty. On one occasion, a man had parked himself at the corner of her bar all night, touching her up whenever she had to bring drinks out to the tables. Eventually he called for another beer for himself, and as she brought it, made a painful grab at her breasts. With her free hand she knocked him flat ('He was so drunk, he was a pushover!') and then with the line, 'Don't forget your beer, *sir*', she poured the pint all over him. To her surprise, she was warmly applauded by another group of men in the bar, who had been following the progress of the incident. The groper staggered out, dripping, and she braced herself for repercussions from above. But the groper did not call the manager. 'I was lucky there,' she said. 'I would have lost my job. We're supposed to put up with it, whatever they dish out. I knew that at the time, but I just thought, to hell with it, I don't have to take this!'

The laugh's on them

Women fighting back are also employing the priceless weapon of humour to demolish the opposition – up and down the world you can hear the rattling of those funny bones that females are supposed not to possess. The surreptitious night-time feminist raids on sexist adverts in London have become a modern art form – particularly offensive ads are wittily defaced with an appropriate comment, and the results photographed for immortality. Favourites are:

> * *A Renault 5 car with the caption, 'If this car were a lady, she'd have her bottom pinched.'* Women's sub-caption, 'If this lady were a car, *she'd run you down.'*

> * *A Volvo baby car with the gushing line, 'To Volvo, a son.'* Underneath: *'Better luck next time.'*

> * *A tool set with the invitation to women buyers, 'Renew his interest in carpentry.'* Invitation below: *'Saw his head off.'*

300

* A Pretty Polly tights ad showing a glamorous
pair of legs with the leering line, 'Where would
fashion be without pins?' The women's answer: 'Free of little pricks.'

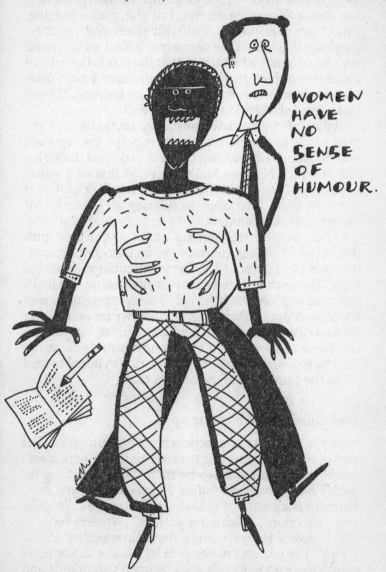

WOMEN
HAVE
NO
SENSE
OF
HUMOUR.

Women are using their sense of humour at work in ways that allow them to assert their sense of their own worth against the constant inroads of ignorant and demanding men. In one major insurance group, women processed the motor insurance claims, but the male claimants would often refuse to deal with them and insist on speaking to a man. One very experienced section head became so annoyed with this, that she was in the habit of transferring them to a totally inexperienced male newcomer whom she was supposed to be training. 'That'll teach 'em,' she used to say. And it did!

Males, of course, will constantly mythologize their own work, and as such are weeping-ripe for exposure and deflation. US feminist Cynthia Ozick sat through a talk at which Norman Mailer asserted that all a writer needs is 'his pen and his balls'. Demurely Ozick asked at question time, 'I've been wondering all evening, Mr Mailer – in what colour ink do you dip your balls?'

Other women recommend as an all-purpose put-down the following, delivered as an innocent observation in a World-About-Us, David Attenborough sort of way: 'The sex life of spiders is very interesting – he fucks her, and she bites his head off.' This was originally said by Robin Morgan, American poet and writer – you won't do as well as Morgan and Ozick straight off, but you can try. Have a go – you don't know how funny you can be till you begin, especially with such rich material to feed on as the comic half of the human race!

Undermining and blowing up . . .

male pretensions and practices is not just fun – it's a vital part of women's asserting themselves in the work place, establishing your right to be there and *dismantling the hostile male dominance values by substituting you own.* Humour is a great way of saying to your male colleagues and 'superiors', 'Come off it, lads!' Women have to break down the prevailing masculine reality in the world of work, and develop in its place a mode more sympathetic to women's lives, women's standards and women's work. Now more than ever is the time to try to *make the system work for you*, to maximize your choices and to push for alternatives to the way that men have always done it and run it. Some of these currently under discussion and trial are:

> *job-sharing
> *flexitime
> *home working

All these potentially offer more flexibility and more control. What are the pros and cons for you?

Job-sharing

Not, as some people think, a fancy modern name for part-time work. Job-sharing means that two employees jointly agree to be responsible for one full-time job. They carve up the attendance between them – Jane works Monday, Wednesday and Friday one week while Joan does Tuesday and Thursday, and the next week they swop round – or Jane always comes in mornings and Joan takes over afternoons at lunchtime. They share the salary and any benefits. Where this differs from part-time work is that

> * *you have a permanent job registered on the company strength as full-time, so you are much less vulnerable to redundancy or dismissal*

> * *the kind of posts full and varied enough to be 'job-shared' are much more interesting and responsible than any part-time work is likely to be*

Job-sharing is now an established reality in areas as diverse as lecturing and banking – the recent Leeds Council advert for an Equal Opportunities Officer specified that job-sharing applications would be considered. If you have a friend with similar qualifications (or lack of!) to your own, consider putting together a job-sharing application for any job you fancy, but which you either could not hold down full-time, or don't want to. *Selling points to the employer* are the inalienable fact that he'll be getting two brains for the price of one, and the proven fact that you'll waste less of his time. Research in the US and elsewhere has shown that job-sharers use their own time, not the boss's, for dental appointments, bits of shopping, and even phone calls! How can he lose?

Flexitime

A genuine innovation too, this is already the work form used by 7·6 million people in the US, and spreading in England. This gives workers the opportunity to establish their own work schedules within the framework of a working day that runs from 7 am to 7 pm. The conditions are that the worker must put in the standard 35 or 40 hours per week; and that all workers are present during one short core period of the day (11 am till 3 pm for example). But otherwise this means that you can work entirely according to your own rhythms of life – if you're a morning person, you can be there with the milk, or if you prefer to finish work when the rush hour is over and the local hostelry has opened its friendly doors, you can do it the other way round.

Flexitime is related to, but different from, another alternative work scheme, *the compressed workweek*. This is a system that permits the employee to work a 40-hour week in four days rather than five. This intensifies your work, but also your leisure – think of a three-day weekend, every weekend! Again, there are real pluses for the organization as well as for the employees in these arrangements. Not only do they get the phones manned, and the place in business for a much longer working day, but all the research has shown that the element of personal choice and control makes for a much more highly motivated and efficient work force. If you know you can leave when you choose/see your gynaecologist at your own convenience/fit in your shopping or an afternoon visit to the cinema at will, you have no reason to resort to lies and subterfuge, or just goof off.

Home working

A dodgy area which combines some very old and oppressive traditions of women's work, with some spanking new but possibly equally threatening moves. Home working can mean for a woman her own personal, privatized sweatshop, where she has to turn out far too many machined pieces, or addressed envelopes, or whatever, to make even a pittance. Home or outworkers are horribly exploited, isolated and unprotected by any union action or state benefit, sacked if they complain and immediately replaced by some other poor woman. Don't touch it! It is a grotesque 19th-century hangover into the modern world and should be made illegal.

But home working also covers a very new development, and one which uncritical technologists say will come for us all, when every home is plugged into every available terminal, and every worker is plugged into his/her own computer. This type of home working applies both to males and females, and is not a solitary personal choice from lack of viable options, but a conscious policy decision of the employing body to deploy workers in this way. In England, Rank Xerox launched a scheme in 1982 to have executives work from home. Norwich Union Building Society has for some years been organizing secretaries to work from home – a van brings round the necessary tapes, and collects the typing when the women have finished. At a different work level, computer programmers, and word processor operators are among those workers who, once wired up, can go into production from their home base.

So far so good – but what's in it for women? First, it's important to grasp that it's only ever introduced as a cost-cutting or cost-eliminating exercise by the employers – i.e., it's not *your* welfare they have at heart. There is also a real danger of exactly the sort of miseries that attend the old-style home worker – isolation, fragmentation, alienation. Considering that the majority of women declare that one of their primary reasons for working is to get out of the prison-house of a lonely home and into the world – that it is not the work they seek, but the company – then home working seems to offer women, under the guise of the new technowizardry, *exactly* what they do *not* want!

Where you stand

Think hard about your work requirements, and your life as a whole. The advantage of these new schemes are:

> * *a real stake in the work force*
> * *a salary*
> * *a chance to use your other days for college attendance, private study, self-development, or fuller leisure and relaxation*

The disadvantages can be:

> * *a reduced stake in the company/system/product like part-timers*
> * *the evolution of a new form of job segregation, as more* women *take advantage of these developments than* men
> * *you lose out to those workers, male or female, who take the traditional 9 to 5 path, and work up and through their careers in ways that you just can't*

Finding the way

Your choice will be constrained anyway by the normal interplay of factors that deny everybody total freedom of movement. Consider your options, and *watch out that you don't give up on any of your basic work rights* – slippery bosses have discovered that they can get round the

Employment Protection Act 1975 by offering less than 16 hours work per week to each half of a job-sharing pair, for instance. But choose on the realistic basis that if you go one road, you cannot go the other. It's no good opting for a flexible, alternative, non-work-dominated lifestyle, and then getting miffed when the one-track-minded rats race past you to the top.

Having made your choice, go to it. Encouragingly those who have tried the newer forms where they exist, or persuaded bosses to experiment with them where they didn't, are enthusiastic about the potential for change and growth. 'It's just something other', said Becky, a US job sharer. 'It's a totally different way of life. I enjoy my work, sure [in university administration]. But this way I can have all the other things I want, too. I can study, read, exercise, see my friends – Renaissance woman, the all-round *mensch!*' Sounds good no?

> *Two roads diverged in a yellow wood . . .*
> *I took the one less travelled by,*
> *And that has made all the difference –*
> Robert Frost

Birds do it!

Women everywhere are making it, woman-style, in a host of different ways and occupations. American Lilli Lenz was among the first women to prove that you can be a carpenter, *and* a lady. Lenz was a graduate teacher until she became increasingly conscious that most women 'have no practical control over their lives'. 'I felt incapable, having to rely on other people', she says. 'I feel I'd like to take care of myself.' She got her breakthrough with Barnhardt Construction Co of California. Ben Walker, who hired her, said, 'She showed up for work when the men wouldn't come out of their houses because of the rain.' Being hired by Barnhardt's enabled Lilli to apply to join the union, and she has become the first woman member of the United Brotherhood of

307

Carpenters and Joiners of America. Craftswoman Anne Graham forms a brotherhood of one in her work as an enameller and jeweller. But she has successfully launched herself in the work she wants to do, hand-making lovely pieces from silver, gold, tortoiseshell, ivory and diamonds, armed only in the first place with a grant from the Scottish Development Agency and her faith in her own talent.

Minding your own business

Have you ever thought that you don't necessarily have to work for someone else? Considered the possibility of setting up on your own? More and more women are going in for this, the ultimate form of Positive Action. Wendy Curme, who has set up her own succcessful PR business in London, says, 'I wanted to work for myself – I'm that sort of person, very self-motivated. I don't need people to crack the whip over me, and that used to rub them up the wrong way. I felt that the time had come.'

If you feel that the time is coming for you, be sure to:

> * research the field very carefully (does your area really need another bijou/bistro/boutique outfit?)
>
> * read all about it – start with the Guardian Guide for the Small Business by Clive Woodcock, plus all the material prepared for hopeful entrepreneurs by the major banks, and go on from there
>
> * winkle out all the advice and funding you are entitled to – ring the Government's Small Firms Service on Freefone 2444 as a first move. Your local council, central and EEC finances are also available under certain circumstances
>
> * get by with a little help from your friends – setting

up with like-minded mates, or forming a co-operative (looked on with increasing favour by banks, etc, as they become more familiar) spreads the load and maximizes the resources. But NB best friends only – a business partnership is a closer relationship than many marriages, with even less tolerance of human frailty or failure. Only go in with those you either know well, or have a good reason *to trust (like their investment of £10,000 in your project!)*

But start by investigating the possibilities. Look into it. What can you lose? The chances are that *either* you will realize that the world of business is not for you – in which case you have done yourself a favour by dumping an impossible dream that would only have come back to reproach you – *or* that you are on to a good thing – in which case, *avanti!* What are you waiting for? Be your own fairy godmother and get going!

Beating the recession

Not an easy task – if it were, all the politicians and economists would be succeeding in doing it! It would be frivolous and dangerous to make light of the severe financial situation throughout the world, and the particular difficulties likely to be encountered by anyone who plunges unwarily into the market place. But paradoxically, the recession has also operated to break down a lot of fixed and old-fashioned business ideas, now the former certainties are losing their purchase. And as the big corporations, industries and even governments flounder, a high premium is placed on individual flair and skill – smaller enterprises can succeed when the giants fail.

'It's wide open now for anyone with a bit of grit and gumption', says a Manchester bank manager. 'The business world is in total disarray. No one can say with confidence any longer what will work. But equally they're more cautious too in saying something *won't*. If you've got a good idea that's a bit way out, you won't get the automatic thumbs-down now you'd have got ten years or so ago'.

Among 'way out' ideas, a prize-winner must be Mrs Pam Murphy's. Left a widow with a dairy farm and 120 head of cattle, she had the inspiration of converting and marketing the 1200 gallons of . . . ah . . . *waste* that they produced *every day*. The result is Cowpact, a solid pong-free garden fertilizer whose successful market impact amply demonstrates the truth of waste not, want not!

> *Don't talk to me about manpower any more*
> *because the manpower question has been solved by*
> *womanpower –*
>
> F. D. Roosevelt

Positive supporting action

In keeping with the newer business ideas, many women are now getting the particular practical support that can make all the difference between success and failure. Dominique and Thérèse were both unemployed when a pregnant friend suggested that they should capitalize upon the French love of children by making high-quality baby clothes. They began in a small way, among friends and contacts, and rapidly expanded into a select boutique in Nice. They readily admit that they found finances a problem, especially at first. But they are loud in their praise not only of their bank, but also of their suppliers and creditors. 'Many times, we have said to one another, *c'est foutu* [it's all screwed up]. But the patience, the help we have had – it saved us.' In Britain, Lloyd's bank recently backed a woman landscape painter for an exhibition in Nassau. Pamela Anderson who had already sold her work in England and Europe, had this chance, and received the cash to take it. Any business can be good business!

Management, woman-style

There are positive advantages for all women in these female initiatives. Contrary to the misogynistic male mythology that no one wants to work for a woman boss, those who have had a chance to try it are warm in their appreciation. In an award for the Best Female Manager run by *Cosmopolitan* magazine and Lloyd's Bank, winners elicited these tributes from their staff:

> *Unlike some male bosses she knows what a secretarial job entails, that it is more than just typing and making coffee.*

> *Julie has all the qualities that you would expect in a male manager, but she is also very female, very supportive. She always praises a job well done, tells me what is going on, and is approachable, with a sense of humour.*

Edith Lowy, Managing Director of her own firm, explains the advantages for women in working for a woman: 'Morale is higher. It's more of a team effort. You all pull together, and there is very much less sickness and absenteeism. My women are covered if they have to go home to be with their children. I know what it is like. They don't have to pretend it's something else. They can turn to me when they have any kind of trouble, and they know it.'

Contrast this with the male boss who was recently hauled (successfully) before an Industrial Tribunal for calling his secretary 'a bitch on Mondays'! Francine Gomez is one of the biggest bosses in Europe, as head of the great pen company Watermans which she has turned around from a £300,000 a year loser in 1969, to today's million-pound earner. She makes a point of giving women a positive boost wherever possible: 'I'm trying to help the weak against the strong, to help an under-privileged category.'

Room at the Top

As this suggests, if you make it upwards, you can take
other women with you. And there's plenty of room for
us all up there, according to Jeanette Lee, Vice-President
of Hallmark Cards Inc. 'In the lower levels, there are a lot
more bright career-oriented women coming up. There
just aren't that many higher-level corporate women to
choose from today, but there will be in about ten years.'
Up-and-coming women have the knowledge that they
won't be going it alone – they have already a number of
successful women as models for their own future
development. Helen Grindrod is one of only 8% of
women barristers in Great Britain; as a 'silk' she is one of

only 14 female QCs; and she sits as a Recorder on the Northern circuit in addition to carrying on her own practice. She began with a degree in English, but 'the Bar crept up on me as an idea', she said. 'I decided to stop moaning, and do it.'

'Doing it' involved studying alone, working with books from the local library and old exam papers, usually in the evening as her son was then under school age. It also meant working through a certain amount of routine and traditional anti-feminism – at one chambers, the Clerk made it abundantly clear that he would not tolerate a woman barrister as a member of 'his' chambers, while the chances of civil work were reduced as insurance companies were not prepared to strike out and brief women. 'You also had to watch out that you didn't get shoved off with the work that you don't want to do,' said Mrs Grindrod. 'I was determined not to do all "women's work" – matrimonial, divorce.' Some of these discriminations have worn away with the advance of women. Formerly 'women were not allowed to be full members of the circuit mess. The men wanted to be able to tell their dirty stories, so they voted against the admission of women. But the passage of time brought the general recognition that you can't go on being rude to half of mankind for ever.'

Like all successful women, Helen Grindrod tends to underestimate her own achievement – 'I just did it,' she says. But hers is a history of hard work and sustained commitment ('slogging on' as she calls it) over a period of time. Her initial enthusiasm for the law has not waned – despite 'great chunks of boredom' at junior level, she still finds the work 'fascinating' and has not become impervious to the drama of the court room: 'I still feel a *frisson* when the jury is coming back, whether I'm prosecuting or defending.' Yet she does not minimize the demands of the job: 'It's physically exhausting. Emotionally, too. The adrenalin keeps flowing, and you can't take five minutes' kip in the middle of the court!'

It is encouraging not simply that Helen Grindrod has made room at the top of a heavily male-dominated profession, but also that she has done it without having to go back on her womanhood. Her version of the legal 'uniform' was an extremely smart black suit, with silk stitching on the lapels, which worn with black stockings created a tremendous effect of restrained elegance and glamour. Her approachable manner, sense of humour, and patience even at the end of a long day in court are in marked contrast to the pomposity, self-importance and irritability of some of her male colleagues in their august profession. She is encouraging, too, about the prospects for women in the law. 'It's discouraging now that more girls are not coming forward. They won't be received with open arms, but they won't be turned down. Those who are coming in have every chance. Younger women stick at it. They've got the stamina.'

Stamina is the name of the game

'I'd rather work 12 hours a day and enjoy it, than 8 hours a day and hate it,' says Bernadette (Brandy) Lawrence, who has established her own metal trading business in the Midlands. 'You have to put the effort in. For six years I worked so many hours in the day that I didn't know what I was doing.' Although she claims to be taking it easier now, Brandy still has a 5.30 a.m. start, and the desk in her beautiful flat is loaded with paperwork. It's all relative!

Brandy began in a traditional female job after A-Levels, as a clerk in an insurance office. She hated it. Looking for a change of direction, she applied for a job in the metal trade. Told on application, 'We can't employ women,' she replied smartly, 'Then you'd better let me talk to someone who can!' Enthusiasm has also been a key to her success – in one scrap metal firm. 'I liked that, I could see the scrap.' She also gets a kick out of being the boss, even though it's a work of constantly educating the customers. 'They still say, "Who actually runs this place, I mean, who *is* the boss?" When I say, "I am," they say, "Well, I've heard it all now".'

One of Brandy's biggest assets is undoubtedly her

sense of humour. 'When I started our business with this fella,' she recalled, 'everyone assumed we were having an affair.' She knew about this gossip, and discounted it, until it was quite deliberately brought out as a 'joke' in front of her. Wide-eyed, she asked the joker directly, 'Why, if any man was paying me £10,000 a year for sex, you don't imagine that I'd bother to come into work *as well*, do you?' And talking about women in industry, she drily recalled a colleague who was all for women's advancement. He would always appoint a woman if he could, because of the following virtues they had over men:

* *he could push them round easier*
* *he paid them less*
* *they didn't threaten him*
* *he could make passes at them all*

Brandy's sense of the ridiculous has helped her to weather her share of the silly and dirty tricks that men can dish out. Working for one international firm early on, she was put on to the job of routing the firm's vehicles which travelled all over Europe – among the most interesting jobs in the company. She was the first woman ever to hold this post, and the job was always done in pairs, to avoid any chance of error. The man she was to work with went to the boss and complained that he should not have to work with a woman – it made him too vulnerable, in case she should decide to complain that he had attacked her! 'Men resent the penetration of their mystique at work', she said, laughing. 'If a woman's doing it alongside them, they can't go home and impress their wives with their mighty male work. It takes down their masculinity.'

Masculinity is a delicate blossom, as it appears. Men continue to expect her to fuss over them and ask if they'd like a cup of coffee. 'You should see their faces when I say, "I'm not buying at that price, I want £10 a ton off it"', she says with a grin. One boyfriend was heard to come out with the immortal line, 'So your work's more important than I am?' Another, working for a competitor, found it hard to cope. 'That was a bit of a trauma – for him!' she remarked mischievously. As a successful woman of today, Brandy has not had to sacrifice her femininity to get where she is. The male head of a metal factory described her with deep admiration as 'the only man in the metal trade – a wonderful girl!', and though she claims to wear 'manky old jeans' at work, her red hair, high heels and personal sparkle leave no doubt about the second half of the equation. Her difficulty is in finding men who are on her level in every way. But she has no desire to get married. 'A *husband?*' she laughed. 'He'd only expect to moan to *me* at the end of a hard day!'

Mr Siddons, I presume?

Today's high-flying women are living with a series of problems that women in the past did not have to face. Until recently they were expected to choose between work and love – the Civil Service actually *required* women to resign on marriage, a policy unofficially pursued in many other occupations too. Remaining single was the price they had to pay. Now, when these barriers are removed, a modern girl is expected, even encouraged, not to pursue her work at the expense of her emotional life. Having relationships with men, balancing work and love, accommodating their demands in a demanding life of your own – that's the price you're having to pay now! Unless you're going to remain celibate – and enough women find this the right choice for you not to reject it out of hand – it's essential that in the endless juggling match of men and work, that you *get it right*. Where difficulties are likely to occur is when your work and love life become entangled. It would be wonderful if these two aspects of life, the primary elements of a normal existence to which Freud said everyone was entitled, would stay in separate compartments. But they won't, and don't. If then like many other women you find yourself in the position of mixing them, the result can be a heady brew with a powerful kick. Go carefully.

You're in the dark . . .

in every sense, since this is a totally under-researched area. Much attention has been given recently to the *negative* aspects of the meeting of men and women in the work place. Numerous studies have established the menace of sex harassment, and the misery of women at the hands of men who crudely foist their unwanted sexual attentions on unwilling victims. But although very important, that is only one side of the case. Many working women look to their job situation for social contacts, especially as newcomers to a town or city. Many hope to find a prospective marriage partner at work, and do so. And many, especially today, expect to meet through their work the kind of men they like, with a view to friendly relations of the *non-marriage* variety. None of this has received any attention from psychologists, social scientists, the CBI, the TUC, the opinion pollsters, or any of the professional observers of the human race. If you want to be positive in the personal aspects of your public life, you're on your own, and have to make it up as you go along. But as in every other significant but unacknowledged area of life, certain unwritten ground rules operate which you should acquaint yourself with.

How to play the game

If your relations with your colleagues are confined to a lunchtime game of basketball and a glass of plonk at Christmas, or if you are deeply into an old-fashioned courtship with the altar already beckoning, you have little to worry about. But the reality for many working girls lies in an attraction for a boss or colleague who for a number of reasons you will not expect to marry. What then? You must be sure to weigh it up, and move forward on your own terms.

Rule number one . . .

is that at work, work must come first. Your employer is

not supposed to be subsidizing your sex life, and you should not be able to draw your salary with a clear conscience if your major effort in the last month has gone into mooning over Joe Bedworthy, making interminable phone calls, dashing off early to meet him and using the spaces in between to drool into letters all the things you still want to say. At work, you only gain respect by how well you do your work. To be seen showing that you don't give a toss makes you wide open to criticism. Many bosses are already convinced that all girls think about is their 'love-life', and need no encouragement on this score. 'I really rated Laura', said one personnel manager of a trainee. 'Then she fell for her boss, and just went to pieces. Never there – and never any use when she was – going round in a daze – and once came back to work after lunch with her jumper on inside out! Well, we couldn't have that sort of thing, even today. Well, could we?'

In extreme circumstances, a wild infatuation could even cost you your job. One couple of love-birds, a girl and the charge-hand at the Midlands factory where she worked, were sacked for their canoodlings in the workshop. Both lost their case for unfair dismissal at an Industrial Tribunal – the court found that they had brought it on themselves by becoming a public nuisance: 'Other girls were being embarrassed by misconduct on the company premises', said the Chairman.

Misconduct by him . . .

is usually treated much more lightly than misconduct by you. That case was unusual in that both parties had to leave. Recognize that even in today's 'enlightened' climate of opinion, you are far more likely to have to get out, or be pushed out, as a result of an affair at work, than your partner will be. 'The girl is expected to go in these circumstances', said a leading Midlands industrialist. 'She can't be really serious about her work anyway if she's playing around – and the bloke is the one we want, after all.' NB *he* can be playing around and still be serious about his work. But she can't. And she's expendable. Because he is a branch of the company tree, and she is thought of simply as a bird resting temporarily somewhere in the foliage. In these cases, all that the birds usually catch is a worm.

*

Love is of man's life a thing apart,
'Tis woman's whole existence –
George Gordon, Lord Byron

*

The balance is against you . . .

in mixing love and work, in so many ways. The chances are that he will be your boss, or otherwise in a more important position in the outfit than yours – a salesman, say, while you're secretarial. That can in itself activate the juices – it's the forbidden fruit/man in authority syndrome, that makes dangerous the lives of vicars, doctors and men of power. Try to distance yourself from the dynamic of the immediate situation, where he calls the shots and you see yourself as having to hop to the crack of his whip. Would you fancy him if you had met him anywhere else? At a party, for instance, or in the pub? Would he still hold the same fascination if it were not for the illicit, thou-shalt-not aspect? Try thinking of him in a pair of long johns, wincyette pyjamas, or some other absurd get-up. I won't tell you how Ed Morrow used to visualize his interviewees, to nerve himself up to deal with world leaders and mighty men on equal terms, but use your imagination! It's amazing how the magic can drop away from a chap when you need it to!

You'll need it to . . .

unless you can be absolutely, totally, 105% *certain* that

he feels as strongly as you do. And you almost never can. Because (forgive the obvious, I know you'll have noticed) they're different from us. Love, sex, 'relationships' – men reckon to do all this with the other hand, so to speak, and *still give their primary attention to their work.* They may like to get things off with a bang – the more stylish men especially will rise to an initial starburst of flowers, tender little meals *à deux*, cards and kisses. But they soon expect it to 'settle down' to a more 'realistic' level – i.e., one of almost minimal maintenance effort on their part. And they will not let it interfere with their work, even though they're usually perfectly happy for it to interfere with *yours*. Someone's got to make the running, after all, and they've elected you. At the ultimate crunch – if it all comes out to maximum embarrassment all round, or if it just breaks up in private distress – they will fall back on their work with much more warmth and zeal than you can, because they have never really left it. They'll always leave you sooner.

Billie had enjoyed what she thought was a 'truly fulfilled' love affair with the sales manager in a large fashion house where she was p.a. to the managing director. She saw her lover several times a week, but worked with her boss every single day from 9 to 5. Imagine her feelings when the sales director told her that her boss had told him that the relationship had to end. It couldn't go anywhere, as he was flying higher than she could. She was a nice enough girl, but better off dumped now, 'before things got serious'. Not a word of this had been mentioned to Billie. The two men ganged up to remove an imagined impediment to his promising career. Loverboy thought it was all good advice. He really appreciated a help forward from a senior man. He reminded her that he'd always said, work comes first. *Her* work there ended with her love, that night.

Work isn't the only thing they put first

A study in progress on adultery, the first of its kind, has already established that while *60% of married men* are having affairs, only 40% of married *women* are. That means that large numbers of married men are having affairs with unmarried women. If he's senior to you, the chances are he's married – and however little he talks about her, or even conversely if he bends your ear for hours with how unhappy he is with her, *married he is*, and you lose sight of this at your peril. This is not on the basis of the morality argument. The days are past since the Elizabethans believed that adultery was a sin twice over, because in committing it you also blasphemed against God. Nor need you take too much notice of the 'pinching another woman's man' charge. If he were really hers, you wouldn't have a chance. It's just one of those devices invented to lay the blame for sexual misdemeanours on women's shoulders, as if men were helpless non-participants in the matter. It's rare for a woman to step in and bust up a warm, close, loving marriage. It takes two to tango, and if his hips start moving, he's been listening already for the music. Don't let anyone get away with thinking that you dragged him onto the dance floor!

> *A married couple is a dangerous machine* –
> Iris Murdoch

The reasons for avoiding married men are much more practical and self-preserving. If your lover has stayed with her for however long, there has to be something in it for him. You'll get his whines and whinges – the charge sheet against the woman will be as long as your arm. But it's a main principle of natural justice that no one shall be tried *in their absence*. Not only is she not there to give her side of the case, but you will never see them on their own together – you will never form any idea of what binds them to one another however loosely – and you will never know the true nature of what you're up against. 'These are your rivals,' said one married lover to Ella, showing her a photograph of his two children. What she couldn't then know, but subsequently realized, was that this family-based attitude fully encompassed his wife, too. He later used to tell her how much he loved his wife, really! In these situations, you can only lose. N.B. it is better to have loved and lost, than to spend your whole damn life with him—London graffito.

All good advice . . .

and like all good advice, usually ignored! Modern career women, rejecting the conventional constraints on female freedom and female lives, often decide that the old double standard is the first thing to get a kick in the works. Women on the move, women moving upward, deliberately choose short-term relationships, and generally find them in the work place. The *opportunity* is there – one survey showed that working women are four times as likely to have affairs as non-working women, for obvious reasons. And the *incentive* is there – women enjoy it. 'It's a great big high, better than booze, better than anything,' said Joy. It's so good – you lose half a stone, feel the old glow, revamp your wardrobe, your hair, your body – it's like a month at Champneys, only for free!'

> *Too much of a good thing can be wonderful –*
> Mae West.

Ground rules for working lovers

Follow as Set One Rules for Not Becoming Lovers, at least as far as:

> * *not making a horse's ass of yourself*
> * *not futzing around in the work place*
> * *not losing out on slutus/promotion/the job itself*

But if you decide that it's for you, *be positive*. Don't swallow the delicious myth that you're just being swept along on a resistless tide of passion, a feather to each wind that blows – 'His hot hard kisses rained down upon her unprotected face; she was helpless before the force of his manhood' . . . Really? Recognize the fact that you are wanting, even willing this affair to happen, and *take an active part in the stage management*. If you don't, you'll find yourself cast as an extra in your own psycho-drama, constantly revolving around the central character – him. All too easily you'll reach a point when you are fitting round *his* work life, you are constantly waiting for him to call, you are sending little notes and gifts to keep things alive while you're apart, which he doesn't even remember to acknowledge when you're together!

Positive Action for lovergirls . . .

means being able to say :

> * *'No,* I'll call you – *possibly Wednesday of next week/month/after this big push at work is over'*
> Subtext: *'I've had enough of hanging around the phone not even daring to go to the loo waiting for you to phone'*

> * *'We need a weekend away together to unwind – can you manage one next month if I book somewhere?'*
> Subtext: *'I'm getting dissatisfied with snatched lunchtimes and abortive get-togethers in the graveyard hour after work'*

> * *'Let's take my car tonight'*
> Subtext: *'I like to drive too, you know, and besides, I drink less'*

> * *'Can we find a new pub for a change?'*
> Subtext: *'I'm up to here with being polite to your goofy gang of local oiks when it's you I want to be with'*

And eventually, *you* choose the cliché to administer the Big E:

* *'I'm afraid we're going to have to call this a day'*
* *'We've come to the end of our rainbow'*
* *'It was great while it lasted'*

or even:

* *'Work comes first'*!

Positive women learn from men

Not the bad things, but the good. It's good to have
control of your life, in love and in work – it's good to
know where you're going, to take decisions and to move
forward for yourself. If you want to be like this, you have
to be positive too about your mistakes and miscalcula-
tions, learn to forgive yourself for your failures, and put
them down to experience. You can't expect to get it right
all the time, and as one of the first female freebooters on
the high seas of sexual adventure, you have to expect a
little shipwreck now and again. Look before you leap –
one legal lady had the misfortune to go to bed with a
promising barrister, and wake up to find that he just had
to have tea, Terry Wogan, and the *Telegraph* crossword
before all else in the morning – 'A little cultural *death*,'
she said with a shudder. 'And a nasty vaginitis too.'

Making the running

If women decide to wrest the sexual initiative from the
hands of men who have monopolized it for so long, then
they have to be prepared to risk, as men do, the possibility of rejection. Never make a pass at a man without
considering in advance how you'll feel if he says no.
Frances had painfully liberated herself as she thought
from the strangulation of a convent upbringing. But she
was devastated when her first tentative approach to a
man received a brush-off. 'I thought they were supposed to jump at it,' she said miserably.

324

They won't always 'jump at it' any more than we will. Brace up for the odd … misunderstanding, muffed pass or dropped catch. But only the odd man out – if you get any more than a very few, reassess your technique. You must be choosing wrong, or doing it wrong. If you find that you're a compulsive dud-picker, see a shrink – horrible little men can be hobbit-forming. What you're after is the guy who can make the earth move, and still have an abundance of fun, tenderness and small talk for the after-times. His large talk should also be good – he must be clean if not decent – and his hair can be of any colour that pleases his mother if he has all these other virtues – the Thinking Woman's Fancy, in short.

> *A man is more than a dildo –*
> Germaine Greer

But always, in the end, fall back on your work …

as men do – learn this from them too. When you come to the end of every rainbow, your work is still there – it's the faithful old partner that never lets you down, no matter how you stray. Be sure to keep true to it in your fashion, so that it will always be there when you need it. If you can think positive about this, you *can* balance your work and your love live to obtain the maximum satisfaction from both. Remember that if a man is entitled to work and to love, as Freud said, *you are too*. It's not too much to ask – it's only just enough. With nerve, skill, a high heart and a sense of fun,

YOU CAN HAVE IT ALL!

8

Having It All

This may look like a tall order at a time when even *men* are being expected to make do with less, rather than go for more. A critical look at women's job situation now suggests that you need to develop your expectations in the light of these external factors:

1) *How real is the breakthrough?* Some of the recent encouraging advances for women may be more apparent than actual. In the last five years the American media have made much of the first woman

rabbi	TV anchorman	ambassador to Ghana
big city editor	sportscaster	supreme court justice
commercial pilot	warship officer	West Point cadet

Amongst other media-event female 'firsts' are the Number One woman to:

> * *install a telephone line*
> * *celebrate communion*
> * *conduct Mozart in Carnegie Hall*
> * *found a bank*
> * *become a State Governor in her own right*

Yet this list of 'firsts in our time' is misleading. The work of US researcher Louise Kapp Howe has thrown up the fact that in the US census of 1900, women were employed in *every one of the 303 occupations listed* except for nine. In what men fondly suppose to have been the heyday of the over-protected female, women were working as:

farmers	lumber-	engineers	police	firefighters
detectives	men	architects	barbers	surgeons
bootblacks	linemen	bankers	miners	journalists
lawyers	trappers	under-	gunsmiths	oyster-
	teamsters	takers		catchers

It looks as if every generation has to rediscover its working women, so deep is the myth that we're all angels at the hearth – and then ballyhoo as adventurous what in fact our *grandmothers* did!

2) *Real advances provoke real reaction.* If you're happily lying back under the impression that the big battles are won, and it's all over bar the shouting, forget it! All over the world men are quietly re-forming in the attempt to win back the ground that they think they've lost. In the history of the age-old struggle for women's full freedom, the 1980s will undoubtedly go down as the Age of the Backlash. Hopes and possibilities which we glimpsed in the Sixties, moved up on in the Seventies, are in the Eighties being whittled away or whisked out of reach by new 'developments', which individual men always claim are beyond their knowledge or control, nothing to do with them, no, no, no . . . of course not. 'I'm not *against* women', explained Jack, a London businessman. 'But you can't have two jockeys on one horse. We've given you girls a crack of the whip, and it doesn't work. It's better all round when men run things.'

As men still run things, it's not too difficult for them to maintain their lead over women in the work force. Consider this earnings profile over a recent twenty-year period in America:

Earnings of women working full-time as a percentage of men's

1956		63%
1970	50th anniversary of	59%
	women's winning vote	
1974		57%

SOURCE: *Women's Bureau 1975 Handbook on Women Workers*

And in this period the US had had a Federal Equal Pay Act *and* an Equal Employment Opportunities Commission! Some backlash, huh?

A similar picture emerges in Great Britain, where some of the key skirmishes have gone our way, but many major engagements remain, and *not* of the romantic kind. As Joan Lestor M.P., Opposition Spokesperson on Women's Rights and Welfare explains: 'In spite of two major pieces of anti-sexist legislation, *job segregation, which is the major obstacle to the advancement of working women, is again on the increase.* In the business world there are now proportionately fewer women managers than in 1979 and women are still the clerks, telephonists and typists who help the men who run Whitehall.'

Technological change is eliminating more jobs for women than Positive Action can immediately create. While some women move up, more move *out*, and the breakdown in traditional job patterns can mean that many more men are taking over what used to be 'women's work' (when men didn't want it) than women are taking over what has always been men's work. And some women are even joining in the backlash – psychiatrist Helen Mayer Hacker reports the formation of the Pussycat league, founded by an attorney, an advertising consultant, and a rich housewife, who believe that 'looking, cooking and smelling good for men are our major responsibilities and result in more than equal rights for us.' Miaouww!

3) *The recession throws women back, and provides the excuse for keeping us there.* A recession severe enough to throw so many working men on the scrapheap is a massive body blow to any hopes for women – steps forward, even leaps, are possible in an expansionist economy when the master race of men, relaxed and in control, can give in to the generous impulse of 'Sure, why not?' But once contraction sets in, women are the first to be squeezed out – because they are at the vulnerable end of the job market, and because they can be victimized with the old lies that they don't really need a job, only work

for pin money, and keep men out of jobs anyway. 'Now be fair', said Les, a Black Country Trades Unionist, 'We can't save jobs for the men at the minute – and men's jobs come first. You can't start on about a woman's right to work when they're putting *men* out. There's a recession on!'

This ignorant, selfish and divisive male attitude has been noted and attacked from the very highest level. In a colloquium on 'Women in the European Community' Dr Patrick Hillery, Vice-President of the EEC, issued this warning:

> *The increasing awareness of women of the injustices to which they are subjected and their justifiable insistence on being accorded their fair role in society is the strongest hope for the movement for the equality of women. It does not help women's cause that the growth of this movement is coinciding with a time of considerable economic difficulty and serious unemployment.* But it must be recognized that a great deal of progress depends not on increased expenditure, but on a more equitable sharing of existing resources.
>
> *Inevitably some aspects of our policy will cost money. We must, however, be on our guard against suggestions that justice and equality are only to prevail in times of plenty. Nor can we accept that any particular group in society should have to carry an unfair share of the hardships. The Commission has consistently taken the line that these hardships must be distributed fairly throughout all the sections of the Community.*

On 15 December 1975 the United Nations Organization adopted a resolution to proclaim the period from 1976 to 1985 'the UN Decade for Women'. This does not mean a decade for women to be conned out of their jobs by or for the benefit of men! Don't fall for it!

Having it all . . .

in fact becomes more desirable, the more difficult it is to achieve. Modern women want a job – and they want to hang on to it when they've got it. They learn to like the money, the independence, the sense of control that it brings, and when Mr Right comes along that's fine too – the liberated girl is determined not to sacrifice her right to be a loving, sexual woman, so she makes room and time for him in her busy life. But if he becomes more than a ship that makes a pass in the night, then he comes to take up more and more time. And if, in a settled relationship, you move on to think about having children, you'll be sufficiently a woman of today to feel that you either shouldn't, mustn't, or can't give up your place in the job market. That's what having it all means – enjoying to the full your potential as a woman, as an individual, as a working girl, as a wife/partner, and for ultimate fulfilment, as a mother.

Sounds familiar?

It should do – it's the theme song of most of the advice dished out to today's girls. And it's right as far as it goes – you have the human right to make the most of your gifts and attributes, which you have no reason to think are inferior to men's (and quite a bit of evidence to the contrary!). And in a society that places as much emotional and financial value on work as ours does, then women must get into that world and assert their right to be there, to have any hopes of winning equality with those who dominate there already.

But this scenario only holds good for the first part of your working life – say the first ten years at most, when you are likely to be free of serious emotional entanglements and all the out-of-work work that they entail. As an ambitious girl pulling yourself up by your own bra-straps, you can handle career demands alongside Mr Right, especially if he too is looking after himself, moving for himself, doing the same thing. But once move into a marriage-type relationship, and it's amazing how the old male/female patterns assert themselves. Even the most 'liberated' of modern men expect the woman to take over the lion's share of their joint domestic management – which is hardly surprising. But even the most 'liberated' of modern girls fall in with this – which *is*. Beryl works full time as an office manager and stoutly defends her habit of ironing all her husband's shirts each week – 'Well, I've got my own blouses to get done, it doesn't make any difference, does it?' *Only twice as much work for her*, on top of the cooking, the shopping, the cleaning. And her job, of course. What difference does it make?

Beryl has remained childless by choice, feeling with some reason that she has her hands full enough already. Even today, many women feel unable to take this choice – they are made to feel 'selfish', abnormal, or butch, by a harsh society totally careless of an individual woman's needs, or the desperation of an overcrowded planet. Many women do not formally 'choose' to have children – they simply let them 'come along', as people say. And many more women, married or single, get caught, because when you have sex with a man, it happens. There's nothing that turns Mr Right into Mr Toad so quickly as having to run, clean, provision and care for Toad Hall, as well as 2·1 little toads. And holding down your job as well – don't forget that. In the magazines, the glossy myth is the high-flying career woman, living the life she has always wanted. In reality, it's likely to be a crack-of-dawn start to get children organized and off to school or nursery, a full day's work broken only by a lunch-hour's frantic shopping, then home for the *other* eight hours. In these circumstances, *'having it all' is simply a con-trick formula which means* 'doing *it all'*.

Even top-level women are not free of these unfair and punishing demands – the financial capacity to buy in the help of other women is the solution that working women dream of, but it can bring greater worries in its train. Vivien was able to afford a good nanny for her little girl, as the highly successful boss of her own business.

But she was called home one day by police, who had found her three-year-old wandering along a main road. The nanny had got on the phone to her boyfriend, and left the front door open. Vivien spoke with deep feeling:

> *Wanting to? I wouldn't want my daughter to do what I've had to do, a business and a home. Children ill or anything, a woman's expected to do two jobs. It's not that they can't do one or the other, but being a wife and mother is a full-time job in itself.*
>
> *Two jobs are too much. It kills you in the end. Something has to go. My health has suffered. I have terrible migraines. You can't go on. And I have only one child. Too much is expected of women if they are married. Men still want their home comforts. There's no great fun in flying off for trips – when you get home you have to sort out all the problems that a man gets done for him.*

A man gets it done for him

And who gets to do it for him? One guess! This may be a workable arrangement if the couple still observe the traditional pattern whereby he goes out and wins the family bread, in return for which she stays home and keeps house. But this comforting picture, at best a reality only for the privileged section of the population, is more and more rapidly becoming a thing of the past. *The single most striking fact about women's work is the steep rise in the number of married women now employed:*

Percentage of married women working in Great Britain 1911-1979

1911	1921	1931	1951	1961	1971	1979
9·6	8·7	10·0	21·7	29·7	42·3	51·3

SOURCE: *Department of Employment Gazette June 1977, April 1978.*

Even this figure, showing that over half of all married women are now working, does not do justice to the extent of women's involvement in the work force. It is artificially lowered by the years that women take out to look after children, an activity which now has become one phase of a woman's life, rather than her *raison d'être*. The majority of married women return to work as soon as they can when the children are off their hands, so that in the 35 to 54 age-group, *70% of married women are working* (see overleaf).

The double burden

In Britain, more married women work in paid employment outside the home than in any other European country. But this does not relieve them from their traditional responsibility for child care and household management. On the contrary, women are just uncritically expected to be able to run all the home work as well. Put that together with the fact that women's earnings are still less than 75% of men's, and you don't have to be Einstein to figure out that women are doing *twice the work of men for only three quarters of their salary!*

Men benefit from women doing it all at home in many different ways, as Trades Unionist Chris Aldred suggests:

* *They get looked after at home, and manage to get out of doing all their share of caring for the children*

* *Without competition from women at work, men get first pick of the best jobs and a better chance to learn a skill*

* *After getting pushed around at work all day, at least they can be boss in their own homes — after all, they are the breadwinners.*

*They may be cushioned from redundancy by en-
couraging women workers back to the home when
jobs are scarce

Women At Work, 1981.

But there's more to it even than this. Men simply could
not do their jobs if it weren't for the unsung, *unpaid* effort
of women to keep their houses and mind their children.
If they had to pay for this work – and it *is* work, however
much you love them (or not, as the case may be!) – *they*

Married women's participation in the work force by age, Great Britain 1971-79

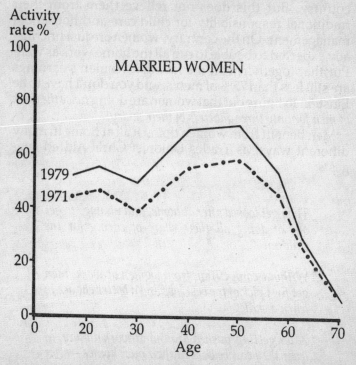

SOURCE: *Department of Employment Gazette, April 1978*

couldn't afford you. A recent article by Dr Ellen Derow in the Department of Employment Gazette demonstrated that if a houseworker claimed comparability with women paid to do similar jobs, she would have to be paid £7,180 p.a. If she claimed comparability with men, the figure rises to £8,400. Try taking *that* out of the average man's wage! Women's home labour subsidizes the whole of the labour market, as one woman expresses it:

> *The truth began to dawn then how I keep him fit*
>   *and trim,*
> *So the boss can make a nice fat profit out of me*
>   *and him.*
> *And as a solid union man he got in quite a rage*
> *To think that we're both working hard and*
>   *getting one man's wage.*
> *I said, 'And what about the part-time packing job*
>   *I do –*
> That's three men that I work for, love
>   my boss your boss and you' –

'The Maintenance Engineer', Sandra Kerr

Parity begins at home . . .

As Hilary Land has argued in a research paper on women's and men's work in the home, and its effect upon their paid employment. Women can never attain equality in the job market while they are shouldering the domestic burden as well: '. . . it would be fundamentally wrong to see the question of combining paid employment with family responsibilities as only of concern to women . . . The question must be raised whether this work, to which men and the economic structures they create accord so little priority, must always be done by women, and valued so lowly?'

Men, of course, always deny this. Apart from the usual masculine ploy to claim that they think women are wonderful ('The ladies, God bless 'em!'), individual males will indignantly assert that they do their work in the house and with the children, and they don't know what these bloody women (speedily demoted from their 'wonderful' status) are bleating about. This is a self-comforting *lie and delusion*. A world-wide study of daily time spent by men and women, conducted by UNESCO, showed a remarkable consistency in men's success in getting out of their domestic responsibilities:

In no country do employed men spend more than half an hour a day on housework, or employed women spend less than a hour and a half, even though women's working hours outside the home are sometimes longer than men's.

Other studies from Europe and the US show that working women not only boost the economy with their individual labour power – they also rely on an increased use of market goods and services to compensate for the smaller amount of time that they can spend on household tasks. *What they cannot efficiently do, however, is to rely on their partner for useful help*. For every twenty minutes devoted to food preparation by a male, a woman can reduce the time input by ten minutes. This holds true for all domestic chores – male time substitutes for female time in the ratio of two to one!

This of course provides the perfect excuse for men to cop out – 'I just can't get the hang of this/I'm not as good at this as you are' are masculine bleats familiar to every female ear. And at the end or the beginning of a trying day, the last thing a working woman wants to do is to endure the irritation of hanging around and watching some dope raise incompetence to the level of an art. The temptation to shoulder them aside and get on with it yourself is so strong as to be irresistible to many women. *Don't do it!* Why should you carry the load he's dumped on you as well as your own? Don't be satisfied with this imperfect substitution of your own time and effort. Teach the guy to shape up and speed up. Introduce the poor thing to the concept of work study. Tell him that increased productivity and efficiency are the order of the day. After all, it's no help to have the dishes washed up 'for you', if in the time he takes to do it you have changed the beds, done the washing, and hoovered the house from top to bottom!

The 'for you' con-trick

Many men sincerely believe that they are more participant in the house than reality shows to be the case – all the studies demonstrate a profound discrepancy between what men do, and what they *think* they do. And even men who are genuinely more helpful still stop short of accepting their share of the responsibility because they are leaving it all in women's hands as the last resort – what they do is 'help', or 'help out'. This unspokenly asserts all the time that the domestic work and child care are *women's work* – men can opt in or out depending on how benevolent they're feeling and how heavy their own work load is. *Women can't*. And the work that men do opt to do is usually of the non-urgent, semi-pleasant variety – gardening, for instance, or washing the car, both of which can be put off if it's raining or the mood's not right. How many men will as a matter of course

> *clean the lavatory
> *change a nappy
> *clear up after a sick baby, cat or dog
> ?

Makes them feel sick to think of it? Of course it does – it's *women's work!*

*

> We have no O-levels, or A-levels either.
> We didn't fight and we didn't win,
> we only ran to get the washing in.

Look out, you just missed us
as you crossed the crowded campus.
We were only there to clean the floors
and hand your morning coffee out –
　　　　'Degrees', Elizabeth Bartlett

*

And as women's work of course, it's largely invisible. No one
notices if you do do it – they only notice if you *don't*. No
matter that they are busily renewing the work on a daily
basis, with their clutter, their washing, their need to be
fed and serviced. It is because this process is so constant,
so relentless and so unquestioned that millions of
women take it as 'natural' that they should just go on
doing it the way their mothers did before them. But for
the sake of your future prospects, your health, and the
welfare of the relationship, if you are in this situation
with a man, *break out of it*. Start by listing all the
household jobs that have to be done in one week –
everything, no matter how trivial – and share them out
equally. Make a rota, and make sure that he has his share
of the dirty jobs, and sticks to them. Then if he can do his
fair share, a genuine 50% of the domestic chores in half
an hour a day as per the UNESCO study, get him to let
you in on his secret!

Equality for men ...

in sharing the work burden of their houses and their
children is long overdue. Women are expected to succeed in two roles, while men's work lives are actually
constructed to keep them *out* of their houses and
families as much as possible. Alan, a London commuter,
leaves his Essex home at 8 am and does not return till 6
pm. 'I never see my children in the week', he says, 'and
you can't just pick up on it at the weekend. They'll be
grown up before I know them' – a reminder that equal

shares for men means an equal part in the good things of life, not just cleaning the lavatory and changing a nappy!

Working women will speak freely and strongly about their unequal load. June works full time as a data librarian for an international company – an interesting and responsible position which she enjoys. 'But the housework's an endless headache, a nightmare some-times', she says. 'It makes you feel so guilty. The problem is keeping on top of it all the time. You mustn't make a religion of it, mustn't let it get you down. But it's hard not to worry.' June declared that her husband was 'very good, quite domesticated, can lend a hand with anything'. Other women have different experiences. 'My husband help round the house?' asked Ethel in-credulously. 'Him? he's the idlest sod . . . he *makes* work, he doesn't *do* it! Andy Capp's a king to him!' Ethel's working day starts at 5 am when she clocks on as an industrial cleaner. She goes from there to a newsagent where she works until 7 pm. Her husband is unem-ployed. But Ethel still does all the shopping, cooking, cleaning and washing. 'I let him put it over on me when we was young', she explained. 'And I've had it now.'

Having it all . . .

Does not mean all of what Ethel has. It *must* not mean *doing* it all, as the price of being allowed out to work in the first place. And it need not mean having it all *at one and the same time* – what is a perfectly workable arrange-ment for you in your twenties may be hopeless in the thirties, and possible again five or ten years later. The killer is trying to keep all the balls in the air simul-taneously, especially if your partner has always refused to learn to juggle!

And while you are taking a very critical look at the 'having it all' deal, and working out the cons and catches lurking under its apparently friendly exterior, work out also what having it all means *for you*. 'All' is no good if in fact it's too much. Of the holy trinity of total female fulfilment – work, marriage, children – you may decide to pass up on one, or more. They're not compulsory.

Current evidence suggests that for many working girls, having it all does not necessarily imply finding the satisfaction through marriage and motherhood – the traditional female base-identity – that is always assumed. An EEC survey of working women found that the female respondents gave these reasons for working:

	%
independence	47
necessity	45
self-fulfilment	39
interesting work	31
security	26
improved living standard	20
to get out of the house	17
inadequate salary of breadwinner	13
to save	6

Yet of these women, who placed independence, self-fulfilment and interest in their work as a high priority, 55% felt that their full potential and their professional skills were not being used in their jobs. Similar percentages declared that their work was not increasing either their chances of promotion, or their professional ability. Yet a total of 96% of these women intended to continue working, and two-thirds of them declared their intention to seek promotion. So despite discouragement, frustration and under-use, they were pushing on in the world of work, where their clear and just demands cannot be staved off for ever. What they are calling for is not more of the traditional women's burden, but a fair share of men's!

How to have your all

More and more men today are asking what Freud called 'the great question', what does a woman want? It is heard more loudly as the old certainties break down to the extent that chicken-sexing, sausage-plaiting and corn-husking can no longer be mindlessly set down as 'women's work', while mining, fire-fighting and bus driving are reserved for men. As Flo Kennedy, US lawyer and activist has declared, '*The only men's jobs and women's jobs are those which can't be done without a penis or a vagina.*'

So when you hear the question, have your answer ready. What women want is

* *wage parity with men*

* *career advancement opportunities*

* *job safety and security*

* *freedom from masculine harassment*

* *realistic childcare support*

* *job-sharing in the home, as well as in the work-place*

You may pass up on one of two of these – promotion chances, for instance, if you don't want a spiral-type career ascent, or child care, if you're not taking that option. But until this total package is available freely and without hassle for all women, there is no real chance of obtaining and holding equality with men at work. These are the issues, and their successful resolution in our favour will transform the workplace in the coming decade, far more than have the struggles of the brave few to break into all-male fields and top positions.

That's all we want . . .

But we won't settle for less. Things will not be easy. There will continue to be masculine mutterings, dirty tricks, resistance and retaliation. Yvette Roudy, French Government Minister for Women's Rights puts it like this: 'In this period of economic crisis, to strive for women to take their rightful place in the world of labour at every level is to row against the current. That is why we have to row even faster.'

We can do it. In the history of women's struggle for civil and personal freedom, the advances have been painfully won in clearly defined stages as each area of oppression was identified, assaulted and taken. One by one the legal, economic and suffrage disabilities have been conquered and withdrawn. Modern women have come to see their part in the age-old battle of the sexes as a cultural struggle – their task as breaking down the barriers which continue to hold women back from their rightful place as equal partners in a society where they are numerically dominant but in every way made subordinate. Current social change is proceeding at an unprecedented rate. It is up to all women to seize the chances for progress that this brings. The moment is now. Old oppositions are weakening, and the newly-spawned have yet to gather their strength. Women are leaning on an opening door –

GET YOUR SHOULDER TO IT, AND PUSH!

USEFUL ADDRESSES

The Equal Opportunities Commission,
Overseas House,
Quay Street,
Manchester M3 3HN
061 833 9244

The National Council for Civil Liberties,
21 Tabard Street,
London SE1 4LA
01-403 3888

The Low Pay Unit,
Poland Street,
London W1V 3DG
01-437 1780

TUC Women's Advisory Committee,
Congress House,
Great Russell Street,
London WC1
01-636 4060

Girls and Maths Project,
University of London Institute of Education,
58 Gordon Square,
London WC1
01-636 1500 Ext 665

National Organisation for Women's Management
Education (NOWME)
29 Burkes Road,
Beaconsfield,
Bucks
04946 2360

FURTHER READING

Women's Rights – Anna Coote and Tess Gill (Penguin)

Taking Liberties: an introduction to equal rights – Jean Coussins (NCCL)

Women's Rights: a series of information pamphlets (NCCL)

Equal Opportunities – A Careers Guide – Ruth Miller (Penguin)

Positive action for Women: the next step – Sadie Robarts with Anna Coote and Elizabeth Ball (NCCL)

Women At Work – Chris Aldred (Pan)

Your Job in the Eighties: A Woman's Guide to the New Technology – Ursula Huws (Pluto Press)

How To Prepare Your Own Case for an Industrial Tribunal (Equal Opportunities Commission)